FROM PUSAN TO PANMUNJOM

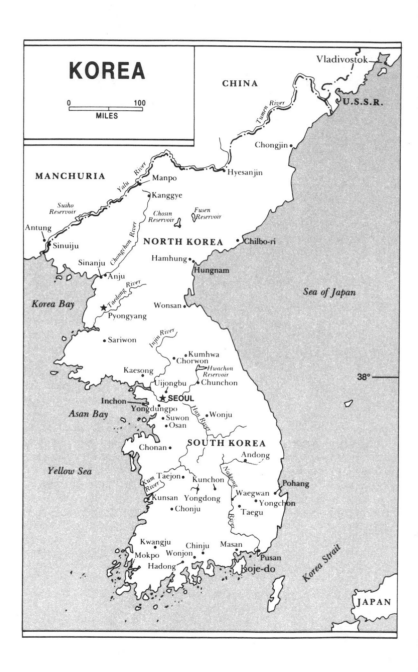

KOREA

0   100
MILES

CHINA

Vladivostok

U.S.S.R.

Tumen River

Chongjin

MANCHURIA

Yalu River

Manpo

Hyesanjin

Kanggye

Suiho
Reservoir

Chosin
Reservoir

Fusen
Reservoir

Antung

Chongchon River

NORTH KOREA

Chilbo-ri

Sinuiju

Hamhung

Sinanju

Anju

Hungnam

Taedong River

Sea of Japan

Korea Bay

Wonsan

Pyongyang

Imjin River

Sariwon

Kumhwa

Chorwon

Kaesong

Hwachon
Reservoir

Uijongbu

Chunchon

Inchon

SEOUL

Yongdungpo

Wonju

Asan Bay

Suwon

Osan

Han River

38°

Chonan

SOUTH KOREA

Andong

Yellow Sea

Kum
River

Taejon

Kunchon

Nakdong

Pohang

Kunsan

Yongdong

Waegwan

Yongchon

Chonju

Taegu

Nakdong River

Kwangju

Chinju

Masan

Mokpo

Wonjon

Pusan

Hadong

Boje-do

Korea Strait

JAPAN

FROM PUSAN TO PANMUNJOM

GEN. PAIK SUN YUP

Foreword by
**Gen. Matthew B. Ridgway and
Gen. James A. Van Fleet**

POTOMAC BOOKS, INC.
Washington, D.C.

First Memories of War edition 2007
First Potomac Books paperback edition 2000

First Brassey's paperback edition 1999

Frontispiece map printed courtesy of John Toland and William Morrow, Inc.

Library of Congress Cataloging-in-Publication Data
Paek, Sŏn-yŏp, 1920–
    From Pusan to Panmunjom / Paik Sun Yup.
    p.   cm.
    Includes index.
    1. Korean War, 1950–1953—Personal narratives, Korean. 2. Paek,
Sŏn-yŏp, 1920– I. Title.
DS921.6.P274   1992
951.904'2-dc20   91-43775
                                                                 CIP
ISBN: 978-1-57488-743-3

Printed in Canada on acid-free paper that meets the American National
Standards Institute Z39-48 Standard.

Potomac Books, Inc.
22841 Quicksilver Drive
Dulles, Virginia 22841

10 9 8 7 6 5 4 3 2 1

Contents

Maps

An AUSA Book

The Association of the United States Army, or AUSA, was founded in 1950 as a not-for-profit organization dedicated to education concerning the role of the U.S. Army, to providing material for military professional development, and to the promotion of proper recognition and appreciation of the profession of arms. Its constituencies include those who serve in the Army today, including Army National Guard, Army Reserve, and Army civilians, and the retirees and veterans who have served in the past, and all their families. A large number of public-minded citizens and business leaders are also an important constituency. The Association seeks to educate the public, elected and appointed officials, and leaders of defense industry on crucial issues involving the adequacy of our national defense, particularly those issues affecting land warfare.

In 1988 AUSA established within its existing organization a new entity known as the Institute of Land Warfare. Its purpose is to extend the educational work of AUSA by sponsoring scholarly publications, to include books, monographs, and essays on key defense issues, as well as workshops and symposia. Among the volumes chosen for designation as "An AUSA Institute of Land Warfare Book" are both new texts and reprints of titles of enduring value that are no longer in print. Topics include history, policy issues, strategy, and tactics. Publication as an AUSA Book does not indicate that the Association of the United States Army and the publisher agree with everything in the book, but does suggest that the AUSA and the publisher believe this book will stimulate the thinking of AUSA members and others concerned about important issues.

Foreword

Combat provides the sternest test of leadership ability. In early 1951, when we first met Paik Sun Yup, he had been tested, retested, tested again, and not found wanting. He continued, while under our command, to perform superbly at division, corps, and higher echelons. He was, without question, the finest operational commander in the Republic of Korea Army. Beyond that, he held steadfast to the basic tenets of the profession of arms: allegiance to country, personal honor, moral courage, abiding concern for subordinates, and the will to win.

American participation in the Korean War has been well documented and analyzed. Heretofore missing has been an authoritative account, in handy English form, from the perspective of the nation that provided the most manpower and sustained the greatest casualties. General Paik's book fills that void. *From Pusan to Panmunjom* is primarily about leadership in combat, written by a man who had no respite during the three years of that vicious conflict. For that reason alone, it merits study by military professionals. Moreover, there is another dimension to the book that makes it valuable to a wider readership. Interwoven with his personal experiences is Paik's insightful, factual account of an army that, utterly unprepared to begin with, had to learn the business of war the hard way—and did so in a manner that gives the lie to the long-held myth that the ROK Army was incompetent.

When the war erupted, Colonel Paik—all of twenty-nine years old—was in command of the 1st ROK Division, positioned on the provisional boundary north of Seoul and astride the main North Korean axis of advance. The violent, surprise attack engulfed his inadequately trained, ill-equipped unit. Yet for three days, Paik's division held fast, and then, its flanks turned, withdrew in good order. Over the next several weeks it conducted a series of delaying actions south to the Naktong River, where a coordinated UN Command defense was finally organized. In the heavy fighting of August and September, the 1st ROK Division was the hinge between American and South Korean forces and shares credit with American units for the successive defeats of the North Korean efforts to capture Taegu. Paik led his division in the breakout following the Inchon landing and the advance into North Korea, reaching Pyongyang—to the surprise of most—simultaneously with our 1st Cavalry Division. In the months that followed the Chinese Communist intervention, he demonstrated how well an ROK division could perform when reinforced by supporting arms to roughly American standards.

Now a major general, he was given command of an independent corps with the mission of eliminating substantial guerrilla forces concentrated in the mountainous terrain of southwest Korea. This brilliant campaign propelled him to the post of chief of staff of the ROK Army and responsibility for managing its wartime expansion, equipment, training, and deployment for operational commitment. Concurrently, he represented his nation's interests in the armistice negotiations. In the space of three years, his prowess as a leader had earned him four promotions and carried him to the pinnacle. Soldier that he was, he opted to step down from that pinnacle to head the first field army to be created.

The pages of Paik's book trace the emergence of an army initially bereft of tradition but seasoned and honed in the crucible of war. For forty years, misconceptions have persisted that the ROK Army did not pull its weight and was woefully lacking in heart and ability. Thanks to Paik, we now have the facts to repudiate that cruel, uninformed judgment. True, that army was no match for the enemy at the outset, when it barely extricated itself and quickly gave up most of its national territory. Yet the ROK Army maintained its organizational integrity, refurbished its ranks, and held where and when it counted most. True, Korean divisions were the preferred targets of Chinese Communist offensives and logically so. The Chinese knew full well the ROK divisional artillery and other support were only a fraction of that of American divisions and knew, too, the rapid force expansion had diluted front-line divisions of battle-wise personnel. Even under these conditions, many young leaders emerged to inspire divisions to fight resolutely.

The wartime challenge confronting the ROK Army was enormous. While fighting, it more than tripled in size; created the entire range of training, school, and logistical infrastructure; steadily improved its capacity for command and control; and developed esprit de corps. It came of age in the battle of White Horse Mountain. It later demonstrated its professionalism alongside American forces in Vietnam.

The alliance between the United States and the Republic of Korea—forged in the joint defense of freedom—has been central to the peace

and stability of Northeast Asia for four decades. Today, it is a partner-
ship of equals rooted in commonality of national interests and nurtured
by enhanced understanding of each other's culture and perspectives.
We are grateful to our comrade-in-arms, Paik Sun Yup, for his notable
contribution to that auspicious end result.

GEN. MATTHEW B. RIDGWAY
Commanding General; Eighth U.S. Army
1950–1951
CinC, United Nations Command
1950–1952

GEN. JAMES A. VAN FLEET
Commanding General, Eighth U.S. Army
1951–1953

Preface

The Korean War began at dawn on Sunday, June 25, 1950, with North Korea's unprovoked military incursion into the Republic of Korea. The republic's army was totally unprepared in strength and equipment and was virtually incapable of deterring the massive North Korean attack.

It was variously called a conflict, a police action, or a limited war, but it was really a brutal struggle for national survival—and a war. However, people under sixty can't remember it. Even in Korea, our commemorations are growing more perfunctory with each passing year. Yet memories of the war pound in us veterans like the beating of a second, massive heart.

I have reached three score years and ten and submit this memoir humbly, less as justification for my life than as a warning to all. Accounts of the Korean War have been published in a variety of books and other forms in Korea and abroad in the years since the war ended. But few if any of these accounts originated from those Koreans who were close to the scene. I am one of the few soldiers left alive who spent the three years, one month, two days, and seventeen hours of the Korean War, from the beginning of the Sunday invasion until the armistice in 1953, as a field commander in the lines. I hope, then, that this book will add in some small way to the literatures of the war and of the Korean Army.

Geographically, Korea has been situated at a pivotal point of geopolitical contest among the powers. In the last weeks of World War II, Russia accepted the surrender of the Japanese forces in Manchuria and northern Korea. The Americans accepted Japanese surrender in southern Korea, below the 38th parallel. Although this line was considered to be purely technical, Russia set up its system in the north, rejecting every mediatory effort made by the United Nations for a unification of Korea. As a result, we were among the first victims of the cold war. Despite a history of one thousand years as a unified nation and our tragic war, Korea has remained divided.

I penned this memoir because I am saddened to consider that so many of my countrymen know so very little about the Korean War or about the role their army played in defense of their homeland, and partly because I thought that many Americans have failed to recognize the important role the ROK Army played in defending Korea. The reader will see in virtually every line the enormous extent of the help that we received from the United States of America, which we appreciate so much. For me, the relationship between America and Korea started with the innumerable combat operations we endured together, and I firmly believe such a close relationship between the two countries will continue to flourish in the future. Thank you, America. We have not forgotten.

Acknowledgments

This book is about my life with the Republic of Korea Army during 1950 through 1953, focusing on the crucial phase of the Korean War from the Pusan Perimeter to the truce talks at Panmunjom. Although I realize the story presented is a fragment of a much larger picture, I attempted to recollect the events that took place in the battlefields to which I was exposed as a field commander during the war. I always felt writing a book of this nature is considered to be a professional privilege as well as a risk, but many American friends encouraged me to undertake this writing. Although I make no attempt here to thank these people individually by name, I am deeply grateful for their willingness to give so generously of their time, knowledge, and suggestions.

My special appreciation is extended to Gen. Matthew B. Ridgway and Gen. James A. Van Fleet for the kind foreword that they jointly contributed. The enthusiastic support and assistance of the late Gen. Richard G. Stilwell contributed greatly to my decision to publish this book including a critical assessment for my final decision for the publication of this book. Likewise, I wish to thank John Toland for his cogent suggestions and encouragement for my writing after we revisited the Naktong perimeter in September 1987.

The most difficult task in this venture was the matter of translation. For this, I am grateful to Bruce K. Grant for providing a complete English translation of my Korean manuscript, by which he displayed the wealth of his linguistic knowledge. I am indebted to Nam Sung In for his sustained support and assistance, critical comments, review of the manuscript, and preparation of maps in the same professional manner that he displayed under my command during the war. I am thankful to Brassey's (US), Inc. for accepting my manuscript, hopefully to infuse additional dimensions to the history of the Korean War that had already been written by many others. My thanks go to my family, which supported me with cheers and patience and helped me keep active for the book.

With the foregoing, I am humbly dedicating this book to the officers and men of the Republic of Korea Army and the U.S. armed forces who sacrificed the bloom of their youth in the Korean War, to the officers and men from many countries who also sacrificed their lives in the war under the banner of the United Nations, and to the Korean people who suffered the hideous agonies of war.

Abbreviations

G-1	Personnel section of divisional or higher staff
G-2	Intelligence section of divisional or higher staff
G-3	Operations and training section of a divisional or higher staff
G-4	Logistics section of divisional or higher staff
G-5	Civil affairs section of a divisional or higher staff
JCS	Joint Chiefs of Staff
KMAG	U.S. Military Advisory Group to the Republic of Korea
LST	Landing ship, tank
NKPA	North Korean People's Army
POL	Petrol, oil, and lubricants
RCT	Regimental combat team
ROK	Republic of Korea
S-3	Operations and training section of a regiment and battalion

1

THE LONG, LONG SUMMER

Kaesong Has Fallen

I picked up the telephone sleepily. "Sir," said a voice I recognized as that of my G-3. "The North Koreans have invaded! They're attacking all along the parallel." Gasping for breath, he rushed on, his words numbing my soul. "The situation in Kaesong is chaotic, and I'm afraid the city may already have fallen." As I hung up, I glanced at the time. It was 7:00 A.M., Sunday, June 25, 1950.

The call was the first I knew that the Korean War had begun. I was then a colonel in the fledgling Republic of Korea (ROK) Army, and at the ripe old age of twenty-nine I commanded the ROK 1st Division, proud protector of Seoul, South Korea's capital. We were stationed ten thousand strong in the western corridor, a north-south invasion route running from Kaesong just south of the 38th parallel to Seoul. The corridor was bounded on the west by the Yellow Sea and on the east by high, rugged terrain.

The ROK 1st Division's assigned sector actually started at the Yellow Sea, ran through Kaesong, and ended just short of Uijongbu, fifty-six miles away.

My 1st Division anchored the western end of a line of four army divisions strung out impossibly thin along the 210 miles of the 38th parallel that cut across the waist of the Korean peninsula. The end of World War II had installed the 38th parallel as a line artificially dividing one country into two: North Korea controlled by communism and the Republic of Korea working to establish democracy.

When I assumed command of the ROK 1st Division, I had examined its defense plan, walking the entire frontline trace to acquire a personal

1

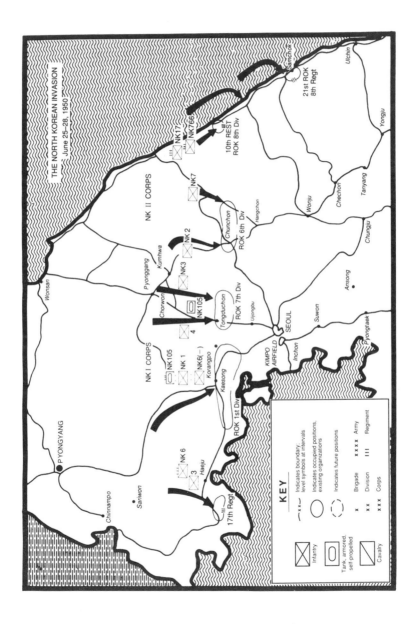

THE NORTH KOREAN INVASION
June 25–28, 1950

KEY

Indicates boundary;
level symbols at intervals

Indicates occupied positions,
existing organizations

Indicates future positions

x	Brigade	x x x x	Army
x x	Division				Regiment
x x x	Corps		

Infantry

Tank, armored,
self-propelled

Cavalry

2

feel for the ground. I had not liked what I saw. The division's forward units were situated along a line that closely followed the 38th parallel. Administratively that may have made sense, but militarily, the resulting dispositions were ludicrous. I changed the defense plan and had the division organize a defense line along the near bank of the Imjin, which ran through the division area of operations south of the 38th parallel.

This move sparked controversy. My critics pointed out that the new defense line implied the abandonment of the important city of Kaesong, which was forward of the Imjin and much closer to the 38th parallel. I realized that, of course, but my concept was simply that excluding Kaesong cut the division's front to a manageable nineteen miles from an impossible fifty-six, vastly improving the chances that the ROK 1st Division would be equal to its assigned defense mission. Another change I made when I assumed command was to move the division reserve, the 11th Regiment, from distant Inchon to nearby Susaek. Once the 11th pitched its tents in Susaek, I breathed a lot easier.

After the Korean War broke out, Gen. Omar Bradley, chairman of the U.S. Joint Chiefs of Staff, characterized it as "the wrong war, in the wrong place, at the wrong time, with the wrong enemy." For me and my troops, it was absolutely the wrong war, and its timing could not have been worse.

The timing was wrong because I had commanded the ROK 5th Division in Kwangju until April 22, 1950, and had yet to learn much about my new division. Moreover, I had received temporary duty orders assigning me to the Infantry School where I was to attend a senior officer training course lasting three months. I had been attending classes at the Infantry School full-time for almost two weeks. I was, of course, excused from my duties as ROK 1st Division commander while attending the school.

A North Korean invasion had been very possible for some time. The North had committed provocations of every kind along the 38th parallel since 1949. The ROK Army G-2 had warned key army commanders at a conference held in mid-June 1950 that "North Korean movements are abnormal. An attack is possible."

I was living in eastern Seoul with my wife and two-year-old daughter and commuting to classes at the Infantry School. After I got my G-3's alarming call on the morning of June 25, I quickly donned my dress uniform and dashed out to catch a cab. I walked impatiently up and down a major street but couldn't find a taxi. There were, in fact, very few vehicles of any kind in Korea in those days. I finally flagged down a passing military jeep and hitched a ride directly to ROK Army Headquarters in Yongsan Ward's Samgakji District. The streets looked just like they did every Sunday, quiet and deserted. Church bells pealed peacefully.

I wanted to learn the details of the invasion at ROK Army and also to determine whether I was to assume command of the ROK 1st Division, since I was still assigned to the Infantry School. I arrived at ROK Army behind the Yongsan post office and went directly to the chief of staff's office.

The office was in a state of bedlam. I shouldered my way past seven or eight officers until I reached the chief of staff, Maj. Gen. Chae Byong Duk, and asked him whether I should return to the division and assume command. A gigantic man, the general yelled back in unmistakable terms, "What are you yapping on about? Get to your division now." I didn't argue.

I needed a vehicle, so I headed for the nearby quarters of Lt. Col. Lloyd H. Rockwell, chief U.S. adviser to the ROK 1st Division. Colonel Rockwell was assigned to the U.S. Army's Korean Military Advisory Group, or KMAG. He hadn't heard a word about the invasion, but luckily he had a jeep. I told him about the urgent call from my G-3, and we jumped into his vehicle. With Rockwell at the wheel, we headed for the residence of Colonel Choi Kyung Nok near Seoul's famous South Gate.

Colonel Choi commanded my 11th Regiment, and as the senior regimental commander, he was acting as division commander while I was posted to the Infantry School. As we pulled up outside his home, he was all ready to go. In seconds the jeep was speeding directly for division headquarters at Susaek, northwest of Seoul.

Seoul's streets had been as quiet as on any other Sunday up till this point, but military vehicles suddenly began to appear everywhere, their growing numbers telling any Seoulite who was awake that something extraordinary was afoot.

We arrived at division headquarters at about 9:00 A.M. Major No Jae Hyun, commander of the division's artillery battalion; Major Kim, division G-3; and my communications company leader were already there. The staff briefed me on the status of the division as I dismounted from the jeep, not waiting for me to enter the headquarters.

Kaesong City had already fallen, they said. The situation there was hopeless. My 12th Regiment under Colonel Chun Sung Ho had been stationed in and around the city, but all communications with the unit had been cut. Meanwhile my 13th Regiment near Munsan under Colonel Kim Ik Yul was engaged in a pitched battle with invading units of the North Korean People's Army, or NKPA. The staff also told me that my 11th Regiment in reserve at Susaek would deploy to prepared defensive positions at the division front as soon as it could recall sufficient numbers of our men who were away from the division on leave or pass.

The staff explained that many division officers and men had been given passes and leaves and previous day, Saturday, so that only about 50 percent of the reserve regiment was present for duty. They said leaves and passes had been forbidden under an alert order issued by ROK Army in early June, but headquarters had lifted the alert. The division had instituted a liberal leave and pass policy, applying it most widely in the 11th Regiment because that unit was in reserve.

If all this weren't enough, my two-week absence from the division left me without an exact feel for the unit's pulse. I was frustrated and angry. "What a hell of a mess this is!" I muttered to myself. The phrase caught in my brain like a broken record, "Hell of a mess. Hell of a mess. Hell of a mess."

After the briefing, I divided the division staff among the available vehicles—jeeps, a communications vehicle, and a three-quarter-ton truck—and we set off at top speed for my 1st Division's forward command post, located in a primary school. I had designated this school as our emergency forward command post because the top of the hill across from the school afforded direct observation all the way to Kaesong, or at least it did when the sky was clear. The sky wasn't clear that day. All I could see from the hill across the entire division front was the smoke from bursting shells. The constant pounding of artillery clubbed my brain, dulling my senses.

The panoramic view of the battlefield triggered a palpable fear in me for the safety of my regiments. The 12th Regiment on the division's west, or left from the vantage point we had, was responsible for a very broad sector centered in Kaesong. I needed to know how much of the regiment had survived and when its remaining elements could pull back via its only avenue of withdrawal, which was the railway bridge across the Imjin River. On the east, my right-flank regiment, the 13th, had occupied fighting positions south of Korangpo. I needed to know how well the 13th was holding up. The 11th Regiment, what there was of it, was in division reserve. I had to know how soon it could finish recalling division soldiers and be ready to advance into Munsan City at the division's front, south of the Imjin River.

In my first hours back with the division, I was consumed with worry about the situation along the front. If my regiments could not find an opportunity to move into the positions we had prepared along the near bank of the Imjin, the invading forces would engulf Seoul literally overnight. Moreover, if my forces couldn't fall back to the Imjin defense line we had built, the division itself would be isolated. The onrushing NKPA would sever our avenue of withdrawal. I was also worried about the situation in the ROK 7th Division, commanded by Brig. Gen. Yu Jae Hung, which bordered us on the east. Communications with the 7th, however, were completely down, so I was frustrated in my need to determine the situation on the division's flank. I simply had no way to find out what was happening next door.

Lieutenant Colonel Rockwell had accompanied us all the way to headquarters at the primary school, but around noon he came up to me and said, "KMAG has issued an order to withdraw. I've got to get back to Seoul."

I was shocked "The U.S. Army said it would help us, but when the situation gets rough, you just pull out, huh? I'm sorry now that I expected anything from the U.S. Army." Tears welled up as I shook Rockwell's hand and bade him farewell. He drove quickly away.

The ROK Army relied on KMAG for almost all of its logistics supplies and equipment. KMAG's withdrawal meant we would be fighting empty-handed.

I needed to take a detailed look at the front, so I drove toward Korangpo. Enemy tanks and large units could cross there because the Imjin ran very shallow in the area. I found that my 13th Regiment was giving a good account of itself. Its forwardmost battalion had managed to delay the enemy for hours and was now withdrawing. By happenstance, another battalion of the 13th had been undergoing field training along the south bank of the Imjin. When the alarm sounded, this unit immediately moved into prepared defensive positions on a nearby hill.

As the hours passed, the officers and men who had been absent from the division began to return, often out of breath from their efforts to get back. The 11th Regiment had paused long enough to collect large numbers of these soldiers but now began to deploy forward, coming up on the division's left. Its men began strengthening positions centered on the railway bridge at what came to be known as the "Munsan Salient." North of Munsan, the river makes a semicircular loop to the northwest, toward Kaesong, leaving a dagger of land pointing at Munsan. This was the salient, an area of immense strategic value because the railroad from Kaesong crosses the Imjin here and leads on to Munsan and then to Seoul itself.

The ROK 1st Division leaped a major hurdle by successfully occupying the positions along the salient, but we then faced the next problem: When should we blow the bridge over the Imjin? A little past noon, the division engineer battalion commander informed me that he was ready. "We're all prepared to blow the bridge, sir. Please tell us when you want it to go."

"Wait a while," I directed. "Let's not blow it till the 12th pulls out of Kaesong and clears the bridge."

Finally, at about 3:00 P.M., the commander of the 12th, Colonel Chun, and thirty or forty his men appeared and crossed the bridge in three-quarter-ton trucks, bumping wildly on the railroad ties. Colonel Chun was bleeding profusely from a facial wound. We evacuated him to Seoul without delay. At age fifty-three, Chun was a very senior field-grade officer and a veteran of the Kwangbok Army, a group of Korean patriots in China before the end of World War II who espoused military force to liberate Korea from Japanese occupation. Colonel Chun recovered from his wounds only to be killed while commanding a ranger unit at the Battle of Yongdok.

We delayed blowing up the bridge for another hour, awaiting more

12th Regiment troops, but only a few stragglers made it out. Suddenly our outpost on the northern approach to the bridge called in, "Enemy soldiers are coming up behind our guys crossing the bridge now!"

"Blow the bridge!" I commanded.

Silence. Nothing. No explosion. The bridge remained intact. "We tried to blow it," the engineer battalion commander reported to me forlornly. "I don't know, maybe fragments cut the fusing cord or something." Before the engineers could begin to inspect the wiring to the explosive charges, enemy troops burst onto the bridge. A fierce exchange of small-arms fire broke out around the structure, with the NKPA on one side, us on the other. Bullets snarled in the air around me.

Our failure to blow the bridge put us in a hell of a pickle. We had no choice but to abandon the strategically important bridge to the enemy, and our casualty toll was mounting sharply. Meanwhile, one of my three regiments had been shattered at Kaesong and remained a regiment in name only. Despite the deteriorating situation, we had been extremely lucky in one regard. The NKPA had not mounted a major thrust across the railroad bridge, choosing instead to attempt to send a tank column through Korangpo, across the Imjin, past the hill defended by the 13th, and on into Munsan from the northwest. NKPA tacticians no doubt calculated that we would blow the bridge. Certainly I thought we would.

Two battalions of reinforcements arrived by train late in the afternoon. Both were demonstration battalions, one from the Korea Military Academy and the other from the Infantry School. Demonstration battalions were maintained at both institutions to demonstrate small-unit tactics to the students and cadets. Because my 12th Regiment was no longer an effective fighting force, the two battalions boosted the division's combat strength significantly.

An enemy tank column crossed the Imjin near Korangpo, and a desperate battle developed as the column entered the 13th Regiment's defense zone. The antitank platoon assigned to the 13th took the column under direct fire, but the platoon's 57mm antitank guns and 2.36-inch rocket launchers could not penetrate the thick armor of the Soviet T-34 tanks. It was disastrous enough that the platoon was undergunned but even more ruinous that the platoon had never been issued armor-piercing ammunition.

Despite having an antitank platoon, ROK Army soldiers did not have sufficient antitank training or weapons and had never even seen a tank. This contributed greatly to the "T-34 disease" that gripped our troops on this first day of war. The symptoms of the disease were straightforward. As soon as the men even heard the word "tank" they fell into a state of terror.

The more courageous soldiers of the 13th Regiment overcame their fear. Acting without orders from their officers, a number of them broke into suicide teams and charged T-34s clutching explosives and grenades. They clambered up onto the monsters before touching off the charges. Although such desperate acts brought tears to my eyes, the bravery of these men prevented NKPA armored units from getting past the 13th all that first day, earning precious time for division troops on leave and pass to return to the 11th Regiment.

As darkness fell over the battlefield on June 25, 1950, I made my way back to the division command post. The ROK 1st Division had held against desperate odds, and I could almost see a stiffening of the spine, a pride of unit, ripple through the division.

The communications officer brought me a cable from my younger brother, Col. Paik In Yup, who commanded the independent 17th Regiment on the Ongjin Peninsula, a solitary claw of land jutting into the Yellow Sea far to my west. The 38th parallel cut so closely across the top of the tiny peninsula that the invasion instantly trapped the 17th, which fell under direct ROK Army operational control despite its relative proximity to my division. "Please convey this to the commanding officer of the ROK 1st Division," In Yup's telegram began. "My officers and men are fighting well, magnificently, but the situation could not be bleaker. This may be the last you hear from me."

For an instant, I was consumed with worry for In Yup, but it was dangerous to allow myself to be distracted, whatever the reason. I was young and green and my responsibilities heavy. The lives of ten thousand men lay in my hands. I must frankly confess that a full day of constant, terrible crisis had robbed me of my usual calm, detached manner. I was shaken. And I had not anticipated the terrible thirst. I drank all the water I could get during the day, yet my throat burned and ached for more. I tried to sleep, but the sound of bursting shells continued long into the summer night, and sleep eluded me. I couldn't get my burning eyes to close.

The first day of a war that would drag on for three years, one month, two days, and seventeen hours and hold in balance the lives of my country, my buddies, and myself had finally ended in darkness. But after the night, the dawn would come again.

The Munsan Defense Line Crumbles

The NKPA's onslaught stunned the unprepared ROK 1st Division, but on the war's second morning, June 26, 1950, we began to fight as if we'd been doing it forever. The division's soldiers ignored the NKPA's superior numbers, daunting firepower, and even the shock effect of its T-34s. We knew the terrain, and we had prepared fighting positions on the strong points. We exploited these advantages to mount a spirited resistance. As our troops emerged from their initial shock at the invasion, we realized that the NKPA was neither as skillful nor as invincible as they looked to us on the previous day.

Contact began early on the second morning. Colonel Kim's 13th Regiment on the forward hill was smothered in the smoke from exploding artillery shells. But the 13th fought stubbornly on its high ground, much better than I had expected.

On the negative side, enemy forces that had deployed into positions around the Imjin bridge the previous night had moved onto the high ground during the night and now threatened Munsan itself. This new menace worried me because if the NKPA seized Munsan, the enemy would be on my 13th Regiment's flank and astride its line of withdrawal. As the pressure built, I committed the reserve, ordering the 11th Regiment to retake the Munsan Salient. I instinctively understood that if we remained exclusively on the defense, the NKPA would end up shoving us into the ocean.

Taking only my driver and aide, I set out to visit all divisional units along the front. Enemy shells burst around the jeep every yard of the way. I would be lying if I said I wasn't terrified, but the need to inspire ten thousand men unfamiliar with battle kept me at the task. My legs trembled uncontrollably the whole time we were under fire, but I don't recall being seriously concerned about being killed or wounded. Although I was barely able to control my fear, I must've appeared fearless to the division's fighters. I think my little show of bravado helped to bolster the newfound confidence the men felt as they faced another day of combat against fearsome odds.

The highway was clogged with streams of refugees trudging south and columns of soldiers marching north. We threw every last trooper who could pull a trigger into the line. My order to retake the Munsan Salient committed the 11th Regiment and the two demonstration battalions to the battle and meant that the ROK 1st Division no longer held a single unit in reserve.

I communicated with ROK Army at every possible opportunity, begging for reinforcements and asking for a replacement for the wounded commander of the 12th Regiment we had evacuated the previous day. I told headquarters that the man I wanted was Lt. Col. Kim Chum Kon. Kim was then assigned as deputy assistant chief of staff, G-2, at ROK Army. He and I had served together twice before, when I was deputy chief of staff for intelligence at ROK Army in 1948 and when I commanded the ROK 5th Division.

Around noon on June 26, the 11th Regiment and the demonstration battalions initiated the counterattack I had ordered. The attack enjoyed the full support of our 6th Artillery Battalion, the sum total of the division's big guns.

The enemy had already dug in on the high ground, however, and doggedly resisted the 11th's attack. An artillery duel developed, one we couldn't win. The NKPA's guns were much superior to our ancient 105mm howitzers, with their limited, 8,000-meter range. My gunners simply were unable to contend for artillery superiority against the large-caliber NKPA guns.

Despite the artillery disadvantage, some of the 11th Regiment's attacking units advanced resolutely amid an absolute rain of shells and succeeded in pushing the enemy out of positions near the bank of the Imjin. But the counterattack finally ran out of steam. I was frustrated as I watched because we had missed an opportunity. Had the counterattack begun earlier, we could have retaken the salient, but by the time the tardy 11th got its attack organized, enemy forces had consolidated their hold on the battlefield.

Around sundown on the second day, NKPA tank units finally managed to push past the 13th Regiment. In its battle to hold back the T-34 columns, the 13th had learned to mass its antitank fire, although even the concentrated fire was pitifully inadequate. Time and again our antitank gunners placed their rounds squarely on enemy T-34s. A direct hit didn't destroy a tank, but it did stop it temporarily. The division's artillery battalion fought hard and well to siow the tanks. The men labored tirelessly to keep the division's fifteen howitzers firing. These brave fighters were destined to maintain their fire until they had no shells left to shoot. With so few guns, they had to select targets carefully, directing their fire onto the enemy's main force and at its onrushing armor.

Our artillery maintained an accurate curtain of fire at the front edge of the advancing armor, forcing the tank commanders to abandon the rapid pace so dear to tankers' hearts. Indeed, the coordinated efforts of the 13th Regiment's antitank guns and suicide teams and the accurate fire and strenuous exertions of division artillery managed to keep the T-34s out of Munsan for two full days.

But time ran out. Free from the 13th's nagging fire, the T-34s charged down the road, advancing ominously on Munsan. Munsan fell as a dozen T-34s burst into the city. The enemy now sat squarely astride the only avenue of escape for units of the 11th Regiment, located as it was on the extreme left flank of the division. The armor penetration into Munsan sent NKPA spirits soaring, and growing enemy infantry pressure began to force the 13th Regiment out of positions it had defended so fiercely. In short order the division's entire defense line collapsed.

Darkness fell, and the rain pelted down. I ordered a withdrawal, directing all units to occupy fighting positions along our second defense line. I had received word that the ROK 7th Division on the other main invasion route, east of my ROK 1st Division, had withdrawn in unseemly haste toward a town east of my boundary, and this was another reason our own withdrawal became inevitable.

I ordered my units to withdraw to a second line of defense extending along a stream that placed us almost exactly halfway between the 38th parallel and Seoul. After I was assigned to command the division, I had designated this area as our final line for the defense of Seoul and had fighting positions dug along it.

The linchpin of the new line was an area where the road from Seoul to Kaesong, now known as the Unification Highway, and the single north-south rail line parallel each other in a series of curves forming the shape of the letter S. The area is bounded on both right and left flanks by low hills that would serve to concentrate any attacker. I had needed only a glance to see the advantages the terrain offered to the defense. The ROK 1st Division didn't have enough manpower to prepare the necessary defensive positions, but students from a nearby middle school had cheerfully grabbed shovels and pickaxes and pitched in. As I issued the order to withdraw to this second line, my heart overflowed with grati-tude for those young students.

Once I had ordered the withdrawal, my anxiety soared. I was irritated and showed it. A number of nagging questions tore at me. Would all my units receive the withdrawal order in the darkness and confusion of the battlefield? Would the 11th Regiment be able to skirt the enemy and squeeze to safety? Was the 13th Regiment able to withdraw; was it even able to avoid encirclement? The 13th's line had crumbled as the armor units growled by, and enemy forces had penetrated south of the 13th's assigned defense zone. Would the division's units be able to bring its heavy weapons and equipment out with them in the darkness? Would our eastern boundary hold?

I had my G-3 and all the headquarters staff officers breaking their backs to be certain every last unit got the withdrawal order. In some cases we called in S-3s and gave them the order in person. In other cases we communicated by telephone, and sometimes a division staff officer had to go find a unit in the field. A withdrawal under such conditions presented such high potential for mass tragedy that my mind went numb. I can't describe the feeling.

At some point during the night, the KMAG adviser to the 12th Regi-ment, Maj. Mike Donovan, appeared at the division command post. He said he had returned because KMAG had canceled its withdrawal order. Donovan brought with him a message that ROK Army was preparing a counterattack. Headquarters planned to throw six regiments into the battle in the corridor east of ROK 1st Division. It was counting on us to support the counterattack by holding where we were in the western corridor. I quickly understood that this meant my 1st Division would be fighting to its death along the stream northwest of Seoul.

In a detached way, as if it weren't me, I noticed that I had lost the heel of my low-top dress boots. The exposed nails had been driven up inside the sole and were gouging my heel. I tugged the boot off to find my heel clotted with blood, but I didn't have time to take care of the wounds. I was too busy getting division headquarters moved to a primary school near the stream that marked our second line of defense, too busy checking to see which units were managing to reach the new line. Just too worried.

The enemy began mounting night assaults on this second night of the war, but despite the attacks, all ROK 1st Division units along the front were able to withdraw with relatively little confusion and deploy to positions along the new defense line by dawn of June 27. This is not to say that things went perfectly. As I feared, confusion arose when a few units didn't get the withdrawal order, and some formations became disorganized when they separated from parent units. But the comprehensive rupture across the entire front that had harrowed my mind for hours didn't happen. I felt like I'd survived an artillery barrage.

During the night we received two battalions of reinforcements and deployed these forces in our new line. Both battalions were from the ROK 5th Division stationed in South Cholla Province under the command of Maj. Gen. Lee Eung Joon. One battalion was from the 15th Regiment, the other from the 20th. They had journeyed from South Cholla through Seoul and on to me in the western corridor. ROK Army, meanwhile, committed the bulk of the ROK 5th Division in the eastern invasion corridor, just to the right of my division boundary. The commander of the 15th Regiment, Col. Choi Young Hi, had been temporarily assigned to the Infantry School for training, as had I, but joined his battalion in Seoul and accompanied it to our headquarters.

Lt. Col. Kim Chum Kon, whom I requested ROK Army Headquarters to assign to my command, also arrived during the night to take command of the 12th Regiment. Very few 12th Regiment troops had managed to get out of Kaesong alive, but Colonel Kim jumped to the task of organizing its remaining elements.

Restless, impatient, worried, I lay on a mat and despite the exertions of the day found that sleep completely eluded me for the second night straight. Despite my physical fatigue, my mind seemed determined to mull the kaleidoscopic events of the past forty-eight hours. Things began to fall into place; I began to see what made the NKPA tick; I began to see what they were and who they were. The ROK 1st Division faced an enemy more than two divisions strong, reinforced with T-34 tanks. The enemy was well prepared for this invasion with a massive military buildup.

I wasn't the only one whose mind was working overtime. During the night the deputy commander of the division's engineer battalion organized twenty-one reinforcement troops into a suicide team to deploy against the expected NKPA night attack. Every member of the team wrote out a will before leaving our lines to dig and man foxholes along the highway leading south from Munsan. Their mission was to ambush the T-34s that inevitably led an NKPA assault. The team was provided with our newest antitank weapon, blocks of TNT fastened around a hand grenade. The plan was for a soldier to pull the grenade's safety pin and pitch the explosive onto a tank. This required the grenadier to expose himself so close to his target that he had little prospect of surviving.

To nobody's disappointment, the T-34s didn't come that night. An enemy patrol did, however, and was annihilated by our TNT squad. The suicide team made it safely back to our lines at dawn, bringing with them about a dozen small arms from the fallen enemy. Our engineer battalion had failed to blow the Imjin bridge, but the courageous spirit of the suicide team had more than retrieved the engineers' honor.

The NKPA seemed to regret the respite from attack it allowed us that night and appeared promptly at first light on June 27, 1950, advancing through the cover of thick foliage to our north. Shortly thereafter, about twenty-five T-34s rumbled down the highway heading straight for us— and Seoul. But the ROK 1st Division was starting on its third day of war. Our units had gradually regained a measure of composure, confidence, and esprit.

My artillery battalion once again laid down an accurate barrage directly in the path of the tanks. Combined with the concentrated fire of our antitank weapons, this was sufficient to bring the onrushing armor column to a halt. Our suicide teams remained active, and even the newly arrived troops of the 15th Regiment joined in this desperate measure. A number of them climbed onto enemy tanks that managed to penetrate the artillery barrage, providing a valiant display of dedication to a free Korea and dying as heroes. Violent attacks continued throughout the day, but the enemy and its mighty T-34s could not breach our line.

In the afternoon Maj. Gen. Kim Hong Il visited ROK 1st Division Headquarters. General Kim came in his capacity as director of the ROK Army's Strategy Supervision Team. General Kim was then fifty-two years old—to my tender twenty-nine—and after I briefed him on the progress of the battle in our sector, he praised our efforts in a characteristically crusty sentence. "I'm amazed the ROK 1st has held out so long." The general went on to tell me, however, that things were going badly in the eastern corridor and that we had no reason to hope for a satisfactory outcome.

General Kim then sought my view on a crucial issue. "You've done about all you can on this line. What do you think about breaking away cleanly and withdrawing south of Seoul, south of the Han River?"

"I think that's out best option," I replied, "but I can't withdraw on my own volition." I asked General Kim to return quickly to ROK Army and ask Chief of Staff Chae Byong Duk for permission to withdraw.

"I'll do just that," General Kim promised and hastily drove off toward Seoul. Late that night an officer in a jeep pulled up to our headquarters with a written order from General Chae. The order could not have been simpler. "Fight to the death in your present positions." This order removed all possibility that the bulk of the ROK 1st Division would ever cross the Han River to safety. All we could do was stay where we were, resist till the last, and hope for a miracle.

I heard later that General Kim strongly recommended withdrawal of the ROK 1st Division, but the chief of staff was reluctant to decide either way. I was told that General Kim held the telephone out to General Chae and begged him to call and order me to withdraw, but General Chae refused to decide. Then Chae received a message informing him that the U.S. Army would intervene in Korea. This instilled in the general the vague hope that the ROK Army somehow could stop the NKPA juggernaut north of the Han, so he ordered me to hold at all costs.

In later days, I was roundly criticized for ignoring General Kim's recommendation to withdraw and for insisting instead on a stubborn defense along our line at the stream. My critics believed that as division commander I should have decided on my own to execute a bold withdrawal southward to and across the Han. But this is merely one of the many "what ifs" spawned by the swirling ambiguities of war. Many a military commander has courted disaster by accepting the recommendation of an officer on his commander's staff, but staff officers are not part of the chain of command. Moreover, abandoning a battlefield in violation of orders is a capital offense in every army in the world. Not that I was afraid of punishment. The issue was a much simpler one. The duty of the soldier is to obey orders.

I could "what if" myself to death. What if I had ignored orders and directed a withdrawal that night, while the ROK 1st Division remained largely intact? Then I could have made a valuable contribution by throwing my division into the defensive operations we were to undertake south of the Han. The weight of an intact and savvy ROK 1st Division may well have prevented the enemy from pushing us all the way to the Naktong River north of Taegu. I'm frustrated to this day over that.

So long as we were under orders to fight to the death, and in view of the old maxim that the best defense is a good offense, I decided to put together a surprise for the NKPA. During the wee morning hours of June 28 I ordered the division G-3 to draw up plans for a counterattack. Our objective was to be nothing less than the recapture of Munsan. The work was done quickly, and in short order the plan had been communicated to the division's units.

At 3:00 A.M. on June 28 I was preparing for a final, decisive confrontation with the enemy, but I knew little about the progress of the war elsewhere. I had no way of knowing that the sole vehicular bridge leading south from Seoul across the Han River had been blown up by friendly forces. I had no way of knowing that ROK Army had withdrawn from Seoul. I had no way of knowing that on this same day enemy forces would stream through Seoul's northeastern suburbs and occupy Korea's capital city itself.

The ROK 1st had been fighting furiously for three days and nights now. We were weary, but we still held our defense line on the morning of June 28. It was noon before we discovered the extent of our isolation. We had sent an ambulance of wounded back to Seoul, but this vehicle now returned with the wounded still aboard. The division G-4 had set out to pick up ammunition at a supply point just west of Seoul, but he also returned, his trucks empty. He got as far as Seoul's northwest outskirts before he heard the gloomy news that the enemy was already in the city, that the Han River's only bridge had been destroyed, that the enemy had freed the convicts in Seoul's West Gate Prison just a few miles farther down the road, and that NKPA vehicles were speeding along the streets of the capital.

I was still reeling in disbelief at this crushing news when my artillery commander reported that we had no more shells for the big guns. His words hit me like machine-gun bullets, draining the strength from my body in a rush. I threw my arms around the major and made no effort to blink back the bitter tears.

Minutes later, I looked up from my headquarters at the primary school and spotted an enemy cavalry unit with about fifty Mongolian ponies working its way through the rugged terrain to our east. NKPA soldiers were riding some of the ponies, while machine guns and mortars were strapped on other horses. They saw us, too. In seconds machine-gun rounds and mortar shells began to strike within the school's perimeter. The enemy had broken through from the east.

We were flanked, and any idea of a counterattack was out of the question. My attack plan disappeared in the smoke of exploding mortar shells before we could execute it. Quickly yelling orders to cancel the counterattack, I joined the division staff in running the few hundred yards that separated our now untenable headquarters from the bank of the Kongnung River. We took cover along the bank at a point where the highway crosses the river over a concrete bridge. At that very moment, a U.S. Air Force aircraft flew over and bombed ROK 1st Division units along our western flank. The American pilot, of course, thought he was bombing the enemy.

The series of shocks had come too fast and too strong for me to handle. I was seized by a strong feeling that I was living out the last moments of my life. I felt like I no longer had control of events, and there wasn't a damn thing I could do about it.

Across the Han by Raft

But I didn't die. I managed to rally enough to call a quick conference to discuss how to react to the flank attack from the NKPA cavalry unit. I summoned the regimental commanders and the staff for what was to be our last meeting north of the Han. The regimental commanders, my chief of staff, the principal division staff officers, and the commanders of other division units all convened at the river.

I remember speaking to them in a rambling manner. I said something like, "You've fought your hearts out for three long days. But this morning Seoul fell to the enemy. The bridge across the Han, the escape valve for Seoul's citizens, is no more. We've seen a U.S. Air Force aircraft, and I assume the Americans have entered the war. The bombing error should have taught us something very clearly, though. The defense of Korea is our job. We must now withdraw to the south and make our way across the Han. And we must preserve as much of the division as we possibly can in the process. Our initial objective is the Infantry School. We will assemble there. If the enemy beats us to the Infantry School, we'll keep going to the Chiri Mountains in South Cholla Province. We'll move into the Chiri, make them our stronghold, and continue to resist as guerrillas. We can survive in the Chiri for two or three years until the situation swings in our favor."

Enemy shells hit the bank of the little river very near our group. We discussed where to cross the Han. We would be withdrawing in broad daylight and would face monumental difficulties. Ten thousand men would have to cross the Han River with the enemy in hot pursuit. I wasn't that conversant with the terrain along the Han and asked my regimental commanders for their views.

The 11th Regiment commander said he thought that a ferry downstream from Kimpo would suffice, while the 15th Regiment's Colonel Choi recommended the ferry at Haengju. Luckily, the two commanders were familiar with the terrain at both locations. I sent the two of them off immediately to reconnoiter the respective ferry sites. I told them to find a place where we could get across the Han and to prepare for a division crossing.

Once the two colonels had departed as the advance elements of the division, a few of the headquarters staff and I struck out for the extreme western reaches of the Han, not far from Inchon. When we got there, I discovered that our advance element had not arrived due to the enemy situation. The Han was very wide at this point, and not a single ferryboat was in sight. About a mile wide, the river was a formidable obstacle.

I immediately turned the jeep and headed upstream to the Haengju ferry. Colonel Choi was already there, busily preparing to cross the river, and about a dozen ferryboats and ferrymen remained at the site. Columns of black smoke poured into the sky from the other side of the river, near Kimpo Airport.

Colonel Choi was an experienced engineer officer and took charge of the river-crossing operation with consummate skill. He put out perime-

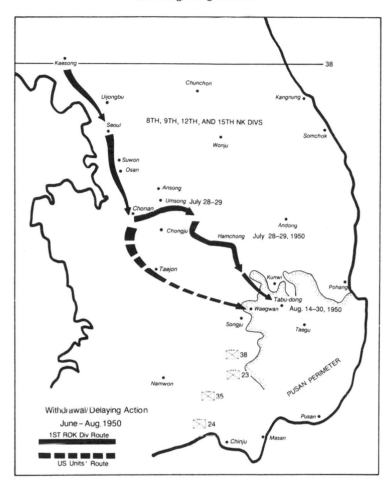

Kaesong

38

Chunchon

Uijongbu

Kangnung

Seoul

8TH, 9TH, 12TH, AND 15TH NK DIVS

Somchok

Wonju

Suwon

Osan

Ansong

Umsong July 28–29

Chonan

Andong

Chongju   Hamchong   July 28–29, 1950

Taejon

Kunwi

Pohang

Tabu-dong

Waegwan   Aug. 14–30, 1950

Songju

Taegu

⊠ 38

⊠ 23

Namwon

⊠ 35

Withdrawal/Delaying Action
June – Aug. 1950

⊠ 24

Pusan

1ST ROK Div Route

Chinju   Masan

US Units' Route

PUSAN PERIMETER

ter guards, tied two ferryboats together, and laid planks across them to make what amounted to a huge raft. The rig was patently incapable of shuttling all the division's withdrawing troops, but we were lucky to have it nonetheless.

The amazing Colonel Choi even found time to surprise us with a meal. I hadn't eaten in three days and was starving, but with thousands of my men facing a trial for their very lives, my Confucian soul wouldn't allow me to presume to enjoy the colonel's chicken. I declined his kind offer.

Our group with its two jeeps was able to cross the Han River safely on the raft, and for that I remain grateful to Colonel Choi to this very day. Yet as we crossed I was in utter despair. I saw no way to rescue the men of the proud ROK 1st Division, scattered as they now were over miles of threatening terrain. Nor could I see any way that a single one of the division's 150 vehicles, artillery pieces, or other heavy equipment would ever get out. So bitter was this medicine that I cried unabashedly, "tears of blood," as we say. I guess you say "bitter tears" in English.

The civilians we encountered on the way, even the ferrymen guiding the craft during the crossing, seemed to stare at me with accusing eyes, making me feel the bitter ignominy of the soldier in retreat. Their faces were expressionless, but I thought I saw resentment and accusations of betrayal in those eyes.

Night was falling as we reached the Han's south bank. We tracked east along the river line, toward Seoul's southern suburbs, and soon heard machine-gun fire from around Kimpo Airport. Black smoke billowing up from Seoul, and the suburbs stood out in bold relief against the pale sky. Somewhere under the smoke were many innocent Seoul citizens, and among their numbers were my own wife and daughter.

The gathering darkness and the near certainty that the road would be impassable obliged us to abandon the jeeps we had worked so hard to bring across. We set out for the Infantry School on foot, walking along the dikes that separated the rice paddies. Forty or fifty officers and men were in the group, including the division provost marshal.

I hadn't eaten since the invasion began, and the march quickly sapped my energy. Within thirty minutes I had trouble maintaining the pace and desperately needed a rest. Yet I knew if I succumbed to fatigue and sat down on a dike, I'd fall asleep till morning. My aide liberated some potable water somewhere in that dark night and brought it to me to quench my parched throat, while the provost marshal took charge of our security and made sure the group maintained a respectable pace. We reached the Infantry School at sunrise on June 29.

As we limped into the Sihung railroad station, I spotted an acquaintance on the platform, 1st Lt. Ray B. May, aide to the chief of KMAG. I was embarrassed to do it, but the first thing I said to him was, "Do you have any sugar, Lieutenant?" To his credit, May found sugar someplace and brought it to us. We mixed it with water and drank it. The syrup immediately revived flagging energy levels and began to restore a sharp edge to our brains.

Lieutenant May told me that the war was going badly, but that the United States was coming into the fight. He suggested that we do whatever we had to do to contain the enemy north of the Han until U.S. ground troops could join the struggle.

I limped over to the Infantry School to find that a new organization, the "Sihung District Combat Headquarters," had taken over the facility. Its commanding general was Maj. Gen. Kim Hong Il, the same gentleman who had visited me two days before at my ROK 1st Division Headquarters. I was escorted into the general's office, where he seemed genuinely glad to see me. He spoke in his usual blunt terms. "Glad to see you made it out," he said, pausing for a moment. "What's the status of your division?"

I briefed the general on all that had transpired since his visit, adding, "Our advance element has only just arrived. I'm afraid it will be some time before we can gather up a significant number of our men and reorganize the division."

General Kim told me the situation around Kimpo could go either way and asked if I could get up there. I had no men, and it would do no good to say I could do something I could not. Trying to put some steel into my tired voice, I answered, "I'll use every means to reorganize the division, but please give the Kimpo mission to someone else." Luckily, an understanding General Kim agreed.

The Sihung District Combat Headquarters had command authority over all ROK forces remaining in the vicinity of Seoul, since the command structure in the city itself had collapsed. The headquarters scooped up withdrawing officers and men and organized them into companies and battalions, which it committed to a defense line running along the south bank of the Han River. The mission was to delay the moment when the NKPA juggernaut would bull across the Han.

Thanks to the kindness of General Kim, I had a few hours to put my exhausted body and mind back together and a few more to rebuild my division. Here in Sihung I finally was able to change into combat fatigues. I still wore the dress uniform I put on before leaving home on the morning of June 25, although my khakis were now filthy with dirt and sweat, and I was still wearing my dress hat. I changed into the olive green combat fatigues with immense relief.

Changing uniforms seemed to symbolize the end of the Imjin River fighting, the first phase of my war. Whatever the reasons, whatever the means, the fact was that I had been defeated. The ROK 1st Division and the units that reinforced it had melded together harmoniously and delivered an excellent account of themselves. Our soldiers were devotedly patriotic, with a keen sense of responsibility, and did not hesitate to sacrifice their lives in their country's darkest hour. They trusted me and followed my commands to the letter.

For my part, I found that I had put every ounce of my being into the task, that I too had fought tenaciously, and that I had shown more patience than I would ever have imagined. Despite my youth and inexperience, I felt I had approached my command responsibilities as resourcefully as I could. On the other hand, I had a number of lessons to learn. I had not paid enough attention to the overall war situation, had not withdrawn at the appropriate time, and had failed to command the front and rear areas as an integrated whole.

Looking back on the early stages of the invasion of the Republic of Korea from the vantage point of decades, I believe two locations were key to the military situation, the Uijongbu area defended by the ROK 7th Division and the Munsan area defended by my ROK 1st Division. The enemy launched its main attack at those areas with the objective of driving through them to reach Seoul. For that reason, the NKPA massed its armored brigade's tanks at these two points.

The ROK Army's antitank weapons were not completely ineffectual against enemy armor. Although our guns could not destroy a T-34, when used carefully they could slow a tank's advance. And when used skillfully our artillery could destroy the NKPA's tanks. The ROK 1st Division destroyed eleven enemy T-34s in our war at the Imjin. Unfortunately, however, most army commanders and their men did not realize that we could be relatively effective against armor. A tank itself is not frightening, but ignorance about a tank can terrorize soldiers. This lesson applied to the military situation today as well. New weapons appear daily, it seems, but when a soldier understands the actual workings of these new weapons, that soldier can devise a way to defeat them.

A debate has flared for years over the question of whether the army possessed an operations plan for the kind of contingency we faced in June 1950. I remember clearly that we did have such a plan. In March 1950 when I commanded the ROK 5th Division, my chief of staff was summoned to ROK Army in Seoul where he was given a defense plan to bring back to the division. That document contained plans to counter a North Korean invasion of the Republic of Korea. The plan assumed that the enemy's main attack would be directed through Uijongbu, and it called for containment of the enemy at the 38th parallel. The plan said nothing about operations south of the Han River.

After I was assigned to command the ROK 1st Division, I developed a new plan, as I have mentioned, in which I established main lines of resistance behind the Imjin River and behind the Pongil Stream. I asked the division G-3 why riverline defense tactics had not been included in the original division plans, in view of their inherent advantage to the defense. Major Kim said he had not had sufficient clout to make such a change, that higher headquarters had not directed that such a change be made, and that simple inertia had also played a role.

The morale of the officers and men of the many broken units who flooded into Sihung hovered at rock bottom. The war situation wasn't pessimistic; it was hopeless. A single rumor, however, completely reversed everybody's spirits. The word was that five-star Gen. Douglas MacArthur himself was to tour the front. At that time General MacArthur was regarded by Korean soldiers and civilians alike as almost a god. He was the hero of World War II and had accepted the surrender of the emperor of Japan. People today can't imagine the extent of his prestige.

As word passed from mouth to mouth that MacArthur had indeed personally inspected the Han River defense line, the morale of the soldiers soared. MacArthur's visit seemed to be the sole subject of every conversation and seemed to add a little steel to the spines of Gen. Kim Hong Il's forces, who stubbornly held the Han River defense line against growing enemy pressure.

We had been told that the Americans hoped we could hold at the Han for at least three days to allow them time to deploy U.S. ground forces from Japan to the front in Korea. In fact, General Kim was able to hold the enemy there for six full days.

During the war, the Republic of Korea faced imminent collapse a number of times. One of the things that saved the nation was the dogged defense of the army at the Han River. Had the Han fallen earlier, the United States would have missed the opportunity to commit its initial ground forces and combat equipment, and the enemy's subsequent drive southward might not have allowed the Americans another opportunity. General Kim's stubborn defense at the Han provided time to both the ROK and U.S. armies to organize, to deploy and realign units, and to prepare themselves psychologically for war.

General Kim's Sihung District Combat Headquarters was very soon to serve as the parent of ROK I Corps, which Kim was to command in a delaying action all the way south to Taegu's Naktong River. General Kim had served as a senior officer in the Chinese Army during World War II and had more experience at commanding large combat formations than any other Korean officer. He served as commandant of the Command and General Staff School after the ROK Army was founded in 1948 and proved to have a very firm grasp on the principles of the delaying action. In view of General Kim's familiarity with higher military tactics, his assumption of command both of the Han River defense line and the subsequent delaying action was immensely fortuitous for Korea.

I got down to the business of rebuilding my division the next day, June 30. First I traveled the seven miles to the Han River to assess the situation there. A violent artillery duel bellowed in full fury across the wide waterway. Somewhere on the south bank I ran into the commander of the ROK Army's armor regiment, who held overall command of the tactical battle. The regiment was firing its halftrack-mounted 37mm cannon across the Han River. Although it had no tanks, the regiment was equipped with fifty lightly armored vehicles and two hundred horses and was the premier maneuver unit in the army at the time. Like everyone else, the commander told me he was inspired by MacArthur's visit and by word that the U.S. Army was to be committed to ground combat in Korea.

"Could you see your way clear," I asked the good colonel hesitantly, "to let me have one of your jeeps?"

"Sure," he said without hesitating a moment. "Take that one." He was a most willing and cooperative soldier to provide me with the vehicle. I encountered his brand of kindness only rarely in the treacherous environment of war. Mobile at last, I drove all over the area between Sihung and Suwon, new home of ROK Army, finding ROK 1st Division officers as I went and putting them to work rounding up our scattered soldiers. This work was greatly helped along by a center for stragglers operated by the military police, who ushered any combat-capable soldier from any unit to this central facility.

During my trips through the area, I found my eyes smarting with tears a number of times at the sight of ROK 1st Division troopers who had managed not only the hellish task of withdrawing as individuals but had also managed to trek those arduous miles with heavy mortars or machine guns still on their shoulders. Some had changed into civilian clothes at some point during the withdrawal and made their way out of the NKPA's trap wearing civilian clothes and *komu-sin*, the ubiquitous rubber shoes worn by civilians at the time.

I stopped by ROK Army at its new home in a primary school in Suwon and had a talk with the Deputy Chief of Staff for operations Col. Kim Paik Il. The army's top operations officer, he was working at a chalkboard labeled "Army Reorganization Plan." Kim was planning how to build new units from forces that had been smashed north of the Han. I saw my chance.

"If it's possible," I asked, "how about combining the ROK 5th Division with my ROK 1st?" The ROK 5th Division held a warm place in my heart because I had commanded it from July 1949 until I had been assigned to the ROK 1st Division a few weeks before the war broke out. Kim agreed readily.

Colonel Kim was a native of North Hamgyong Province in North Korea and was senior to me. He and I fled Pyongyang, the North Korean capital, together in 1945 to start a new life in the South. When the war broke out, he was deputy chief of staff for operations, filling in for Brig. Gen. Chung Il Kwon, who was in the United States. Kim later commanded ROK I Corps on the eastern front and took his unit into Hamgyong Province—his own home area—when the army advanced across the 38th parallel into North Korea. Kim compiled a brilliant combat record before he was killed in an air crash in March 1951.

2

RETREAT TO THE NAKTONG: 200 MILES OF HELL

Delaying Actions

As June turned to July in 1950, the NKPA pressure on the Han River defense line built to a crescendo. Weakened by the loss of manpower and equipment from main-force units, ROK Army reached the limits of its ability to resist. NKPA units in Seoul mounted a fierce attack to seize control of the railroad bridge across the Han River that friendly air raids had failed to destroy. Meanwhile, enemy forces cut off near Chunchon by the ROK 6th Division under Col. Kim Chong O finally broke free and advanced southwest to capture the city of Suwon. As the situation deteriorated, the ROK 1st Division received its first combat order since withdrawing south of the Han.

Our mission was to march northeast of Suwon and delay the enemy at a small river. We were the ROK 1st Division, all right, but in name only. I had been able to assemble only about two thousand of our original ten thousand personnel, so we went into battle at less than regimental strength. We took up defensive positions in a valley near the site of what is today the Suwon Country Club.

Shortly after we deployed across the valley, ROK Army attached about one hundred additional men to the division. I say "attached" because strictly speaking they were not replacements. All the men had been cadets attending the Korea Military Academy, Korea's West Point, as members of Class 10 when the war erupted. The cadets had participated in an earlier battle and had withdrawn across the river on a ferry. The psychological shock of Seoul's capture and the series of defeats in-

23

flicted on ROK Army had reduced these cadets-turned-infantrymen to a fiery state of resentment and anger. They let me know in no uncertain terms that they were done running. "This valley," they told me, "is where we die."

I had no sooner assigned these young cadets to the line, however, when I received a message from ROK Army. "In present circumstances, every officer we have is crucial to the cause," read the message. "Please evacuate the academy cadets to Taejon, where they will be commissioned and used as line-officer replacements." I had to summon every ounce of persuasive power at my command to convince these young men who had committed themselves so intently to battle to let me send them on to Taejon.

I set an ambush for the NKPA, deploying my unit across the valley in the shape of a V, with the open end of the formation facing north, toward the enemy. I had learned this tactic while fighting communist guerrillas in the Chiri Mountains before the war. An enemy unit appeared and marched right into the trap. I waited until they were completely inside the V before I gave the command to fire. The unit was annihilated before it had time to fire a single shot. It was a small victory, but it helped to settle accounts for the defeat we suffered at the Imjin.

The main body of the army was still located north of Suwon at this time, so our victory contributed to the army's withdrawal. Unfortunately, however, a U.S. Air Force aircraft once again bombed us in error, killing several of my men and wounding one of my regimental commanders, who had to be evacuated.

The same day ROK Army Headquarters withdrew from Suwon to Taejon, my 1st Division marched through Pyongtaek, bound for points south. Late that afternoon we encountered a group of U.S. soldiers preparing artillery positions on a road outside Osan. The Americans told us they were part of Task Force Smith (named for its commander, Lt. Col. Charles Smith) from the U.S. 24th Division stationed in Japan. I had mixed feelings as we marched past the Americans. On the one hand, I was finally convinced the Americans were going to join us in the war. But I also envied their guns, for Task Force Smith was equipped with the new M-2 105mm towed howitzers. Still, I had seen with my own eyes that the United States had not left Korea to its own devices. I learned later that the 17th Regiment under my brother, who had somehow fought his way out of his peninsular death trap in the first days of the war, accompanied Task Force Smith in its advance.

The bulk of the ROK 1st Division boarded a train at Pyongtaek and arrived without incident at Chochiwon. I chose to travel by jeep and encountered Col. Kim Paik Il on the way. We were deeply involved in a discussion of tactics while ignoring basic battlefield caution when a Yak fighter appeared out of nowhere and made a strafing run at us, catching us in the open. Grand tacticians that we were, we managed to escape death by the narrowest of margins by employing the simplest of tactics. We dived ignominiously behind a tree. Once the division commander was safely in Chochiwon with his troops, we were assigned to the newly established I Corps, commanded by Maj. Gen. Kim Hong Il.

Based on lessons learned in the early days of the invasion, ROK Army keenly felt the need for intermediate units between itself and the divisions. Senior army leaders created ROK I Corps from the ROK 1st, ROK 2d, and ROK Capital divisions, reducing ROK Army's overextended span of control.

General Kim called me in right away. "Maj. Gen. William Dean, the commander of the U.S. 24th Division dispatched on an emergency basis from Japan," he said, "has deployed a battalion each in Pyongtaek and Ansong, but I'm not satisfied that will get the job done." General Kim then ordered me to march the ROK 1st Division northwest to Umsong and establish a defense line there.

This move resulted in a de facto division of areas of responsibility between the ROK and U.S. armies. The U.S. Army, the 24th Division in this early case, assumed responsibility for the area around the Seoul-Pusan Highway, on the western margin of the peninsula, while the ROK Army took responsibility for the central and eastern fronts. With this partition arranged, we began a war of delay. The ROK Army lacked the forces necessary to counterattack, so all we could do was buy time. We were limited to mounting a strike here and a strike there in an effort to weaken and tire the enemy while awaiting reinforcements from the United States and the United Nations.

The ROK 1st Division's long march had begun.

The division began the withdrawal with about two thousand of its original complement. As we slogged south, we faintly heard the sound of enemy and friendly artillery firing from Chinchon directly to our north, in a sector where the ROK Capital Division had taken up blocking positions. When I heard the artillery, my first thought was, "Hey, it sounds like the ROK Army's getting itself back together." But then I remembered the situation in my own division, where many of the men didn't even have uniforms to wear, and the gloom descended again.

When we reached Chungpyong, we found that the ROK 6th Division had arrived before us, set up a headquarters, and was ready for business. Division commander Col. Kim Chong O and his division G-2 were full of pep and raring to go. Kim's G-2 had served with me when I was assistant chief of staff, G-2, ROK Army. "We hit the NKPA hard at Chunchon and again at Umsong," he told me, "and the men's morale is sky high." Not only had the ROK 6th Division managed to hold on to its trucks, but it also had requisitioned some Japanese-made trucks from a mining company, adding significantly to the division's mobility. Moreover, the ROK 6th had preserved its artillery battalion intact, keeping its combat capability high.

I conducted an inspection of the ROK 1st Division while we were at Chungpyong and discovered that our numbers had increased to about five thousand. We have more than doubled in size during the withdrawal. This unusual circumstance resulted partly from the added strength we picked up from the ROK 5th Division and partly from the inimitable Korean private soldiers, who were not content with the arduous withdrawal over the Han River but continued trekking southward until they found their mother unit.

On July 8, the ROK 1st Division was ordered to cross White Horse Pass and replace the ROK 6th Division's 7th Regiment at Umsong. The 7th was fresh from a decisive victory at the Battle of Tongnak-ri, and its commander fairly brimmed with self-confidence.

"As you can no doubt see for yourself, Colonel," I began to lay out for him my own situation frankly, "my men are exhausted. Our artillery is gone, and we have no heavy weapons. If we replace your regiment in our fragile condition, I think we'll actually weaken the line. Could you lend us a hand until we're ready?" The regimental commander said he'd be pleased to help all he could.

The 7th Regiment stood shoulder to shoulder with the ROK 1st Division in the actions that followed. Its artillery provided protective fire to our front, while its infantry combined with ours to mount determined joint attacks against the enemy. We held our positions until ordered to continue the withdrawal.

The ROK 1st Division withdrew from Umsong on order and passed through several towns before arriving at the foothills southwest of Mount Songni, in North Kyongsang Province. We had marched over a rugged pass in driving rain to get to our new headquarters, and after we arrived we found that the 17th Regiment, which had defended the Ongjin Peninsula at the 38th parallel, was also bivouacked nearby.

A few days before and a few miles to the north, the 17th Regiment had ambushed the NKPA 15th Division under the command of Park Song Chol. The NKPA 15th had bypassed ROK Army units and succeeded in getting ahead of the bulk of our withdrawing army, a most dangerous turn of affairs, but the 15th had then run into a trap set by the 17th Regiment. The ambush had been so successful that the three thousand officers and men of the 17th were rewarded with a special, across-the-board promotion. The regiment also had been refitted with new uniforms and equipment so that the outfit looked every bit as well equipped as a U.S. Army unit.

The 17th was mentally tough. Every man in the regiment had written out and signed on oath. "Even if Korea falls," it went, "we will resist to the death as guerrillas." As a symbol of their intent, all the soldiers in the regiment had shaved their heads bald.

At this bivouac, we joined the 24th Regiment of the U.S. 25th Division and, for the first time, conducted combined operations with American ground forces. I was well acquainted with the commander of the 24th,

Col. Horton White, and exchanged warm greetings with him when we met. White had come to Korea at the end of World War II, serving as deputy assistant chief of staff, G-2, XXIV Corps, which was stationed in Korea on occupation duty. Since I was deputy chief of staff, G-2, at Korean Constabulary Headquarters at the time, I had frequent, official contact with Colonel White. The constabulary was the forerunner of the Republic of Korea Army. Our friendship deepened partly because we shared last names; his was "White," while the Chinese character for my last name also means "White."

Apart from its commander and a few others, the U.S. 24th Regiment was composed completely of black soldiers and had a long tradition in the U.S. Army as the "black regiment." The regiment's artillery included towed 155mm howitzers, and when my regimental commander, Col. Choi Young Hi, got a look at these huge weapons, he came running breathlessly up to me. "Hey!" he shouted. "I've never seen anything like those monster guns they've got over there." We both went over to get a closer look.

Colonel White gave me a batch of 1:50,000 maps, acetate overlays, and grease pencils, and I made my staff ecstatic for a while with these items, so indispensable were they to operational planning. The division staff had been making do with a "Complete Map of the Republic of Korea" they had found hanging in a classroom of a primary school somewhere along the way.

My ROK 1st Division and the 17th Regiment conducted a combined operation with the U.S. 24th Regiment, ambushing the NKPA 15th Division as it advanced through Kallyong Pass on July 23, 1950, inflicting serious losses on the enemy.

ROK I Corps's commanding general, Kim Hong Il, directed the ROK 1st Division to transfer our operational area to the U.S. 24th Regiment on July 25, to assemble in Sangju for a period of reorganization, and then march on to Hamchang.

The U.S. 24th was due to replace us early in the morning, but still hadn't made an appearance when night fell on July 25. We occupied positions in hills flanking the road that led from Kallyong Pass, and it required a serious effort to climb to our lines. We believed the American regiment simply needed a long time to make the climb. Colonel White arrived before the main body of his unit, and I drew the impression that he was having trouble getting his subordinates to follow orders. "Korea has so damn many mountains," Colonel White, who was in his fifties, told me. "Its really rough on an old man like me." Obviously distressed, he added, "War's a game for the young."

The tardy arrival of the U.S. 24th made us more than a day late getting under way. General Kim called, and he was fuming. "What the hell's holding you guys up?" He demanded that we get on the march immediately.

When we arrived at Sangju on the morning of July 26, still behind schedule, I found Youth Defense Corps troops and the 20th Regiment waiting for us. These forces were assigned permanently to the ROK 1st Division, raising our strength to about seven thousand soldiers. The 17th Artillery Battalion also was assigned to the division, and an M-1 rifle or carbine was provided to every man in the division who did not have an individual weapon. The ROK 1st finally looked like a real infantry division again, if a rather light and malnourished one. I had hoped for some rest for the division in conjunction with these changes, but we were immediately deployed along the Yong River, a tributary of the Naktong, and given the mission of defending against NKPA units advancing near Hamchang.

We began to suffer a steady stream of casualties at this location, and morale dropped. Spirits soared again, however, when the U.S. Air Force for the first time provided impeccable, by-the-book air support and when our new 105mm howitzers furnished excellent fire support. I lost two battalion commanders in the desperate fighting around Hamchang, but the enemy failed to dislodge us. We held the line until directed to take up new positions along the ROK Army's Naktong River defense line.

On July 27, Minister of Defense Shin Sung Mo and the new ROK Army chief of staff, Maj. Gen. Chung Il Kwon, stopped by unannounced at my headquarters in a post office. I puffed out my chest and confidently ran through the quick briefing I thought they came for, ending with the words, "Gentlemen, the division has been reinforced and reequipped. We can lick anybody now."

I was shocked by the response. "Congratulations, General Paik, on your promotion!" The emphasis was on the word "General." They shook my hand and pinned the single star of a brigadier general on the collar of my combat fatigues. Korea's top military men also informed me that the ROK 1st Division was being transferred to the newly created ROK II Corps under Brig. Gen. Yu Jae Hung.

As a soldier, I was undeniably pleased to be promoted to flag rank, but the war made it impossible to see more than an inch into the future, so I regarded the promotion as an additional burden to carry.

No Place to Run

I stood at last on the bank of the Naktong River. I had fought north of Seoul, withdrawn across the Han, fallen back two hundred miles in a tortuous version of the long march, and at last reached the Naktong. There was no more room to withdraw.

The front started at the southern tip of the Korean peninsula, near Pusan, and went almost straight north, passing Taegu before it turned northeast at Hamchang. The ROK Army was responsible for the fifty-five miles of front on the northern boundary of the Pusan Perimeter, and the U.S. Army was responsible for the seventy-five-mile western

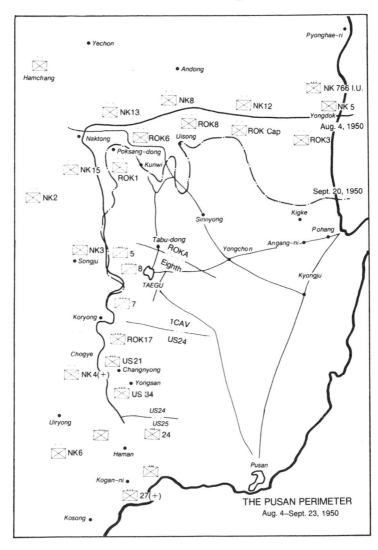

THE PUSAN PERIMETER
Aug. 4–Sept. 23, 1950

flank. The Pusan Perimeter was bounded on the south and east by ocean. Lt. Gen. Walton H. Walker was overall front commander, having been appointed commander of the Eighth U.S. Army on July 8, 1950, and having been granted operational control of Republic of Korea forces.

I remember the month we spent in the protracted withdrawal to the

Pusan Perimeter as the most painful period of the entire war. Paradoxically, the withdrawal was the most deeply meaningful experience of the war for me as well. We never knew the next day's destination, yet we plodded on, leading exhausted men in an endless march. The withdrawal was day after endless day of painful, continuous foot sloughing, interrupted only by the four battles we fought along the way. Yet to me the withdrawal was not sheer monotony but rather perpetual stress and fear, for I knew that the enemy was always nearby, always ready to strike.

Division operations were vastly complicated by the need to accomplish everything while on the move. We started greatly understrength and bereft of heavy weapons and equipment and were obliged to reorganize, replenish, and even rearm while keeping ahead of a pursuing enemy and riding herd on soldiers whose exhaustion caused them to spread out over great distances. In what I regard as one of the minor miracles of the war, some four or five thousand of the men we lost crossing the Han rejoined the division during our withdrawal to the Naktong. I don't know how they found us, but men who were mere stragglers somehow ran down the division and rejoined their original units.

I am more positive with each passing day that these returnees were the reason we were able to counterattack the enemy successfully, reversing the tide of war. I'm not sure we could have done so had our formations not benefited from these toughened troopers, with their store of combat experience and the physical and psychological rewards of succeeding at a two-hundred-mile withdrawal on foot over rough terrain in the terrible heat and humidity of a Korean summer.

We elevated the delaying action to the delaying campaign. By the time the campaign ended, a solid month after it began, our soldiers had gained much. They understood the nature of war. They had learned patience, and they had honed their patriotism and fighting spirit. Our soldiers learned to sleep anyplace, seemingly oblivious to the voracious clouds of summer mosquitoes. They learned to eat anything with their rice ration, picking unripe hot peppers or anything green growing along the roadway to eat as the side dishes indispensable to a rice-centered diet. Their uniforms fell to tatters; their feet swelled with blisters. But nobody complained, and no one collapsed. During the withdrawal I saw for myself that the Korean aphorism "No one stops by the pharmacy when the situation is desperate" is based on an insightful grasp of human nature.

As for myself, it was far beyond the capabilities of one individual to command an entire division in a protracted foot withdrawal. It was all I could do to be sure my direct subordinates executed their responsibilities. Of course, we strictly observed the orders coming from ROK Army, but I found it impossible to command scattered men constantly on the move by simply issuing an order. No commander can control men who

are not in his sight. As division commander, I personally had to preserve the division's lattice of command by controlling the regimental
and battalion commanders and the division staff officers.

I can't deny that in our situation more times than not the ROK Army
found itself approving the orders given by a subordinate commander
who was actually doing the job rather than specifying the orders a subordinate commander should give. I think it accurate to say that in those
weeks an ROK Army division commander played a role similar to the
independent generals who typified ancient China's era of Warring
States (450–222 B.C.).

Brig. Gen. Kim Suk Won, who served in the Japanese Army and retired from the ROK Army before the war broke out, was recalled to
active duty in early July 1950 and given command of the Capital Division. Officers and men throughout the army tried to win assignments
to his division because of his renown as a soldier.

Among my own subordinates, both my G-3 and the commander of
my 11th Regiment petitioned to transfer to the Capital Division. I could
have denied their requests, but in view of the difficult nature of war, I
felt I owed them the courtesy of allowing them to fight beside a respected senior officer.

Lt. Col. Mun Hyong Tae, 5th Division G-3, was extremely close to
General Kim. "What's it like soldiering with me?" I asked him one day,
trying to determine which way he was leaning. It turned out that Mun
wanted to stay with me in the ROK 1st Division. "If you don't mind,
General Paik," he responded, "I'd like to fight with the 1st. So long as
the Americans are in this war, I want to fight with a man who can conduct combined operations with them." As it turned out, Mun was fore-
telling the future face of the Korean War.

During our long withdrawal, the ROK Army had almost no mode of
communications except long-distance telephone lines, which surprised
everyone by remaining intact. Long-distance trunks had been installed
only at post offices before the war, so ROK Army units favored post
offices as field command posts.

A major frustration for me during the withdrawal was realizing that
the men of the ROK 1st and 5th divisions would never fuse. The officers
and men of the two units congealed into groups reflecting the original
units to which they had belonged. Like water and oil, they didn't mix.
War removes the promise of tomorrow from men's lives, dictating a
stark rule that both individuals and groups become singularly egocen-
tric.

The ROK 1st Division had occupied defensive positions around Hamchang when we received orders to deploy directly into the Naktong
River line. On August 1, 1950, we crossed the Naktong and took up
defensive positions behind the waterway. With the Naktong River to
our front, our right flank abutted the village Nakjong on the north, and

our left flank extended to Waegwan on the south. We moved into this line to support Eighth Army Commander General Walker's notion that we could not let the enemy continue to shove us back, that we must hold firm on the Naktong line, and that we might change the nature of the war by going over to the offensive.

Three U.S. Army divisions—the 1st Cavalry, the 24th, and the 25th—held the Naktong line from Waegwan almost directly south to Masan at the southern tip of the peninsula. Our division tied in with the Americans where the line made a ninety-degree turn near Nakjong, and headed almost due east to the Sea of Japan. The front in the rough, mountainous, eastern leg of the line was held by ROK Army divisions—the 6th, 8th, Capital, and 3d.

Unlike other Korean units, my 1st Division enjoyed the advantage of defending behind a waterway, the Naktong, but we had been saddled with a lengthy, twenty-five-mile front, putting us at a distinct disadvantage from the start. The ROK 1st had been assigned the wide sector as the adjacent U.S. 25th Division had been pulled out on an emergency basis to help stem an attack on Mason. The NKPA had streamed west of the Pusan Perimeter through the Cholla provinces, turned east, and after capturing Chinju, had attacked Masan, literally on Pusan's doorstep. When the 25th pulled out, my division had been assigned responsibility for its sector of the line, stretching division assets dangerously thin.

We had encountered difficulties while crossing the river at Nakjong, getting entangled with a flood of refugees and sorting things out only with the invaluable aid of ferrymen and local residents. Once we settled into our sector of the defense line, the U.S. 1st Cavalry Division under Maj. Gen. Hobart Gay was situated on our left flank, and the ROK 6th Division commanded by Col. Kim Chong O was on our right.

We had no sooner taken up our sector than NKPA units, pursuing us doggedly, appeared and began preparing to cross the Naktong in several places. The ROK 1st Division's seven thousand men were arrayed paper thin along our sector, and I foresaw a desperate battle in the offing as we faced a confident, victorious enemy three times our size and boasting ten times our firepower. We could hold the line in the daytime when U.S. air support was available, but we were vulnerable at night.

The North Koreans' objective was to end the war—the "War of Liberation" they called it—by August 15, the anniversary of the end of World War II and a day celebrated in both North and South Korea as "Liberation Day" to commemorate independence from the last Japanese occupation. The North Koreans took the objective of whipping us by Liberation Day most seriously, mounting a furious offensive to achieve that end.

NKPA units discovered shallow stretches in the Naktong, massed their troops, and attempted to bull their way across the Naktong using human-wave tactics. We responded with massed fire and annihilated the leading men in the assault groups, their bodies piling up on the white sandy flats along the river, which literally ran red with their blood. But the NKPA's political watchdog units literally beat the survivors, driving them back into the river and back to the attack.

The bulk of the NKPA assault units was composed of so-called Volunteer Army troops that the North Koreans had dragooned for service in the Seoul area. Knowing these men to be fellow South Koreans, our soldiers found it intensely painful to cut them down on such a scale.

On August 4, NKPA units managed to cross the Naktong and began to open cracks in the ROK 1st Division's Naktong River defense line. Freed by the cover of darkness from the danger of U.S. air attack, the North Koreans built up the river bottom at shallow points with sandbags and oil drums, building what amounted to underwater bridges. On August 8, they sent their T-34s across the river on these bridges.

Meanwhile, the job of defense was complicated in the extreme by immense numbers of refugees crossing the Naktong in endless columns. During the day my units had to protect the refugees crossing the river, and at night we had to beat back attacks, mounted by the NKPA under the cover of darkness and at unpredictable locations. We knew we were not to withdraw from these positions, but our situation deteriorated by the hour.

Around the end of the first week of August, the ROK 1st Division began to receive a new antitank weapon, the 3.5-inch rocket launcher, or bazooka. The Americans provided the bazookas with an injunction. "We request that the 3.5-inch rocket launchers be supervised directly by the division commander, since in no case must these weapons be allowed to fall into enemy hands." Each regiment received two or three launchers, and after undergoing very abbreviated training in their use, we threw them into the battle. Each regiment formed special tank-hunter teams armed with the bazookas, and we went T-34 hunting with a vengeance. Some teams even crossed the Naktong and infiltrated into the NKPA unit areas in search of prey.

The 3.5-inch rockets penetrated the armor of the Soviet T-34. The 12th Regiment was the first to use the launchers successfully, destroying three tanks and capturing another, which was later put on display in Taegu. The division destroyed about ten enemy tanks on this line.

Confidence and morale soared, my troops vying with each other to win a place on the special tank-hunter teams. It was here along the Naktong while employing our new antitank weapons that the ROK 1st Division learned that a tank without accompanying infantry is vulnerable. It was here, too, that the troops recovered from the "T-34 disease" that gripped them when they heard the terrible sound of approaching tanks.

Word spread that the army had destroyed a number of enemy tanks. Colonel Naya—an Indian representative to the United Nations Commission on Korea—and two British journalists, Ian Morrison of the *London Times* and Christopher Berkeley of the *Daily Telegraph*, boarded a three-quarter-ton truck and set out for our sector to verify the kills and write articles about them. Most unfortunately, they all lost their lives when their truck hit an antitank mine. Foreign journalists had begun to arrive around the first of August. Retired American Gen. Carl Spaatz visited ROK 1st Division headquarters as a correspondent for *Newsweek* during the first week of the month. Spaatz had commanded U.S. Air Forces in Europe during World War II.

As the first days of August passed, reinforcements and supply of all types of equipment and material smoothed out dramatically. Our new recruits, however, were grossly undertrained. None of them, for example, had fired more than ten rounds of ammunition during individual weapons training. This visited a substantial burden on frontline commanders who had to meld the untrained men into fighting units.

I was worried about Hill 303 near the railway bridge in Waegwan, where the ROK 1st Division tied into the Americans. I visited this area and held discussions on how to improve cooperation with two representatives of the U.S. 1st Cavalry Division, Col. William Rodgers and Lt. Col. Harold Johnson, who commanded the battalion in the area. Johnson was G-3 of U.S. I Corps when that unit advanced into North Korea from the Chongchon River and served as U.S. Army chief of staff during the Vietnamese War years.

We decided to cover a vulnerable approach to Hill 303 by swapping the positions of a U.S. platoon with those of a platoon from my 13th Regiment, including telephone lines and the artillery fire grids that went with each. This was the first time this had been attempted in the war, and it resulted in some confusion and perplexity among our troops, as indeed we had anticipated, because of the language barrier. We watched with interest as the men of the two different cultures used hand gestures—and even foot gestures—to make the swap, but they accomplished the task in short order, and we were able to relax.

I set up my command post at Osang Middle and High School along the highway that runs into Taegu. I had to select a "final containment line" for the division in this area. Eighth Army Commander General Walker had established the first defense line at the Naktong and called it "Line X." The final defense line was to be "Line Y." Line Y stretched south from Waegwan along the Naktong and curved east from Waegwan to the east coast, including within its boundaries the great cities of Pusan and Taegu. This was the final line. We would withdraw no farther. We would fight here as if the sea were at our backs, for indeed it was.

Bloody Fighting at the Naktong

I went looking for terrain that would support the defensive concept behind Line Y and provide the ROK 1st Division an edge in the looming fight. We did not have detailed 1:50,000 military maps of the area, so I had to rely on hanging wall maps, which did not provide enough detail for a commander to recognize terrain features in the field. In a reconnaissance of the area, however, Kasan Castle and Tabu-dong caught my eye. Kasan was a ridge extending westward from Palgong-san. The ridge served as a defense line twice during the sixteenth-century Japanese invasions under Hideyoshi, and ruins of an ancient fortress familiar to all Koreans still stood on the ridge.

I located terrain very advantageous to the defense north of the hamlet of Tabu-dong, where a long ridge juts northwest along a line of hills. The site was only sixteen miles from Taegu, and the mountains in this range gave way to the valley that is home to Taegu itself. The ROK 1st Division would rise to victory or sink to defeat in these ridges.

After I completed my reconnaissance, I called in division chief of staff Suk Ju Am and division G-3 Mun Hyong Tae.

"Up till now," I told them, "you two have selected the terrain we were to defend. You've done a good job, but this time I'd like to choose the ground myself. We'll fight to the last from the new line. Reconnoiter the terrain between Kasan and Tabu-dong and draw up a plan to defend that chunk of real estate." They looked surprised but said they'd go take a look right away.

The two returned several hours later and said they agreed that the area was the best possible location for a divisional defense line. I called in my subordinate commanders and explained that this was to be our final line of containment. I gave them the following counsel.

"This will be our final defense line. If we can't hold this line, Taegu will fall. If that happens, the U.S. Army defense line along the Naktong will collapse. That means the fate of the nation itself rests squarely on the back of the ROK 1st Division, squarely on this line. I chose this line personally and will take full responsibility for failure. I hope and pray that we will be victorious and share in the honor and happiness of victory." On August 12, 1950, the ROK 1st Division moved into positions on Line Y, our final defense line.

At this critical juncture of the war, I was in some distress from malaria, which I had contracted during the summer. The chills and fever struck me as if they were conspiring with the deteriorating war situation to make it difficult for me to control either mind or body. Headmaster Kim Dong Sok, founder of Osang Middle School, and his family helped out around division headquarters. His son Kim Yoon Whan, a future National Assembly floor leader, brought me rice gruel and nursed me back to health as I lay sick in his father's living room.

I suffered severe attacks of malaria on three occasions during the war, in early August 1950, in October 1950 when we advanced on Pyongyang, and in May 1951 during fighting along the east coast. Even now I have lumps as big as chestnuts under my skin from taking quinine injections.

I think there were two reasons the relatively small number of men in the ROK 1st Division were able to defend our very broad front at the Naktong River line. First, each regiment employed its reserve unit to mount immediate counterattacks to take and hold the high ground around enemy penetrations. Second, we enjoyed efficient air support, courtesy of the U.S. Air Force. Once we requested air support, U.S. fighter-bombers took off from Japan's Itazuke Air Force Base and arrived in the airspace over the division within thirty minutes. The aircraft executed ground-support missions, bombing and strafing enemy positions, for up to two hours before returning to their bases.

American air superiority forced the NKPA to hide its tanks, artillery, and main-force units in the apple orchards that seemed to be everywhere in the Taegu area, coming out to attack only in bad weather and at night. I assigned Lt. Nam Sung In, assistant operations officer, G-3, to interpret for the U.S. air-ground liaison officer, and he labored around the clock, gathering reports of enemy movements from division observers along the forward edge of the battle area and translating them into English before conveying them to a U.S. Air Force officer.

As the staff prepared yet again to move division headquarters, this time from Osang Middle School to a primary school halfway between Tabu-dong and Taegu, I noticed that Lieutenant Nam had disappeared. I went looking for him, but no one knew where he was. Almost by accident I opened the door to one of the classrooms and found him so soundly asleep on the wooden floor that he might as well have been unconscious. I managed to shake him awake and made sure that he accompanied us to our new headquarters, but we almost left him behind. The lieutenant had collapsed from fatigue after working three straight days and nights. But he had plenty of work still to do; our new division front extended twelve miles, way too much for the mountainous terrain.

The NKPA's main-force 3d Division commanded by Maj. Gen. Lee Yong Ho had charged along for weeks now with unstoppable momentum, piercing like an awl through leather down the main north-south highway leading from Seoul to Pusan. The NKPA 3d had knocked aside the defensive efforts of the U.S. 24th Division as it went, starting with the decimation of Task Force Smith. Now this division was supported by the NKPA 15th Division under Maj. Gen. Park Song Chol and the NKPA 13th Division under Maj. Gen. Choi Yong Chin. The three enemy divisions together had sufficient strength to gobble up Taegu and do it quickly.

The ROK 1st Division's final defense line ran from Tabu-dong to Waegwan. It tied in with the U.S. 1st Cavalry Division holding about the same amount of line running south from Waegwan. Both divisions faced a desperate situation. At the time I did not know that three crack NKPA divisions and supporting forces were surging toward our positions, and I think it quite lucky that I did not know. Had I been aware,

I would've been obliged to hide my fear, adding another burden to my load.

My plan was to deploy my regiments evenly across the division front, with the 13th Regiment on my left flank abutting the U.S. 1st Cav and occupying Hill 328, from which my men could see the Naktong River itself. I was to spread out my 11th Regiment right and left of Kasan and the other hills bordering the Chonpyong Valley, a natural tank approach. My 12th Regiment was to occupy Mount Yuhak (839 meters) and Suam Hill (519 meters), but my plan went awry.

The 12th Regiment withdrew from positions at In-dong, site of the Chang Clan's head shrine, and turned right on the road running to Tabu-dong, intending to occupy the summits of the hills, only to discover that the NKPA had used shortcuts during the night to move in quickly and secure the two hills at the very center of the ROK 1st Division's final containment line. We were off to an inauspicious beginning.

The NKPA was accomplished at night fighting and at combat in mountainous terrain, and its commanders concentrated mercilessly on our vulnerabilities and shortcomings. The enemy had turned the tables on us. We were forced to begin a defensive campaign by going on the offensive, instead of conducting defensive warfare from our final containment line.

The enemy had not expected to be held up so long at the Naktong, and the NKPA now streamed forward on every front, its commanders brooking no delays. We had forced the North Korean high command to abandon its "Pusan by Liberation Day" objective, but even local newspapers in the South carried news about North Korean dictator Kim Il Sung's new order to "take Taegu by Liberation Day," August 15. The deadline was only hours away.

With Mount Yuhak safely in hand, the NKPA mounted a general offensive concentrated at the sector of our line held by my 13th Regiment. The NKPA persistently targeted ROK Army units because its firepower was superior to ours; by the same token, it avoided sectors of the line held by U.S. units because American firepower was superior to its.

After heavy fighting, the enemy ejected my 13th Regiment from Hill 328 overlooking the Naktong River. The loss of the hill came as an urgent report to me at division headquarters, and I rushed to the scene. The 13th was retreating southeast. "Damn," I said to myself. "I've got big trouble now." The words had barely formed in my mind when a projectile suddenly burst in front of the retreating men. Regimental commander Col. Choi Young Hi had fired a 57mm antitank recoilless rifle round ahead of them, bringing the men to a quick halt. Before they could get under way again, Choi ran to the front of the unit and, yelling at the top of his lungs, ordered the men to turn around and counterattack. The officers and men of the unit obediently turned in their tracks and started off to assault the hill they had just lost.

As their counterattack gained momentum, I saw a battalion-sized force join the original unit, adding significantly to the energy of the assault. There were no units in reserve anywhere in the division, and I knew it better than anybody. Where the hell had these new troops come from? I cornered the regimental commander. "What battalion is helping in that counterattack?" I demanded.

Colonel Choi looked embarrassed. "Fact is, sir, I set up a personnel section in Taegu without telling you, and I've been doing a little recruiting on my own." By way of justification, the colonel reminded me that I had assigned his 3d Battalion to the 11th Regiment's sector, leaving him with insufficient troops to accomplish his mission. Saying that he had no other choice but to resort to this unorthodox solution, Colonel Choi apologized. "I'm very sorry, sir."

I couldn't censure him, and I couldn't praise him. But I can say that he could not have retaken that hill without his unorthodox reinforcements. In any event, the 13th's counterattack lasted forty-eight hours and even then barely managed to recapture Hill 328.

Meanwhile, the 11th Regiment also faced a growing crisis on the division's right flank. The NKPA massed tanks and heavy artillery along the road to Tabu-dong and surged forward to crush the 11th's lines. The regiment responded with 3.5-inch antitank rockets and with every other weapon in its arsenal but was driven back almost two miles by the sheer weight of the attack, surrendering the terrain from the road junction at Chonpyong all the way to Chinmok-dong.

The 11th's withdrawal resulted in enemy and friendly forces facing each other at extremely short range, with the NKPA occupying the hills on the south side of the road, and ROK 1st Division forces cut off in ridges north of the road, triggering a melee of combat with the offense and defense each facing the wrong direction.

The 12th Regiment, meanwhile, faced a heartbreaking predicament, since from the very first instant of the battle its soldiers were obliged to climb the most precipitous terrain imaginable to engage in mortal combat with an enemy dug in at the top of a seemingly endless series of ridges, ridges that should have been in our hands before the battle began.

Thus, when Liberation Day dawned on August 15, the battle had reached a crisis. Each of the division's three major fronts was locked in hand-to-hand combat with the NKPA. The two sides were so close that even rifles could not be used, and combat along the entire twelve-mile front degenerated into a bloody, life-or-death struggle based chiefly on the exchange of hand grenades.

The fighting continued day and night, neither side asking for quarter. Bodies piled up around every hill. The living used the dead as shields behind which to continue the fight. The entire line looked like a scene straight from hell. Such a battle is painful for a commander who cares about the integrity of his division and the lives of his men. The situation was growing untenable, and I was obliged to request reinforcements. Forced to this desperate measure, I pulled out all the stops, asking for emergency reinforcement from Eighth Army through Capt. Ray B. May, an adviser to the division, during the daylight hours of August 15 and repeating the request through my division chief of staff to ROK II Corps Headquarters.

My requests were answered instantly. The U.S. 25th Division's 27th Regiment and the ROK 8th Division's 10th Regiment would be dispatched to reinforce the ROK 1st Division. Until these units arrived, a message said, I was ordered to hold, employing all the firepower at my disposal.

A second message contained another bit of good news as well. The next day, August 16, a carpet bombing raid by the U.S. Air Force would be executed about noon along the Naktong River bank on the division's flank west of Waegwan. Units in nearby frontal areas were to ensure that their men deepened their fighting holes and kept their heads down.

The battle had reached a crucial stage, but I thought I glimpsed the first rays of hope. By dawn on August 16, the only portion of the final defense line that remained under ROK 1st Division control was Tabu-dong and a portion of Suam Hill. Everywhere else the line was a melee of close combat that was grinding us inexorably to the verge of annihilation.

The news of reinforcements and carpet bombing swept along the grapevine, raising the men's morale. On the morning of August 16, I ordered an attack. In the order, I said, "If we are suffering, then the enemy is suffering more. However difficult our circumstances, the fact remains that personnel and ammunition resupply are unbroken, and we continue to receive air support. Let us all turn now to the assault!"

I thought a counterattack might catch the enemy off balance and deliver us from our moment of crisis. Before the morning was over, the 13th Regiment retook Hill 328, and the 12th seized the eighth and last ridge leading up to Mount Yuhak's summit west of Tabu-dong and was engaged in a hand-to-hand struggle for the summit itself. The 11th Regiment repulsed NKPA units that had infiltrated along the ridges of Kasan, and although it didn't regain any lost territory, the unit managed to hold its place, not allowing the enemy to push it any farther down the Chonpyong road.

At two minutes before noon on August 16, a huge formation of B-29 heavy bombers appeared in the sky over Waegwan. I watched as a massive swarm of bombs floated down, followed shortly by the rumble of the earth itself as it shook beneath the mighty weight of the bombs.

The bombing lasted exactly twenty-six minutes. In that brief span, five formations of B-29s flying out of Kadena Air Force Base on Okinawa, a total of ninety-eight aircraft, dropped more than nine hundred tons of bombs, 3,234 individual weapons. The explosions turned a rectangular area 3.5 miles wide by 7.5 miles long west of the Naktong into a moon-scape.

The strike was a rerun of the combined carpet bombing operation car-ried out at St. Lo during the World War II landing at Normandy in 1945. As it turned out, the enemy's main force had already crossed the Nak-tong and was fighting in close proximity to us, so the air strike failed to deliver a fatal blow to the enemy. Subsequent interrogation of enemy prisoners of war revealed, however, that the raid had dealt a crushing blow to NKPA morale.

After sundown on August 17, 1950, a handsome U.S. colonel with piercing eyes arrived at my headquarters. John H. Michaelis, com-mander of the U.S. 27th Regiment, was to rise to the rank of full general and serve as commander in chief of U.S. Forces Korea. Michaelis arrived at my headquarters as commander of the reinforcements promised ear-lier by Eighth Army. His 27th had fought at the Yongsan Salient farther south on the Naktong and had then been sent to help the ROK 1st Divi-sion in our desperate defense of Taegu.

"How much combat strength do you have?" I asked the colonel.

"I have three completely organized infantry battalions," he replied. "And a 105mm artillery battalion with eighteen howitzers, a tank com-pany, a company of 155mm guns—six of the monsters—and all the am-munition we can shoot." He told me that the U.S. 23d Regiment would be deployed to our sector later as a follow-on reinforcement.

I had been fighting with so little artillery that we had been assigning missions to individual howitzers. The colonel's casual mention of pos-sessing an entire battalion of 105mm guns astounded me. In addition to this daunting firepower, Michaelis's regiment had its own air-ground liaison control team, leaving the U.S. regimental commander with no worries about coordinating air support.

I couldn't contain my excitement at the thought of such firepower. "Let's attack in the morning!" I snapped.

"We haven't received orders to attack," Colonel Michaelis demurred. "My orders say only to defend a strip one thousand yards wide down the main highway northeast of Tabu-dong, five hundred yards on each side of the road."

By the morning of August 18, the U.S. 27th Regiment had moved into Tabu-dong and deployed along the road in an area of open terrain al-most directly in the center of my 11th Regiment's defense line. The ar-rival of the U.S. unit shifted the balance of the battle, putting us in a position for a decisive fight on relatively equal footing with the enemy. My 1st Division held the high ground in the hills and fought NKPA infantry, while the U.S. 27th Regiment held the road in the valley and fought NKPA tanks.

The NKPA ceased all activity for a whole day after the B-29 strike, but as August 18 dawned, the enemy charged back to the attack as wildly as if it were thrashing about in the throes of death. Concentrating all the men and firepower they could muster, the NKPA forces threw themselves at us as if they were demented.

The fighting degenerated once more into a seesaw ebb and flow of hand-to-hand combat, attack and counterattack, with grenades and bayonets doing the killing at close quarters. Many of my men developed painful, swollen shoulders from hurling so many hand grenades. The battle continued with such intensity that neither side could find an opportunity to remove its dead from the field.

My men noticed and reported that the breaths of NKPA prisoners and wounded smelled of alcohol. The enemy was giving liquor to the youthful "volunteers" and committing them to the assault.

Meanwhile, enemy special forces had infiltrated behind our lines, where they now conducted raids and harassment operations against our rear-area forces and facilities. On the morning of August 18, enemy forces infiltrated into the outskirts of Taegu via the foothills of Kasan and fired seven mortar rounds into the downtown area, hitting the Taegu railway station among other places. Taegu citizens assumed the explosions meant the NKPA had encircled the city and was advancing into the downtown area. They became greatly agitated. Many residents hastily made for the road leading south out of the city, seeking to flee as refugees, and the situation there degenerated into panic.

On the night of August 19, a company-sized enemy force attacked my division headquarters in our primary school. We had no warning. I was sound asleep when the attack began. My aide shook me awake, and as I got to my feet my fuzzy mind suddenly grasped that the sounds of enemy burp guns, machine guns, and exploding grenades were originating from very near the headquarters building itself. Division staff officers and KMAG advisers were crawling on their hands and knees down the halls of the school in an effort to escape. An American communications soldier and a number of others were already dead, and the headquarters was in chaos.

Luckily for us, a battalion of the ROK 8th Division's 10th Regiment was billeted on the school's playground, having arrived as reinforcements at 5:00 P.M. the previous afternoon. I quickly hunted down the unit commander. "Major Kim," I yelled above the din. "Hurry, hurry. Get your battalion into an assault." Kim got his unit into attack formation in double-quick time and soon repulsed the enemy.

According to subsequent information, the NKPA unit had conducted the raid with the specific mission of capturing the division commander. A division headquarters usually is not heavily defended, but the chance overnight bivouac of the battalion of reinforcements in the headquarters area saved my skin. Later, I recalled that the division G-3, Lt. Col. Mun Hyong Tae, had waited anxiously for the arrival of the battalion the previous day. "Should we send the new unit right on up to the line?" he asked me. "Or should we wait till tomorrow morning?" The battalion had marched many miles in the sultry summer heat and looked exhausted to me.

"Feed them and bed them down for the night," I told Mun in one of the luckiest decisions of my life. "They can head out at first light in the morning." The fates of war touch every fighter, and in this case, I was very fortunate to survive.

The day after division headquarters was hit, the U.S. 23d Regiment commanded by Col. Paul Freeman also arrived to reinforce us. Freeman was a quiet officer, but all grit. As we shook hands he asked, "*Jan jungguo hwa?*"

"*Wo hui jungguo,*" I responded. Yes, I spoke Chinese.

In fluent Mandarin, Freeman suggested that we converse in that language in the future. Somehow, the idea of an American and a Korean dealing in Chinese struck me as a bit silly. "Let's stick to English," I suggested. The key to success in war, certainly to success in combined operations, is lucid communication. Indeed, clarity of communication may be more valuable than combat skills.

Colonel Freeman had gone to Beijing as a foreign student in 1931 and spent four years there, so he spoke Chinese fluently. His service record was to sparkle from his meritorious exploits in the famous battle of Chipyong-ri, and Freeman was later promoted to four-star general rank and served as commander in chief of U.S. forces in Europe.

As soon as the U.S. 23d Regiment arrived, I sent it as division reserve to an area south of Tabu-dong. The only time in the Korean War that two major American units were assigned to a ROK division was during the battle at Tabu-dong, underscoring the importance of the battle for Taegu.

The ROK 10th Regiment also arrived to reinforce the ROK 1st. I assigned the unit to positions at Kasan on the division's right flank and gave it responsibility for the area where the ROK 1st tied in with the ROK 6th Division.

Colonel Michaelis's 27th Regiment deployed its tanks forward and repelled the NKPA's night attacks, reducing the threat of a breakthrough by enemy armor coming straight down the "Bowling Alley" road. The Americans called the 2.5 miles of straight roadway running from Chonpyong to Chinmok-dong the "Bowling Alley," because of geography and enemy tactics. NKPA tanks and artillery surged forward and fired down the road, the shells exploding with sharp cracks on the ridges behind friendly forces on the valley floor. The NKPA attackers not only gave the impression of bowlers approaching a lane, but also the sharp cracks of exploding shells reminded observers of the sharp "crack, crack" sounds made by flying bowling pins. I must say, at the time I found it difficult to understand the Americans' humor when they referred to a grisly battlefield with such a lighthearted term.

On August 20 the 13th Regiment on Hill 328 on the division's left flank was barely managing to hang on to its hill; the 12th Regiment in the middle had attacked the summit of Mount Yuhak but had not been able to take it; and the 11th Regiment on my right flank had been strengthened by reinforcing units and was maintaining contact with the ROK 6th.

That day the enemy suddenly became passive on all fronts. I learned later that the NKPA's elite 15th Division withdrew from the battle and marched toward Yongchon to initiate an attack there. The fighting in our sector had proved too tough.

At the time, however, I thought the drop in activity indicated that the NKPA was running out of steam, and after discussing the situation with Colonel Michaelis, I decided to mount an attack with the objective of seizing all of Line Y. Just as the division was about to kick off the attack the next morning, however, the enemy began its own attack, beating us to the punch. One unexpected lesson I learned in the war was that when we attacked with determination, and the enemy responded with the same determination, we would trigger a round of furious firefights.

The enemy laid down an explosive curtain of hand grenades and mortars to contain our attack and then threw human-wave attacks back at us. The U.S. 27th Regiment was unable to get its assault off the ground; the enemy pressure forced the Americans to remain on the defensive.

I received a report at this time that a battalion of my 11th Regiment, which was holding a ridge to the left of the U.S. 27th Regiment, lost the initiative in the initial shock of the enemy assault. The report said the NKPA force had thrown my battalion off the ridge and that my men were retreating toward Tabu-dong. Immediately after receiving that report, I got an angry telephone call from Eighth Army Headquarters. "What the hell's wrong with the ROK Army?" began an irate, rebuking voice. "Do you intend to fight or not?"

My battalion's retreat exposed the flank of Colonel Michaelis's regiment, and he had instantly called Eighth Army. "The ROK Army is bugging out," he said. "And I must withdraw before my line of retreat is cut." Michaelis also called me. "I'm going to withdraw," he announced firmly.

"Don't do it just yet," I urged. "Hang on until I can get up there and see what's going on." I jumped into a jeep and took off for Tabu-dong. I found the 11th Regiment troops retreating in a state of utter exhaustion down a hill west of the road leading to Chinmok-dong. The NKPA unit that had seized the ridge was already beginning to lay scattered flanking fire onto American artillery positions. I found the commander. "What happened here, Major Kim?"

"We're exhausted from fighting day and night, sir," he answered. "And that's not all. The ridge is completely cut off, so the supply people can't get food or water up to us. The men haven't had a drop to drink in two days."

I ran to the front of the retreating troops. "Let's everybody sit down

right here and listen up," I began. "I want to thank you for fighting like
you have. But we just don't have room to retreat any more. The only
place left for us to go is into the ocean. If we run now, Korea is done
for. Look at those American troops over there. They're fighting because
they trust the ROK Army, and if we retreat, we bring shame down on
the entire ROK Army. We are men of Korea; let us fight for this land.
We're going to turn around and kick the enemy off our ridge, and I shall
be at the front. If I turn back, shoot me."

I issued the assault order to the unit and made very certain I stayed
at the front when we jumped off. I sure as hell didn't want to get shot
from behind. The yells of the charging men echoed off the surrounding
hills. Major Kim commanded his unit with great bravery, also from the
front of it. In what seemed like only moments, the battalion had retaken
the hill. So different was the morale of the unit as it attacked the hill
that the NKPA force must have thought the assault came from a totally
different outfit altogether.

Colonel Michaelis came up to me later. "Sorry about that call to Eighth
Army, General," he said, obviously impressed. "When I saw the divi-
sion commander himself leading that attack, I knew the ROK Army was
God's own force."

I learned in this first combined ROK-U.S. operation that success depended on mutual trust. If the NKPA kicked us out of the hills, the
Americans would be trapped in the valley. And if the NKPA punched
through the Americans, we would be isolated in the hills. Thus, if the
men of each army did not trust the other, neither would have the confidence to fight. It is no easy task for human beings to trust each other,
even in the course of daily living. To trust others when our lives are at
stake on the battlefield is a great deal easier said than done. When the
war was going well, everything was "Okay, okay" to the Americans,
but when combat was going badly, they became cold and aloof. If ROK
Army units could not accomplish their assigned missions, failing to
earn the Americans' trust as "buddies worth helping," then combined
operations did not succeed.

The Tabu-dong battle reached its climax on August 21, 1950. Truly it
was "an eye for an eye, and a tooth for a tooth," as we answered attack
with attack and assault with assault, leaving piles of dead on every hill
and ridge. The fighting was so heavy that in many squads and platoons
not a soldier who had started the battle still fought at its end, every
original member of the unit having been killed or wounded and his
place taken by a replacement. On the night of August 21, the NKPA
mounted an all-out attack aimed straight at the U.S. 27th Regiment. The
Americans brought every available weapon to bear and repulsed the
attack after five hours of heated combat.

The tide of battle turned our way at last on August 22. I felt rather
than saw that the fighting had reached an apex and was about to swing
our way.

The 12th Regiment had been in a tough position from the outset of the fighting. It had to attack straight up to the peak of the mountain, but that night it took a page from the enemy's book and drove home a surprise night attack that annihilated the enemy on the summit of Mount Yuhak. The 12th had mounted seven previous assaults on the hill's summit, all unsuccessful, before the eighth effort carried the objective. That same night, after a desperate battle, the U.S. 23d Regiment repulsed NKPA forces that had infiltrated through the ridges of Kasan to attack friendly artillery positions.

The main force of the ROK 10th Regiment arrived to reinforce us at this moment, and I sent it to attack the Kasan ridge. We owned the summit by the following day. The 10th Regiment was commanded by Lt. Col. Ko Kun Hong, a graduate of Class 1 of the Korea Military Academy, then an officer candidate school, and an exceptionally brave officer. As a commander he was the very embodiment of initiative and displayed rare intrepidity in operating jointly with the 11th Regiment in the battle for Kasan. As we advanced into North Korea in late 1950, Ko was listed as missing in action and presumed dead.

It was not until August 24 that we were able to occupy all of Line Y. All hills and important ridges were in friendly hands, and we now were able to take the north slopes under direct observation and mop up enemy pockets of resistance.

On August 25 Colonel Michaelis wrapped up eight days of intense combat and moved his regiment to a hot spot near Masan. This was General Walker's so-called fire brigade strategy. When a front was critical, he sent in Michaelis's regiment as a regimental combat team to support local units, quench dangerous fires, shore up the line, and help prepare for a counterattack.

The ROK 1st Division had no trouble executing the defense mission alone on the battlefield during the final days of August. We turned the area over to the U.S. 1st Cavalry Division and moved to the adjacent sector on August 31.

The Battle of Tabu-dong came to be recognized as the toughest action of the Naktong River line. In addition to my ROK 1st Division, one ROK and two U.S. regiments participated as reinforcements. We also had air support from the U.S. Air Force, and civilian residents had slung A-frames on their backs and came out to help, carrying ammunition, food, water, and supplies up frontline hills while under enemy fire. The Tabu-dong victory belonged to the ROK Army, to our allies, and to the Korean people themselves.

The ROK 1st Division lost 2,244 men and 56 officers killed in action in the battle. The NKPA lost more than twice as many, 5,690 dead. Indeed, ROK 1st Division losses were so great that I just wanted to fall down and bawl. The medals bestowed upon those who survived lose their luster when compared with the sacrifice of the many who died. At least during the fighting, from a military standpoint, the division's personnel gaps were soon filled by rear-area youths and students volunteering for the front. These young people were sent to the lines so quickly they were not fully trained. They had to learn the ropes the hard way, by participating in actual combat.

The fight at Tabu-dong cost the ROK 1st Division so many personnel, in fact, that ROK Army felt compelled to conduct an investigation. When it came time to turn over our positions to the U.S. division, the American soldiers adamantly insisted, "We won't replace you until you bury all the bodies up there."

During the early stages of the Tabu-dong fighting, I didn't realize that the battle was all that important. My own ego had long since been submerged by the need to do my utmost to deal with the daily emergencies wrought by the war.

As the fighting continued, however, I gradually realized the great significance of the battle, as the NKPA flooded forward without surcease, the U.S. Army reinforced us with two major units, and I received a series of important visitors. Army Chief of Staff Maj. Gen. Chung Il Kwon visited, as did Eighth Army Commander Gen. Walton H. Walker, and even U.S. Army Chief of Staff Gen. J. Lawton Collins. They all observed the battle and offered encouragement.

The battle for Tabu-dong was over. Or so we thought. But the curtain would rise a second time.

Reversing the Tide of War

The U.S. 2d Division landed at Pusan from the United States in the last week of August, and the British 27th Brigade arrived from Hong Kong about the same time. For weeks, the Korean War had been a race against time. Would Pusan fall first, or would a U.S. infantry division arrive first? The UN won this race when the U.S. 2d Division disembarked.

About the time the U.S. 2d was landing in Pusan, the Americans' superior firepower succeeded in containing the NKPA at the Naktong River line, and the enemy turned its main attack to the east, mounting a sweeping offensive against the less-formidably armed ROK Army units defending the northern sector of the Pusan Perimeter.

We responded by expanding the sectors of the front held by U.S. units and reducing the areas assigned to the two ROK corps, I Corps at Kyongju under Brig. Gen. Kim Paik Il as of September 1, 1950, and II Corps at Hayang commanded by Brig. Gen. Yu Jae Hung. Another reason for the changes in frontages was the assumption that such a move would aid us in going over to the offensive if the Inchon landing succeeded.

The ROK 1st Division passed control of the area around Tabu-dong to the U.S. 1st Cavalry Division and moved to an area north of Palgong-san, adjacent to Tabu-dong on the east. Our new sector had been the domain of the ROK 6th Division and extended from Kasan to the road connecting Sillyong and Uisong. The entire 7.5-mile sector was a series of precipitous ridges that fed up into the higher reaches of Palgong-san. I moved the division headquarters to a hamlet on a road half way to Sillyong.

A delegation of village elders soon paid me a visit. "Palgong-san," they stressed, "is a holy mountain. If this mountain is protected, the nation itself will be secure, but if Palgong-san falls, the nation will collapse."

"Well," I said as comfortingly as I could, "We are the division that defended Tabu-dong to the very last. You need have no worries about the sacred mountain." I deployed the 12th Regiment on the division right at Palgong-san, the 15th on the left, and held the 11th in reserve.

When the Tabu-dong front cooled off in the last week of August, ROK II Corps ordered me to send Col. Choi Young Hi's 15th Regiment to repulse enemy forces that had infiltrated between the ROK 6th and 8th divisions. Choi completed that assignment and returned to the division. Until that time, the regimental designation had been the 13th Regiment, rather than the 15th, but when the unit returned from its mission for ROK II Corps, Choi requested that the unit be officially redesignated the 15th Regiment. Choi had formerly commanded the 5th Division's 15th Regiment and retained a fondness for the old regiment and its designation. I contacted ROK Army, which approved the change.

The NKPA didn't allow us much respite, launching its next offensive on September 2, 1950. The very recent "great victory at Tabu-dong" had fully revived the self-confidence among the personnel of the ROK 1st Division, but our neighboring units had in fact experienced a further decline in morale. The enemy's great September offensive overran defense line after defense line, returning us overnight to the state of virtually perpetual crisis we had endured for so long.

On September 3, one day into the new offensive, the U.S. 1st Cavalry Division retreated six miles, surrendering all the high ground we had turned over to them. Kasan, Mount Yuhak, Suam Hill, and Hill 328 all fell into enemy hands, as did the village of Tabu-dong itself, which the ROK 1st Division had never lost to the enemy. The NKPA's net around Taegu tightened another six miles on the northeast.

The NKPA 15th Division broke through the ROK 8th Division on ROK I Corps's right flank, capturing Yongchon at daybreak on September 6.

The collapsing battlefield situation was viewed so seriously that rear-area organizations like the Defense Ministry and ROK Army Headquarters moved to Pusan from Taegu on September 6. The Eighth Army rear echelon removed to Pusan the same day, and I heard that Eighth Army was seriously considering abandoning Taegu and the present defense line and withdrawing to what was designated the "Davidson line." The

Davidson line stretched from Mason to Ulsan by way of Miryang, about half way between Taegu and Pusan. It was named for the Eighth Army chief engineer, Brig. Gen. Garrison Davidson.

American advisers at ROK 1st Division Headquarters had been talking about the Davidson line since the Tabu-dong battle. I regarded the Davidson line as a temporary holding line and not a true defense line at all. It would serve as a temporary bulwark behind which U.S. and UN forces could withdraw safely to Japan. The line itself was so abbreviated that it did not provide enough space for existing units to deploy, and the interior road net south of Davidson could not maintain even minimal resupply of personnel and material to defending forces.

Even the front we held north of Taegu was serviced by barely 8 percent of all Korea's roads, meaning that any major withdrawal from current positions would prove disastrous.

The ROK Army and Eighth Army both maintained their forward command posts in Taegu, and General Walker himself remained in the city and continued to exercise active command of the front. The perception that the war had reached a crisis heightened to the point that some people began to make preparations for escape by sea. Both soldiers and civilians are exceptionally sensitive to perceptions in wartime, immensely complicating the task of leading them. Taegu's peacetime population was three hundred thousand, but the city was swollen with refugees, and its population now stood at seven hundred thousand. It was unthinkable to consider abandoning so many people to their fate.

The ROK 1st Division responded to the September offensive in a number of ways. We strengthened our defense around Todok-san north of Kasan, contained an enemy attack all along the Palgong-san front, and committed the reserve 11th Regiment to an attempt to wrest Yongchon back from the enemy.

The ROK 8th Division was holding a line about fifteen miles north of Yongchon when the NKPA 15th Division broke away from the fighting at Tabu-dong and made straight for them. The NKPA 15th broke through the unfortunate ROK 8th Division, mounting furious night assaults and attacks spearheaded by T-34s. The Corps commander, Gen. Yu Jae Hung, ordered the ROK 6th Division commander and me to send a regiment each on detached duty to help retake Yongchon and to restore the ROK 8th Division's line. Neither of us was anxious to comply, because we both faced growing pressure all along our own lines, but ultimately we each sent along a regiment.

My 11th Regiment under Col. Kim Dong Bin had no sooner arrived in the area around Yongchon on the morning of September 6 than it became commingled with friendly and enemy units in a bulge in the line and was caught up in a battle best described as a free-for-all. The 11th fought against bitter odds day after day. I was informed that General Yu made an emergency request through Eighth Army Headquarters for armor support from the U.S. 1st Cavalry Division to help resolve the situation at the bulge, but Yu received no immediate response.

When the enemy breaks through a neighboring unit, the situation must be resolved by an immediate counterattack, even if it means committing one's own troops. But no commander in any army can be pleased when the he suffers serious losses accomplishing what amounts to the mission of the adjacent unit. Whether in the ROK Army or the U.S. Army, desires and hopes precede duty.

The enemy took Yongchon twice, and we took it back twice, but only after intense fighting, after which the situation on that front gradually quieted. Ultimately, a platoon of U.S. tanks supported the effort there.

As I watched the fighting at both Yongchon and Palgong-san through the first week of September, I began to see that the NKPA offensive had reached a high watermark. The North Korean formation maintained their unrelenting pressure, to be sure, but my experience at combat command over the weeks led me to suspect that their offensive shared a similarity with the September weather. It was still hot in early September, but the heat lacked persistence.

At this point, a rumor began to fly around the headquarters that the Americans were going to conduct an amphibious landing at Inchon. I had been waiting impatiently for the day when we could undertake a massive counterattack against the enemy, and I hoped with all my heart that this particular rumor was true.

The NKPA attacks on Palgong-san grew noticeably weaker, and when I went up to check on the situation at Yongchon, I found that the enemy's T-34s were useless. The North Koreans literally had run out of gas.

Even when the enemy was able to break through our positions clearly, it lacked both the reinforcements and the resupply to exploit the breakthrough, and our forces quickly surrounded the salient and routed the enemy. The enemy was crumbling. My 11th Regiment completed its mission for ROK II Corps and returned to divisional control, but the 11th had suffered heavy losses in the bitter fighting.

I received a top secret communication from Eighth Army at this time. "Proceed immediately," the message read, "to Miryang and meet there with an important American general officer." I proceeded at the appointed hour to Miryang Primary School to meet with the anonymous officer, but when I arrived I was told he had already left for Taegu.

I received another message the following day and, acting on its instructions, drove down to Taegu and was led to a tent pitched in an apple orchard on the city's outskirts. The American flag officer was short, seemed mild mannered, and had a pet dog with him. Introducing himself as Maj. Gen. Frank W. Milburn, he asked, "Are you General Paik?" I said I was. "I've heard that your ROK 1st Division is giving a good account of itself," he said, adding that the time had come to go on the offensive. Milburn explained that he would be the commander of the U.S. I Corps that would be created from three divisions, my 1st, the U.S. 1st Cavalry, and the U.S. 24th.

Noting that the firepower of the ROK 1st Division was unacceptably low, Milburn said that to compensate he would attach corps artillery assets to the division to bolster our firepower and would provide maximum support in other areas. Before coming to Korea, Milburn commanded the U.S. 1st Division in Europe and had been slated to become commander of U.S. IX Corps. When it became obvious, however, that the Inchon landing would change the nature of the war in the South from the defensive to the offensive, General Walker selected Milburn to command the new U.S. I Corps, which would lead the offensive northward. General Walker appointed Maj. Gen. John Coulter to command U.S. IX Corps.

Despite his unimpressive first appearance, General Milburn proved to be a bold and aggressive soldier. His service record included command of the U.S. 7th Army's XXI Corps in its landing at Marseilles and during the offensive that liberated the Alsace-Lorraine district along the border between France and Germany. Milburn had operated with de Gaulle's French forces during that offensive.

I seized the moment to make a request of my new boss and left with a jeepload of operations maps, the first three-color maps I had seen since the war began. Place names appeared on the maps both in Chinese characters, which Koreans also use, and in English, and military coordinates were printed right on the map. This latter feature proved to be a godsend in later operations because it vastly simplified the problem of requesting air and artillery support. I had no choice but to become a "map beggar" with every U.S. officer I met during the early part of the war. It was lamentable that the ROK Army was obliged to conduct modern warfare without even passable maps.

The atmosphere at division headquarters brightened considerably when I returned, not only with plenty of modern maps but also with news that we would be moving to the offense and that the ROK 1st Division would be assigned to the U.S. Army for the drive north. Days and weeks of desperate battle had left us all dissatisfied and full of anxiety, but these emotions now disappeared. We all seemed to be walking on clouds of hope.

As good as his word, General Milburn attached the U.S. 10th Antiaircraft Artillery Group to the ROK 1st Division. The U.S. 10th had been charged previously with the antiaircraft defense of Pusan. The arrival of the 10th, with its 78th Antiaircraft Artillery Battalion (eighteen 90mm guns), 9th Field Artillery Battalion (eighteen 155mm guns), and 2d Heavy Mortar Battalion (eighteen 4.2-inch mortars), provided the ROK 1st Division with firepower equivalent to that of a U.S. division. The group was commanded by a senior colonel, William Hennig. "The infantry makes all the plans," this truly humble officer told me. "The job of the artillery and the other combat arms is absolute support of the infantry.''

Colonel Hennig urged me not to be stingy with requests for fire support. ''We've got plenty of ammo,'' he said, ''seventy or eighty trucks' worth, in fact.'' Every time the ROK 1st Division faced a combat crisis thereafter, Hennig provided every practical cooperation. For my part, I placed highest priority on seeing to the needs of these invaluable American gunners, and I'm proud to say that we maintained an agreeable relationship even amid the rigors of warfare. The secret to success in combined operations lies in scrupulously caring for the needs of foreign supporting units. Any number of combined operations go awry because of unnecessary friction between host-country and foreign troops. I was pleased years later to hear Colonel Hennig recall that ''the 10th fought its finest battles during the period we supported the ROK Army's 1st Division.''

The news of the September 15 amphibious landing at Inchon got to us even at the front. Division morale shot up. ''Now we finally get to kick some butt!''

General Milburn's U.S. I Corps wasted no time in sending down orders to the ROK 1st Division. ''You will attack from Palgong-san to Kasan and destroy the NKPA 1st Division there. You will prepare to cross the Naktong River and attack in concert with the U.S. 1st Cavalry Division toward Sangju.''

The orders set H-hour for 9:00 A.M. on September 16. The curtain was about to rise on the second act of the battle for Tabu-dong. Combat had continued in the Kasan area every day.

The morning of September 16 arrived with thick fog and torrential rain. My troopers couldn't see an inch in front of their faces. Artillery support was out of the question, much less air support. We jumped off anyway, only to run headlong into an attack the NKPA had undertaken to exploit the lack of air support. The two offensives clashed head on, and very shortly it was impossible to tell who was attacking and who was defending.

I lost all communications with the 15th Regiment on the division's right and was unable to determine the situation in that sector for forty-eight long hours. This situation, of course, was a matter of great concern to me, but to make it worse, higher headquarters kept pressing me for information. It was a very nervous two days.

The 12th Regiment spearheaded the division's main attack but could not break through, while my 11th Regiment bogged down on the Kasan front. The divisions on our flanks experienced the same difficulties. General Walker was fit to be tied, because if we failed to break through the enemy units quickly, we would be late linking up with the forces that had landed at Inchon, far to the north.

General Walker paid me a visit on the morning of September 17 at a brewery near the airport at Tongchon where I had moved division headquarters. The general was touring all his divisions to encourage them to fight more vigorously. I explained our situation. "General Paik," Walker said. "You've been through Leavenworth, haven't you?" Fort Leavenworth was home to the U.S. Army Command and General Staff College, and I had never attended a U.S. military school, of course.

"Well, according to Command and General Staff College doctrine, the thing to do in a case like this is to bypass the enemy," the general said encouragingly. "When you run into strong enemy resistance to the attack, you must turn to the right and left and get by him. Just how you go about slipping by is a question for you and your commanders to answer."

We still had no communications with the 15th Regiment, which was invisible in the fog and, as it turned out, was locked in hand-to-hand combat with the enemy all the way up to its regimental command post, but I was able to verify that the regiment was intact and fighting well. The 11th regiment's battle at Kasan remained a melee.

On the afternoon of September 18 I received a communication from Lt. Col. Kim Chum Kon saying his 12th Regiment had advanced onto the strategically crucial high ground at Komae, a full seven miles north of Tabu-dong. I simply couldn't believe Kim's report that his 12th had penetrated so far through the enemy's positions. I checked. It was true.

Colonel Kim noticed that the main force of the NKPA 1st Division was caught up in the melee at Kasan with my 11th Regiment and had allowed a gap to open between it and the NKPA 8th Division. Kim aimed a concentrated attack at this vulnerable area and broke through into the enemy's rear, where he undertook to chew up NKPA supply lines.

I reported this information to Eighth Army Headquarters only to receive a number of telephone calls from General Walker and his staff officers. "Are you sure? Are you positive? How did you break through?" They couldn't bring themselves to believe it either. For my part, I instantly ordered every available man from the 11th and 15th regiments to bypass the enemy on the right, leaving only enough men to hold on at Kasan.

The enemy now found its lines of retreat cut and its flank compromised. The NKPA began to crumble as we attacked the encircled troops. The U.S. 10th Antiaircraft Artillery Group maintained the closest possible coordination, supporting us magnificently with its big guns.

The U.S. 1st Cavalry Division had lost Tabu-dong and faced stubborn enemy resistance on a line between Waegwan and Hangmyong, but it now seized the opportunity and moved in coordination with us to tighten the circle from the left. This meant the three enemy divisions—the NKPA 1st, 3d, and 13th—positioned between Kasan and Waegwan were now under attack from four different directions. The enemy that had fought with such ferocity now vanished like fog under a burning sun.

Interrogations of enemy prisoners revealed that the enemy troops in our sector had heard absolutely nothing about the amphibious landing at Inchon on September 15. The supreme NKPA leadership had elected to hide this information from their men, forcing them to remain on the offensive. Indeed, enemy machine gunners in every fighting position on every important strong point were chained in place by their wrists, condemning these men to continue firing until they were killed and ensuring a merciless resistance. We smashed these nests too, so many, in fact, that my men became disgusted with the killing.

On September 19, four days after our attack began, I stood north of Tabu-dong on the road to Kunwi—which, appropriately enough, means "military dignity" in Korean. A solemn spectacle spread out before me. Countless enemy bodies were piled up at the bottom of every hill, and the bodies of horses and cows were scattered everywhere. The stench of putrefying flesh, human and animal, assaulted the nostrils. NKPA artillery pieces, T-34s, huge numbers of weapons, and ammunition were strewn all over the battlefield.

I have no idea what the face of hell looks like, but it can't be more hideous that the battlefield at Tabu-dong. The NKPA 1st Division under Maj. Gen. Hong Rim had defeated me and my ROK 1st Division at Korangpo on the Imjin, but here at the Naktong, the NKPA 1st had suffered not just defeat but utter destruction.

An extraordinarily large number of men from Maj. Gen. Choi Yong Chin's NKPA 13th Division defected or surrendered, and the division itself was annihilated. On August 29 the commander of the NKPA 13th Division's artillery regiment, Lt. Col. Chung Bong Wuk, surrendered to the ROK 1st Division, followed on September 2 by the surrender to the U.S. 1st Cavalry Division of the NKPA 13th's chief of staff Senior Col. Lee Hak Ku. After that, the lower ranking officers and men of the division surrendered in droves.

The NKPA 3d Division, commanded by Maj. Gen. Lee Yong Ho, was the first NKPA unit to enter Seoul, and North Korea's dictator Kim Il Sung himself named the division "Seoul's Third." This honor didn't seem to help much, though; the NKPA 3d bugged out during the fight at Waegwan, when more than a thousand of its men took to their heels in panic.

After his defection, NKPA Col. Chung Bong Wuk repudiated communism and was allowed to enter the ROK Army, where he served as commanding general of the Second Training Center and eventually reached the rank of major general. The highest ranking defector, NKPA Sr. (Senior) Col. Lee Hak Ku, was treated as a prisoner of war rather than a defector and was incarcerated on Koje Island, where he led North Korean prisoner-of-war riots that inflicted more damage on UN forces than if Lee had stayed and fought with the NKPA.

The second victory at Tabu-dong served as a primer for the advance of allied forces back up the Korean peninsula and represented one of the war's major turning points.

The destruction of three main-force NKPA divisions in the battle dealt such a fatal blow to the NKPA that de facto recovery was not possible until after the armistice in 1953. As for the ROK 1st Division, our greatest battle started at Tabu-dong and ended at Tabu-dong.

When I look back on the battle at Tabu-dong today, the soldier in me is proud on two counts. First, I'm proud of the real trust and cooperation I enjoyed from my subordinate commanders in the ROK 1st Division. These officers displayed all the patriotism, all the fighting spirit, and all the ingenuity that anyone could expect, and we were victorious because of it. My commanders trusted their men and fought bravely in situations in which they didn't even have time to stop and catch their breaths. The NKPA forces were superior to us in numbers, firepower, and equipment, yet we were able to contain and destroy them because the ROK 1st Division was built on a foundation of mutual trust that melded us into a team devoted to our cause.

The second reason we succeeded was the opportunity we provided for the U.S. Army to trust us. In the battle, the ROK 1st Division was reinforced by two U.S. Army units, assigned to a U.S. Army corps. Later, when we advanced northward, we contributed as a main attack unit of the corps. U.S. Army units didn't help out because of the goodness of their hearts, or merely because we asked for support. U.S. Army units do not support units they don't trust. Why? Because supporting units put their own safety first, and they resist fighting on behalf of units they can't trust with their lives.

In early 1971, Gen. John H. Michaelis returned to my country as commander in chief of U.N. forces in Korea, and I had an opportunity to meet with him again. "American commanders," the general said as he reminisced about the Tabu-dong battle, "kept a very sharp eye on the combat capabilities of ROK Army units and their commanders in those days because we knew that at some point we were going to have to conduct combined operations with you. If I hadn't trusted the combat capability of the ROK 1st Division and of you, General Paik, I could not have taken my regiment into the Tabu-dong Valley."

I may be a bit boastful when I say that it was an epochal event that the ROK 1st Division was the first ROK Army unit given firepower equal to a U.S. division and assigned to combat operations under General Milburn, commander of U.S. I Corps. Indeed, it's downright astounding in view of the skeptical attitude prevailing among U.S. commanders at the time about the combat capabilities of the ROK Army.

The glory won by the ROK 1st Division spread through the ROK Army, resulting in very capable officers gathering to my side.

3

WE LEAD THE WAY NORTH

Back the Way We Came

If you look out your windshield as you cross the Naktong River bridge at Waegwan on today's Seoul-Pusan Freeway, mountains stretch into the distance on both sides of the road like an Oriental screen. These mountains witnessed the intense battles that determined the fate of the Republic of Korea. Exploding artillery shells tore and screamed at these mountains for two months, until not a blade of grass remained. Today thickets and copses grow in profusion around the base of the mountains, and the observer will be hard-pressed to discover evidence of the gruesome battles fought here four decades ago.

The ROK 1st Division had destroyed the enemy forces it faced in the Tabu-dong battles, and the 1st now conducted mop-up operations against pockets of NKPA troops as we awaited orders to pursue the NKPA, which was broken and streaming northward.

We were in our third day of the mop-up when I ran into a U.S. unit at a crossroads on September 22, 1950. Task Force 777 was composed of the U.S. 7th Cavalry Regiment, 7th Tank Battalion, and 7th Artillery Battalion. It was commanded by Maj. Gen. Hobart Gay, commanding general of the U.S. 1st Cavalry Division. Task Force 777 was heading north. "We're pushing north to the Osan area," General Gay told me, "to link up with U.S. X Corps that landed at Inchon." As Task Force 777 revved up, General Gay yelled out, "See you in Seoul!" The American unit moved out at a furious pace.

General Gay had served as Gen. George Patton's chief of staff in the U.S. Third Army during World War II and was said to have been riding in the sedan in which General Patton was killed in a traffic accident after the war ended.

All I could do was stare in frustration at the column of U.S. tanks and trucks as the dust it kicked up wafted skyward like a beckoning cloud marking the road to North Korea. I could do nothing about the U.S. Army leading out in the pursuit of the North Koreans, of course, because we lacked the river-crossing equipment the Americans had. Still, my pride smarted. The ROK 1st Division had blasted open the bridgehead that led to this new offensive, and now I had to stand helplessly and watch the wind snatch away the glory of victory like the dust dissipating behind Task Force 777. As the sound of their engines dimmed in the distance, I have to say I was downright envious. When would the ROK 1st Division be allowed to go to Seoul?

I was never bashful. As soon as the U.S. 1st Cavalry Division passed us heading north after the fleeing enemy, I called U.S. I Corps Headquarters and recommended in the strongest terms that my 1st Division be freed to advance on Seoul. U.S. I Corps was adamant: the ROK 1st Division, it directed, shall "continue mopping-up operations and advance through Kunwi and Chongju."

I accepted the order, but when I directed the 12th Regiment to proceed to Kunwi to continue mop-up operations, the men reacted strongly. The order ran counter to their expectations. Why, they wanted to know, were we not dashing for Seoul instead of sidetracking from that major objective? And anyway, they said, no enemy forces were foolish enough to have remained in Kunwi. My subordinate units normally jumped to follow my orders, but they couldn't hide their disappointment this time because they felt we should be at the vanguard of the attack rather than consigned to duties in the rear.

When the war broke out, only a few American advisers worked in the division, but our complement had grown to almost twenty by the time of the Tabu-dong battles. In addition to the chief adviser to the division, who was Lt. Col. Lloyd H. Rockwell, American augmentation from both KMAG and U.S. I Corps included a communications (commo) team; advisers for operations, intelligence, logistics, and communications; a corps liaison officer; an air-ground liaison officer; an adviser for each of the three regiments; and of course, administrative members of the advisory headquarters staff. I found the supply and communications people and the air-ground liaison officer to be especially valuable.

This was still the period, of course, when the ROK Army relied heavily on the U.S. military. Lt. Col. Rockwell was replaced by Lt. Col. Robert T. Hazlett. Colonel Hazlett came from a cultured family, was the son of a U.S. Army major general, and helped me in the ROK 1st Division until the January 4, 1951, withdrawal from North Korea.

As the ROK 1st Division entered Kunwi per our orders, we found the hamlet utterly destroyed. The ruins provided no place for the enemy to hide, and the NKPA was long gone. We crossed the Naktong River and proceeded northward, along the same route the enemy had pushed us down three months before. For an entire week we dutifully conducted the despised mop-up operations throughout the district around Mount Songni.

Enemy forces defeated in both the Cholla and Chungchong provinces converged on the Mount Songni region in an attempt to flee north in the relative safety offered by the peaks of the Sobaek Mountains. A great number of defeated enemy soldiers were scattered throughout the area.

I formed a special commando team from my engineers before we entered the Mount Songni area and named Lt. Ahn Chong Hun as its commander. Ahn was later to rise to the rank of lieutenant general. I directed the commandos to advance swiftly on Chongju, and I myself hurried toward that city ahead of the bulk of the division.

Refugees packed the roads, desperate to return to their homes. Large numbers of defeated NKPA soldiers had donned civilian clothing and mingled with the refugees. They stood out like so many sore thumbs, but I didn't want to waste time on them, so we just continued north, passing them by.

Rice stood ready to harvest in the fields, and the country villages showed very little war damage. Indeed I saw few signs that the war had passed through the verdant countryside at all. If one can feel relieved by something as deleterious to human life as a counterattack in wartime, I felt relieved now. My eyes traversed miles of rice fields, dry now, and undulating in heavy waves of golden grain. Had we delayed our counterattack only a few days, the invaluable rice would have fallen into enemy hands.

Talking to farmers along the way, I found that even during the brief period of enemy occupation, the North Koreans had issued production quotas to the farms, not only for rice but even for lesser grains such as sesame. The farmers said they had been abused badly by the enemy, passing each day as if in a nightmare as they were forced into heavy manual labor, like carrying war materiel on their backs. Without exception the farmers along the way warmly welcomed the return of their own army and the UN forces as well.

My party was ambushed by NKPA stragglers as we drove at night in a jeep and a half-ton truck near Chongju, but luckily no one was hit. At Chongju we learned from local residents that NKPA Front Commander Kim Chaek and his party had fled only hours before toward Chochiwon. I immediately got a mop-up operation under way in an attempt to run the NKPA leader to ground. I sent our commando detachment under Lieutenant Ahn to dog his path and, requesting artillery support from the U.S. 1st Cavalry Division's 5th Regiment, commanded by Col. Marcel Crombez, which had arrived in the area ahead of us. Unfortunately, however, we failed in our attempt to nail Kim.

I turned my party south again, reunited with the division proper, and headed north a second time, arriving in Chongju on October 2. I ordered my three regiments to assemble in the city. As they settled in, I set up division headquarters in North Chungchong Province's capitol and awaited further orders.

As my 1st Division reached Chongju, got ready to bed down, and awaited instructions, our colleagues in ROK I Corps across the peninsula were advancing swiftly northward along the east coast. On October 1, they punched across the 38th parallel and into enemy territory. I was beside myself with impatience. We spent several uncomfortable days fidgeting in Chongju. I ran into Colonel Michaelis again there. He had completed a circuit through the Cholla provinces and was just arriving in Chongju. Michaelis and I decided to have our own private victory celebration. I acquired some village *makkoli,* thick rice wine, while Michaelis brought some Western whiskey and empty ration cans for goblets. We even managed to round up a few meager snacks to chase down the liquor. The commanders and staff officers of our two units had a good old-fashioned drinking party. I hadn't had a drop of the grape since the war started, and as soon as I had thrown back a few drinks, my mind spun instantly back to the wife and daughter I'd left in Seoul. I wanted to see them very, very much. On this score, at least, I suspect the division commander and the lowliest private in the division felt exactly the same.

On October 5, U.S. I Corps Headquarters in Taejon called the division commanders in for a conference. I flew up to Taejon in a tiny L-5 liaison aircraft kindly made available to me by a U.S. Army artillery unit.

U.S. I Corps Headquarters occupied the south Chungchong Province capitol. The other major commanders had already come and gone. These included the U.S. 1st Cavalry Division's Major General Gay, the U.S. 24th Division's Major General John Church, and Brig. Basil Coad, commander of the British 27th Brigade.

I met with the corps chief of staff, Rinaldo Van Brunt; John R. Jeter, the G-3; and the G-2, Percy W. Thompson, whose daughter was married to General Eisenhower's son. The three staff officers presented me with a thick envelope containing orders for an attack on the North Korean capital of Pyongyang. As I paged through the order, I couldn't help exclaiming happily, "Great! We're going to attack Pyongyang!" But I was disappointed as I got into the details.

The 1st Cav Division was to lead the offensive, dashing north along a main axis paralleling the Seoul-Uijongbu Highway, with the U.S. 24th Division advancing east of the main axis before attacking Pyongyang.

The British 27th Brigade was to follow in the wake of the 1st Cav as I

Corps reserve, while my ROK 1st Division was relegated to an advance in the west, nearest the Yellow Sea, along a line running through Kaesong. This route did not lead to Pyongyang, and operations along it amounted to nothing more than more mop-up work.

The overall operations plan called for ROK II Corps on the east to attack northward in parallel with U.S. I Corps; Pyongyang was to be encircled by the 1st Cav pushing up from the south while the U.S. 7th Division barreled in directly from the east, after landing at Wonsan on North Korea's east coast.

The plan's chief weakness was that it excluded all ROK Army units from the attack on Pyongyang. I found that absolutely unacceptable. The North Koreans started the war by capturing our capital. Now that it was time to return the favor, I believed that any attack on the enemy's capital that excluded the ROK Army was meaningless. On the other hand, I could not have cared less whether the U.S. Army exercised complete operational control or whether my division was subordinate to an American unit.

I immediately asked the corps chief of staff, Van Brunt, to schedule an appointment with the corps commander. Van Brunt hesitated, explaining that General Milburn was in bed with a very bad cold. I got mad and raised my voice. "Are you telling me that a division commander can't even see his corps commander?" Van Brunt picked up the telephone and asked for the commanding general.

General Milburn was in fact in bed in his private quarters, a van pulled by a dedicated vehicle. He greeted me with a present, a bottle of whiskey, and congratulated me on our breakthrough at the Pusan Perimeter. I presented him with a Soviet pistol my men had captured.

"I've read the operations plan, General Milburn," I said bluntly. "I can't accept the idea that no ROK Army unit will participate in the attack on Pyongyang." I requested that he reconsider.

General Milburn asked me how many vehicles were in the ROK 1st Division inventory. I told him we had sixty or seventy. "U.S. divisions," he said in an effort to dissuade me, "have hundreds of vehicles. I don't think the ROK 1st Division can lead a major attack with your existing level of mobility. General MacArthur wants Pyongyang taken right away. What I want to do is grab the city in the shortest possible time, utilizing the superior mobility and firepower of a U.S. division by putting it at the point of the attack. I sympathize with your feelings, General Paik, but you've got to understand my position."

I couldn't relent. We had to be at the front of the battle for Pyongyang. I wanted to restore the honor of my living comrades, who had known only the gall of defeat since the Imjin River battle, and of my dead comrades, who had given their lives fighting to defend their country. And I had a single-minded determination to stand at the vanguard of any battle to liberate my own hometown, which I had left five scant years before as a refugee but to which I would now return as a general officer in the army of the Republic of Korea to take retribution for a war the communists had started.

"We don't have the trucks," I acknowledged. "But we are tough, and we can march day and night on our fighting spirit. Give us this chance. Korea is carpeted with hills, and our roads are bad. I think we can march around the clock and beat an American unit to Pyongyang. Pyongyang is my hometown, and I know the terrain around the city like the back of my hand."

I explained to General Milburn that as it happened his plan for capturing Pyongyang was based on virtually the same concept used by the Japanese to take the city during the Sino-Japanese War in 1894. I stressed my familiarity with the history of that war. I told the general that in the Sino-Japanese War, the Japanese 5th Division, the Sangnyong Task Force, and the Wonsan Task Force had closed on Pyongyang from three sides, surrounding and seizing the city. I told General Milburn that I wanted my ROK 1st Division to emulate the role of the Sangnyong Task Force, advancing north through Singye.

As I argued passionately for the need of Korean participation in the offensive, I realized at one point that tears were coursing down my cheeks. Still, my historical account had caught General Milburn's interest, and he unfolded a map to follow my explanation. I could not guarantee the general, I said, that the ROK 1st Division would beat all other units to the enemy's capital, but the situation afforded the ROK 1st Division a unique opportunity to compete with the world's strongest military force, the U.S. Army.

When I finally ran out of arguments, General Milburn just sat silently for what seemed like hours. "General Paik," he said finally. "Go for it. I'll give you the chance. I'll swap your mission with that of the 24th Division. You go up the east, on our right wing."

General Milburn picked up the telephone and asked for his chief of staff. "Give General Church's mission to General Paik," he directed. I was flabbergasted that General Milburn could grab a telephone and change an operations order involving division-scale units with a single sentence, without convening conferences and making explanations. Watching him in action, I concluded that General Milburn's command style was uncommonly decisive.

Van Brunt promised to send me a revised version of the operations order without delay, but I was afraid something else would come up and cause General Milburn to change his mind, so I waited at corps headquarters for two or three hours until I got the amended orders safely in hand. I flew back to ROK 1st Division Headquarters a happy man. I walked into the headquarters building with a huge smile on my face. "We lead the attack on Pyongyang!" As my meaning dawned on the headquarter's team, the room dissolved into a chorus of happy shouting.

We decided the best way to break through the 38th parallel was to concentrate at Korangpo. The ROK 1st Division left Chongju on October 6.

Attacking Pyongyang "Patton's Way"

In two days we reached the place across from Seoul's Mapo ferry where we were scheduled to cross the main trunk of the Han River. We were very near Seoul, and the roads in the area were tangled with military traffic, some heading north, some south. The U.S. 7th Division had landed at Inchon and was now heading south for Pusan, while the U.S. 1st Marine Division that had recaptured Seoul was now moving west, back to Inchon.

As we came up from the south, the Han River crossing sites were masses of congestion. All bridges over the Han had been destroyed, and the only way to cross from Youido into Seoul's Mapo District was a pontoon bridge supported by twin rows of rubber boats. Despite the limited crossing facilities, units managed to cross in an orderly manner and in accord with the strict priorities established by U.S. I Corps.

U.S. divisions were burdened with heavy weapons and bulky equipment and required a very long time to cross the river, so we suffered a substantial delay as we waited our turn to cross. U.S. I Corps Headquarters published a detailed crossing schedule and exercised strict control over subordinate units during the river crossing. Crossing water in the field always proved to be a serious challenge to commanders of major units.

The U.S. 7th Division and the U.S. 1st Marine Division had successfully conducted an amphibious landing at Inchon and retaken Seoul. In accord with General MacArthur's plan, however, the two units were now on their respective ways to Pusan and Inchon to reembark for an amphibious landing at Wonsan on North Korea's east coast.

A serious problem developed as each of these massive divisions closed on their respective port cities and monopolized the docks in both locations with preparations for their amphibious assault on Wonsan. The resulting delay in off-loading supplies destined for forces advancing overland into North Korea was exceptionally detrimental. Meanwhile, the ROK I Corps on the east coast advanced far ahead of allied forces on the west, captured Wonsan itself, and robbed the amphibious operation of any usefulness whatsoever.

Had the two U.S. divisions not been shunted aside for the Wonsan landing but joined I Corps in our overland push into North Korea, I believe the course of the war would have been altered drastically. I have been told that Eighth Army Commanding Gen. Walton H. Walker, in fact, envisaged these divisions as support for the overland attack into North Korea but dared not recommend this course of action to General of the Army MacArthur, who had been further apotheosized by the success of the landing at Inchon. This was a most frustrating turn of events.

While waiting to cross the Han, I met with ROK Air Force Chief of Staff Kim Chung Yul at the Youido airfield, and we swapped war stories. I was sure to tell him, "I'm on my way to Pyongyang."

I set up a temporary division command post at the township hall north of the Han and northwest of Seoul and awaited the ROK 1st Division's turn to cross the river. I learned that my younger brother Paik In Yup was in Seoul, so I took some spare time to go into the city and run him down. Much of Korea's capital lay in ruins, and Seoul was virtually deserted, except on its western fringe in the Mapo area where U.S. trucks moved in a steady stream northward. I found my brother at a primary school.

In Yup had replaced Gen. Kim Suk Won as commander of the Capital Division and fought at Angang and Kigye before being wounded and evacuated. He recovered quickly and was assigned once more to command the 17th Regiment, which had been selected to participate in the amphibious landing at Inchon. His regiment landed shoulder to shoulder with U.S. units at Inchon, and when I found him, the 17th had just wrapped up the operation to retake Seoul.

In early July, In Yup's 17th Regiment had participated in an operation in the Kochang sector designed to relieve the U.S. 24th Division, which was cut off and isolated by the NKPA in the area. That was the first instance in the Korean War that Eighth Army requested a ROK Army unit to come to the aid of an American unit. In Yup's 17th was an elite regiment, and its combat strength was second only to that of a fully filled division.

I had been wounded twice myself over the months of fighting and fancied myself a warrior, but my brother's tale of his valorous combat exploits filled me with pride. Then, too, In Yup didn't deflate my soaring spirits any when he told me the marvelous news that my wife and daughter had survived the invasion.

With the Han River at last behind us, the ROK 1st Division marched to its assembly area south of Korangpo, arriving on October 10, 1950. We were two days behind the U.S. 1st Cav Division, which had crossed the river ahead of us. The ROK I Corps on the eastern front, commanded by Brig. Gen. Kim Paik Il, meanwhile, reached North Korea's Wonsan that same day, while ROK II Corps in the central front under Maj. Gen. Yu Jae Hung had advanced to Chorwon and Kumhwa.

The distant thunder of artillery told us in the ROK 1st Division on the western front that American units of our own U.S. I Corps already were attacking north of Kaesong. We were marking time at the Imjin River, exactly where we had started the war, and felt left out.

As we waited at our assembly area, I encountered one of those unexpected incidents that tries a commander's wisdom. About a hundred ROK 1st Division officers and men who had fought with us in the original Imjin battle at the start of the war suddenly appeared out of nowhere and rejoined the division. They claimed they had been unable to get across the Han during our great withdrawal and had hidden in Seoul. They now joined the division in a "delayed reunion."

I was pleased to have the extra hands, to be sure, but I was troubled, too, and couldn't hide it. Each man had faced his own set of difficulties, of course, after failing to find a way to cross the Han and rejoin the division during our long withdrawal and subsequent advance. But these men, especially the officers, should not have stopped trying to rejoin the division even if their efforts resulted in death. As strong as my personal views on the matter were, my staff's views were even sterner. They believed we had to investigate the circumstances surrounding each man's failure to escape and also determine whether each had collaborated with the enemy.

I thought the matter over and finally convened a staff meeting to announce my decision. "We face this problem now," I began, "because the war has visited great calamity upon our nation. In such a situation, who shall blame whom? Let's wash the past away in the waters of the Imjin. Let's be one again. Let's be concerned only with serving our country. We must put the past behind us and charge ahead to capture the enemy's capital."

I directed the division G-1 to reassign each of the returnees to a position commensurate with his original posting in the division. Most of these men served faithfully and with redoubled effort, and, in fact, after the war, many were to rise to positions of influence in every field of human endeavor. Even today I think my decision was the right one.

Morale was sky-high as we kicked off our assault on the morning of October 11, 1950. We were jumping off from Korangpo, and at last we would penetrate the 38th parallel and fight on enemy territory rather than our own. The 11th Regiment under Col. Kim Dong Bin led the division's left, attacking toward Pugu. Lt. Col. Cho Jae Mi's 15th Regiment led our right and attacked toward Sangyong, while Col. Kim Chum Kon's 12th Regiment attacked straight up the road toward Kuhwa.

The first day of the offensive punctured our morale. The problem wasn't the NKPA. The enemy resisted as stubbornly as always, to be sure, but the former excellence just wasn't there. A high percentage of the NKPA formations were composed of inexperienced reinforcements who were brought in as fillers after main-force units had suffered terrible casualties in the fighting in the south. Our problem was sheer distance.

As the first day ended, I conducted a field check of each regiment and found that each had advanced only about 3 miles. I was in a gloomy state of mind as I rode back to the division command post in a township capitol at Korangpo. At three miles a day, how long would it take our 1st Division to cover the 105 miles that lay between us and the enemy's capital?

My artillery commander Colonel Hennig happened by and noticed my black mood. "General Paik, you don't look so good. What's wrong?"

"Our attack is just too slow," I answered. "Much slower than I anticipated. I promised General Milburn we'd be the first into Pyongyang, but we'll never make it at this rate."

"Are you familiar with Gen. George Patton?" Hennig asked.

"I've heard of him," I acknowledged. Hennig went on to explain that Patton had led infantry, tank, artillery, engineer, and air assets as an integrated force in a bold dash aimed squarely at the center of the enemy's lines.

"Let's use the Patton approach," Hennig suggested. That sounded good to me, but the heart and soul of Patton's approach to warfare was the tank. We had no armor. Colonel Hennig advised me to go directly to the corps commander and request armor support. Speaking confidentially, Hennig told me that General Milburn had great confidence in me and would accede to the request.

Hennig proposed using his existing ammunition transport trucks to set up a "shuttle march," under which his artillery drivers would transport the infantry forward, return for the artillery ammo, and then repeat the process. Using this approach, Hennig felt that all the ROK 1st Division needed to emulate Patton's lightning advances was to get our hands on some tanks.

The U. S. Army was extremely reluctant to provide armor support to ROK Army units at this early point in the war and in fact had not done so unless the armor was accompanied by U.S. infantry units who could support the tanks. Tanks operating with Korean units were thought to be at risk because ROK Army forces had neither training nor experience in joint infantry-armor operations.

I telephoned General Milburn and requested armor support. He listened to my explanation noncommittally and hung up, promising to call me back in a few minutes. Half an hour dragged by before he called. "Okay," the corps commander said. "I'll send you a company of tanks."

True to his word, twenty M-46 Patton tanks roared up to division headquarters the next morning. Even the ear-splitting thunder of the tank engines failed to drown out the cheers from the officers and men in ROK 1st Division Headquarters. For the first time in my career, I was in direct command of tanks, Company C of the 6th Tank Battalion. I must confess I couldn't hide my excitement either.

"You must observe one prerequisite when you fight like Patton," Colonel Hennig had warned me in all seriousness. "The division commander must ride on the lead tank and command the division from there." Command and control were exceptionally complex in a unit where soldiers from two nations fought side by side. The armies of Korea and the United States had different protocols for cooperation, different languages, sharply diverging training methods, and cultural differences in problem-solving techniques. Colonel Hennig's point was that I could solve these barriers to command and control only if I, as division commander, rode with the tanks on division point.

The ROK 1st Division knew nothing about using tanks. We had to detach a battalion from the 12th Regiment and conduct joint infantry and tank training near Korangpo in full view of the enemy. I left nothing to chance in this crucial training cycle, even doing the interpreting myself. After several hours of yelling over the roar of the tank motors, though, my throat was too hoarse to continue.

After a lunch break, we geared up to repeat the training. I assigned Assistant G-3 Maj. Park Chin Suk to interpret for the second round, since my voice was completely gone. Park spoke excellent English. By the end of the day, our officers and men had joint armor operations down pat. The captain who commanded the American tank company reported to me the next morning that our boys had done so well at the training session he saw no reason to hold up the assault any longer.

I climbed onto tank number one and was about to issue the order for the division to jump off when my new chief adviser, Lt. Col. Robert T. Hazlett, told me he opposed my riding on the lead tank. Hazlett argued that the division commander would be an easy target for enemy sniper fire during an assault if he were riding on the division's lead tank. He wondered aloud who would command the division if I were to be killed in this manner. His point was well taken, but I would not be dissuaded. My very bones ached to take Pyongyang, and now that the time was near, I was not about to let my personal safety be an issue.

A company of engineers equipped with bulldozers had been assigned to the ROK 1st Division from the corps engineers, and now they, the forward air controller team, and each of the varied arms that made up the divisions reported that they were ready for the assault.

On the morning of October 12, the ROK 1st Division boldly began a very fast advance northward. We projected an imposing military bearing that General Patton himself would have envied. We seized Kuhwa immediately and charged on toward Sibyon without missing a beat. Our fight at Kuhwa was the northernmost penetration on the western front at the time. The ROK 1st Division charged along madly. When we encountered the enemy we called in close air support, showered the target

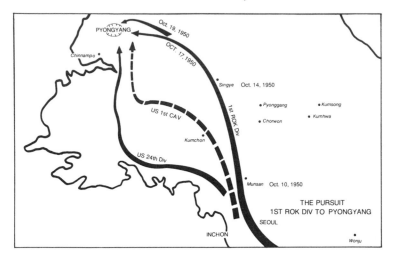

with barrages from our own artillery, and then our armor-infantry team would break through the NKPA defenses and swiftly establish mastery over the enemy. We changed the division's motto to "We advance," and soon the Americans were calling us the "We go" division.

I sent the 15th Regiment on a parallel route farther to the east, routing it through Sangyong and issuing orders for the regiment to rejoin the division at Sibyon. A commander should split his forces only for good reason, of course, and mine was that the ROK 1st Division was punching through enemy defensive positions as if they were paper. Employing the elements of speed and shock, we had no trouble breaking through NKPA defenses in column formation, but this tactic alone did not allow us to inflict sufficient casualties on the enemy. We adapted the technique by conducting small-scale envelopments as we advanced, striking the enemy from two sides in a kind of "moving pincers" tactic. This had the desired effect.

Choi Young Hi had been promoted to brigadier general and now served as my assistant division commander. Lt. Col. Cho Jae Mi replaced him as commander of the 15th Regiment. Cho commanded the 15th Division when President Syngman Rhee was overthrown in 1960 and brought his unit into Seoul during that incident; he retired as a brigadier general. Cho and his regimental S-3 executed the moving pincers tactic to perfection.

As we advanced along the Sami River between the hamlets of Komisong and Pugu, a U.S. Army mechanized unit tore through our area of operations in a tremendous cloud of dust without so much as a "by your leave." The unit turned out to be the 5th Cavalry Regiment of the

U.S. 1st Cav Division, and it was heading north right through our assigned area of operations. Intruding into the operational zone of a friendly unit was a military faux pas of the highest order, since such an action could easily lead to misidentification and a tragic exchange of fire. Moreover, we were competing with the 1st Cav to be the first unit into Pyongyang, and our nerves were on edge.

When the cavalry unit tore into view, I was talking with the U.S. I Corps assistant G-3, who happened to be visiting my unit on official business. I asked this officer to intercede with the intruding 5th Cav Regiment and have it get out of my area of operations.

"General Paik," the American officer responded. "I'm only a lieutenant colonel, and that regimental commander is a full colonel. I think it would be a good idea if you told him yourself."

His answer underscored for me the respect for rank and the primacy of position that prevailed in the U.S. Army, characteristics I had already noted. Well, I was a brigadier general, and I ran down Colonel Crombez, the commander of the offending regiment, and told him to clear the heck out. His explanation was that his 5th Cav had run into a concentration of NKPA units at Kumchon. The enemy units had mounted a dynamic resistance, so on order from his division commander General Gay, Crombez had undertaken to bypass Kumchon and in the process had inadvertently charged into our area of operations. The 5th Cav Regiment was massive. In motor march formation, the column took an hour and a half to pass a given point.

I let Colonel Crombez and the 5th pass on through without further comment, but the Americans working with my 1st Division were infuriated, claiming that the 5th Cav had "violated the order of war." In a twinkling, the thoughtless act of a U.S. Army unit changed my own American commanders from loyal members of the U.S. Army into loyal supporters of the ROK 1st Division. My antiaircraft artillery group and my tank company had joined the team.

Despite the rashness of the 5th Cav intrusion, the bypass tactic worked. The NKPA 19th and 27th divisions massing at Kumchon were annihilated before they could establish serious, organized resistance, an extraordinary battlefield feat.

Night caught up with us just as we were about to cross the border into North Korea's Hwanghae Province. After advancing almost twenty miles that day, our tank company ceased the attack to turn aside and establish an overnight encampment. "Come on, let's keep going," I pressed the American officer. "It's not time to rest yet."

"Let us rest at night. We need hot food, and we've got to shave," the American replied with disarming frankness. "Tanks are tigers during the day but pussycats at night."

I remembered that these Americans had crossed half the world to fight in a foreign land and decided not to insist. I let them billet for the night and posted a guard to protect the tanks. But neither I nor the other officers and men of the ROK Army had time to rest. Yelling, "Catch up in the morning," we continued northward in a night march.

The Greatest Day of My Life

We took Sibyon on October 13, 1950. The city is a crucial transportation hub in landlocked Hwanghae Province and served as a key supply point during the NKPA's invasion of our country in June.

The enemy mounted a spirited resistance at Sibyon, but our tactics carried the day. We attacked from two directions. Our tanks and the 12th Regiment assaulted from the south at the same time the 15th Regiment, which I had sent on a bypass to the east through Sangyong, hit the city from the east. The success of the operation greatly boosted our confidence in our skill at employing the joint armor and infantry team in an assault.

Indeed the ROK 1st Division earned a reputation among U.S. units for outstanding coordination of armor and infantry. Perhaps for this reason, Company D of the U.S. 6th Tank Battalion was also attached to the division even though I had not requested more tanks. The commander of the 6th, Lt. Col. John Growden, accompanied his company and brought his headquarters company with him, further adding to the ROK 1st Division's considerable armor assets. The ROK 1st Division now owned 50 tanks.

We smashed with irresistible force through Singye, Suan, and Yul-ri and pushed northward into South Pyongyan Province, seizing the hamlet of Sangwon on October 17. The ROK 1st Division had driven to within a scant twenty miles of the outskirts of Pyongyang and was poised for the final assault. The closer we pushed to Pyongyang, however, the more starch we found in the enemy resistance.

Just outside of Sangwon our armor people had the scare of their lives. The tanks at the division point were growling along a winding, narrow road set in terrain that severely limited their vision. As the lead tank rounded a bend, it came face to face with an enemy T-34, the first of a column of five enemy tanks heading south down the road to counterattack. Neither of the leading tank crews had seen the other, and both were astonished. The respective drivers threw on the brakes to avoid an actual physical collision.

I was riding on the lead tank. The shock and tension of the sudden encounter momentarily stunned the tank crews. I managed only to jump off the tank and take cover in a ditch.

The young tank platoon leader who commanded that lead tank didn't fall victim to shock, however. The officer instantly used his radio to contact the friendly tanks following in his wake. Five of his tanks sped backwards at top speed to form a staggered line across the road and ditch in such a way that all had clear visibility. On the platoon leader's command, the Pattons all fired a volley of direct fire from their main weapons that knocked out the enemy tanks where they sat. In an instant the T-34s were burning, and bewildered crewman spilled out of the monstrous vehicles with their hands raised in surrender. As in this case, tank battles between NKPA armor forces and U.S. tankers usually underscored the vastly superior capabilities of the Americans, with their long experience in World War II.

As we advanced, we found that village houses sheltered many civilians, although all the young men were gone. The women, children, and old men often came out to line the lanes and greet us, waving our national flag called Taekukki.

Everywhere now the NKPA was surrendering or melting away, but we could not spare the time to stop and process prisoners. "Stay put, the next echelon will take care of you," we solemnly directed surrendering enemy soldiers. We were concentrating our minds on the dash for Pyongyang.

Near Sangwon we came across a ghastly scene. A large group of twisted, blackened enemy bodies lay as they had fallen on a hill that had been subjected to a U.S. Air Force napalm attack. We had seen the results of napalm before, but it was always gruesome.

As we closed on Pyongyang, I decided to hit the city with a pincer movement, or enveloping attack. I split the 15th Regiment off from the division at Yul-ri and sent it along a separate route with orders to cross the Taedong River west of Kangdong and attack Pyongyang from the northwest as the bulk of the division hit the city simultaneously from the southeast. I regarded it as unwise for an entire division to attack from a single direction and didn't want to provide grist for criticism by future tacticians.

As the sun set on October 18, the ROK 1st Division marched into Chidong, a hamlet a mere nine miles from the outskirts of Pyongyang. The low ridges to the right and left of Chidong afforded excellent defensive positions for the enemy. Our reconnaissance units reported that the NKPA manned strong defensive positions along both ridges. The enemy had built tough, Soviet Army–style pillboxes over a deep, wide area. The approaches were protected by barriers and thick mine fields. The North Koreans were ready for a decisive contest, but if we could break through here, we had level terrain all the way into Pyongyang.

We laid heavy artillery concentrations on the positions but saw no indications that the fire had fazed the dug-in enemy in the slightest. I convened an operational conference in a house along the road, calling in my commanders, staff, and U.S. advisers. This was to be our final discussion before the attack on the enemy's capital, and its purpose was to decide how to crack the tough defensive nut we faced so we could charge into Pyongyang, winning the race.

The key issue was a simple question of timing for the attack. Should we ignore the danger and mount an immediate night attack, or should we play it safe and wait until daylight threw some light on the problem? We also had to decide the route each unit would follow in the attack and determine which unit would carry the weight of the main assault.

The 11th Regimental commander Kim Dong Bin, the 12th Regimental commander Kim Chum Kon, and the 6th Tank Battalion commander Lieutenant Colonel Growden were of one voice in urging that we maintain our momentum and push on through the enemy positions, forcing a quick conclusion. Colonel Growden gave unrestricted play to his decisive personality and even explained a tank maneuver he thought could carry the defenses, suggesting that the infantry follow his tanks in the attack.

My two regimental commanders, meanwhile, had been classmates in the Korea Military Academy and now maintained a thinly disguised professional rivalry. Neither was willing to let the other undertake the main attack. Col. Kim Dong Bin was especially insistent that his 11th Regiment, which had never worked with the tanks, now be allowed for that reason to take division point and operate with the tanks on this occasion. Kim was most adamant, and I faced a difficult choice.

Growden spoke out in favor of the 12th Regiment, asking whether it was wise to "change horses in midstream." At this decisive point in the discussion, Growden said that he found it difficult to accept the idea of working with the 11th Regiment because he had established a close working relationship with the 12th during the course of our dash through North Korea.

The words were no sooner out of Growden's mouth, however, when Colonel Hennig suddenly yelled, "Shut up!" Hennig shouted so forcefully at Growden that every Korean officer in the tiny house jumped an inch off the floor. Hennig then sharply reminded Growden of the principle that combat plans were determined by the infantry and that the mission of the other arms was to support the plan. Growden didn't utter another syllable. I don't know why he bowed out of the conversation so completely, although I've wondered if it was because Hennig had been Growden's instructor at West Point when the latter was a cadet there.

In an attempt to accommodate all my commanders, I directed that we immediately mount a night attack. Once through the NKPA's defensive positions, the 12th would share division point with the tanks, guiding our main attack to the Taedong River bridge leading into Pyongyang.

The 11th would divert to capture the Mirim and Pyongyang airports and then cross the Taedong River into Pyongyang at Mount Chuam.

I stressed to my commanders that we were not to shell any of the cultural artifacts of the city. My mind's eye surveyed some of these even as I spoke. I saw vividly in my memory the ancient Taedong Gate, the Yongwang Pavilion, Ulmildae Observatory, and the Chongyu Wall. The names of prominent civil servants were carved at this site, and one of these was the name of my maternal grandfather, Bang Hung Ju, who had served as head of logistics for Pyongyang Province in the Royal Army during the Chosun dynasty. I knew, of course, that collateral damage was unavoidable during combat in an urban area, but if I were to destroy cultural monuments deliberately in my hometown, future generations would scorn me forever.

I was surprised when Colonel Hennig accepted my instructions to protect Pyongyang's cultural heritage with more equanimity than my Korean commanders. Hennig knew of previous examples of such orders, such as the declaration of Rome as an open city during World War II and excluding Kyoto from U.S. bombing raids because as an ancient Japanese capital the city was replete with cultural artifacts.

The 12th Regiment led the division's night attack on the NKPA positions. As our artillery fires lifted, the 12th started up the ridges, driving home the attack throughout the whole of the night. If we failed to breach the defenses here, our dream of being the first unit into Pyongyang would clearly go up in smoke.

Just before dawn, the enemy broke and ran, abandoning its positions. The men watched eagerly as the morning fog lifted to reveal the vast plain rolling from our position across the last miles into Pyongyang. Scattered hillocks dotted the plain, which seemed otherwise to be a patchwork of dry rice paddies. The great plain could not have provided better terrain for armored operations. The tankers had struggled for weeks with the unpaved, winding, narrow mountain roads, and now they practically jumped for joy. "This," they exulted, "is real tank country."

We had but a single worry. How close was the 1st Cav to Pyongyang?

As it grew light, a Mosquito light observation aircraft flew back and forth between the ROK 1st Division and the U.S. 1st Cav, reporting each division's position at regular intervals. The situation resembled nothing so much as a sports event. The 1st Cav was passing through Chunghwa, and U.S. Air Force bombs were already raining black smoke over Pyongyang.

I shall remember our final assault on Pyongyang to my dying day. My two regiments attacked in line abreast across the vast plain, supported by fifty tanks and no fewer than four battalions of artillery—more than one hundred howitzers and mortars. This was my moment in the sun.

I would never be treated to a greater spectacle as a division commander. The sight of the ROK 1st Division in assault was the grandest panorama I shall behold in my lifetime. No spectacle in a Hollywood war movie could run even a close second to the reality of our charge.

The youthful, homeless refugee who had fled North Korea only five years before was now returning as a general officer at the head of fifteen thousand American and Korean troops poised to capture his own home, Pyongyang, the enemy's capital. No words can convey the emotions that swept me. Those moments were the most exquisite of my life. The villagers on the city's outskirts had already hoisted dozens of South Korean national flags. The center of each was marked by the red and blue interlocking commas symbolizing the great ultimate philosophy, or heart, of the Oriental belief in the dualism of the cosmos, as it was the heart of our flag. The flags fluttered proudly in the breeze as we rode by on our tanks.

During the assault, the division communications officer discovered and monitored an enemy telephone line, only to be shocked when a North Korean soldier came on the line from the NKPA General Headquarters. He rushed over to find me. "Sir. I don't speak North Korean dialect," he said. "Can you talk to this guy yourself?"

I could, and I grabbed the mouthpiece. "Comrade," I asked in a thick Pyongyang accent. "What's the situation now?"

"Hundreds of U.S. Imperialist tanks are bearing down on us," he answered.

"Comrade," I ordered. "You must resist to the end!"

"What the hell are you talking about?" came the response. "If we're to survive, we've got to retreat right this minute!" My conversation with the frightened NKPA soldier made it clear to me that the enemy's situation verged on chaos.

As our assault wave was about to reach Chuul, we suddenly came under intense machine-gun and mortar fire, much of which seemed to be directed right at my head. It was a close thing. The fire was coming from a large barracks the Japanese had built there. I jumped down quickly from my tank and flopped unceremoniously down in a ditch along the road. The tank returned the fire, making short work of the enemy pocket.

The rest of the attack went smoothly, although the innumerable land mines gave us some trouble. Enemy mines were boxlike affairs made of wood rather than metal, defeating our mine detectors, which keyed only on metal. We had to remove the mines individually, with bayonets, and I had to put infantry on the task because my engineers alone couldn't accomplish the job in the time we had. We were indebted to NKPA prisoners in the business of clearing the mines. The former NKPA soldiers not only knew exactly where the mines were buried but were exceptionally skilled at removing them. The mine operation was remarkable indeed, with enemy prisoners of war working for my engineers to remove their own mines.

As we neared the Taedong River bridge and prepared to enter East Pyongyang, a jeep following close behind me hit a mine and overturned. Division chief of staff Suk Ju Am was riding in the vehicle and suffered a serious head injury. Colonel Suk had the bad luck of being evacuated to the rear with Pyongyang literally in front of our noses. Division G-3 Mun Hyong Tae was riding in the back seat of the same jeep, but luckily he escaped injury.

At 11:00 A.M. we arrived at the intersection that led onto the bridge. We had agreed that we would meet the U.S. 1st Cav Division at this intersection, but it was nowhere to be seen. The ROK 1st Division had beaten everyone to Pyongyang.

As our lead vehicles pulled into the intersection, an ear-splitting explosion came from the direction of the bridge, and chunks of flying iron filled the air. The enemy had welcomed us to Pyongyang by blowing the bridge. The bridge's central span dropped neatly into the river.

As we awaited the arrival of the 1st Cav, some U.S. soldiers in my 5th Tank Battalion put up a sign. "WELCOME 1ST CAV DIVISION," it said. "FROM THE 1ST ROK DIVISION. PAIK." I spotted the sign and thought it was a bit insulting. I told the U.S. officer at the site that I wanted it taken down. He wouldn't do it. "I'm a member of the ROK 1st Division," he responded, growing red in the face. "And our team won! I'm proud of the sign."

We waited about forty minutes before the lead element of the U.S. 1st Cavalry Division pulled into the intersection. The unit was accompanied by a lot of brass: the division commander, Major General Gay; the corps commander, Maj. Gen. Frank W. Milburn; and Major General Low, a special envoy of President Truman.

The lead element was followed by a veritable throng of foreign war correspondents, their camera shutters clicking like so many automatic weapons. Americans and Koreans alike shared the pleasure of the moment, and we congratulated them on their entry into Pyongyang. I noticed a number of American and Korean soldiers from the two divisions hugging each other, and not always with dry eyes either. But forty minutes was all the rest the ROK 1st Division was to have. We were ordered to deploy immediately for the job of mopping up the city's streets. The 12th Regiment took charge of East Pyongyang, the area east of the Taedong river; while the 11th crossed the Taedong at the ford at the foot of Mount Chuam and advanced into West Pyongyang. Although all three bridges over the Taedong had been destroyed, I had known since I was a boy that the river beneath Chuam Mountain was shallow enough to ford.

I soon learned that my 15th Regiment had earned the honor of being the first friendly unit to enter downtown Pyongyang. As the main body of the ROK 1st Division was arriving at the first bridge, the 15th advanced on Moran Peak and Kim Il Sung University and then proceeded into downtown Pyongyang proper.

We had not foreseen the speed with which the 15th would press home its role in our double envelopment. As we began the difficult task of clearing the enemy from prepared, in-depth defensive positions stretching east from the bank of the Taedong River, the 15th attacked the same area from the rear. The NKPA soldiers threw down their weapons and surrendered en masse. On the other side of the ledger, the 15th Regiment experienced difficulties with its communications gear and couldn't contact us. The regiment leaders were in a state of near panic because they were unable to identify themselves as we crossed the river. They feared, of course, that we would send artillery fire plunging down on them before they could identify themselves.

The Taedong River in the vicinity of the Taedong Bridge leading to Pyongyang is four hundred fifty yards wide and very deep at that time of year, and the Americans regarded the ROK 1st Division's crossing of this water barrier as something of a miracle. The 1st Cav was obliged to hold up its advance into downtown Pyongyang until engineers had constructed pontoon bridges across the Taedong.

Colonel Crombez, a cavalry regiment commander in the 1st Cav Division, asked me how we had done it, obviously more than a little curious. "Shucks, Colonel," I answered with a broad smile. "I learned to swim in the Taedong River." That was true enough. "I know the terrain on the bottom of the river as well as I know it on top." That was stretching it a bit.

Pyongyang Is Free

The NKPA had erected barricades at key points throughout urban Pyongyang. The barricades were built of sturdy, earth-filled bags woven from rice straw and pierced with wood-lined firing ports. The NKPA urban warfare tactics involved resisting from behind these barricades and sniping from hidden positions in buildings. The major NKPA units had withdrawn from the city, however, so the defenders could not offer organized resistance despite their otherwise effective tactics. We had little trouble destroying each enemy position in turn.

We pursued the grim task of mopping up the city until after dark on October 19. The operation was marred by only one major incident. I got a call from a Colonel Kim, and as I picked up the handset, I was astonished to hear an enraged man yelling at me through the wire. "What the hell are you doing in my area of operations in a combat zone?"

I calmed the gentleman down enough to learn that he was Col. Kim Yong Ju, commanding the 8th Regiment of the ROK 7th Division, assigned to ROK II Corps. Kim was attacking along an axis parallel to that of my 15th Regiment, and his assault had carried him into West Pyongyang. Kim explained that he had been ordered by his corps commander, Maj. Gen. Yu Jae Hung, and his division commander to abandon his original route of advance and divert to attack Pyongyang. I learned later that ROK Army Chief of Staff Chung Il Kwon wanted a Korean unit to be the first to enter Pyongyang and had ordered Yu Jae Hung to send a force to accomplish this. Whatever the circumstances of the 8th Regiment's unannounced presence in Pyongyang, only good luck prevented a tragic clash between the ROK 1st Division and Colonel Kim's forces.

The ROK 1st Division's numbers looked good to me. We had kicked off an attack that started at Korangpo on the Imjin River above Seoul and ended at Pyongyang. We had averaged between seventeen and eighteen miles per day. German armored forces of World War II were famous for the lightning speed of their attacks, yet the average speed of our push on Pyongyang exceeded that of the German forces that advanced deep into the Soviet Union to surround Stalingrad.

During our attack, the men of the ROK 1st Division had sometimes marched, sometimes ridden, but we always pushed forward, and we seldom stopped for long, even at night. We beat a very tough competitor, the U.S. 1st Cavalry Division, which had already established a glorious tradition during World War II by being the first U.S. Army unit into both Manila and Tokyo. I will be grateful all my life to the officers and men of the ROK 1st Division, who carried heavy packs while also lugging cumbersome machine guns and mortars across their shoulders, and who with blistered, bleeding feet and all manner of afflictions maintained their desire to unify the Korean peninsula.

I was shaken by something that happened as we mopped up Pyongyang. I was in my jeep bumping toward East Pyongyang to see how the work was going. My vehicle rounded a corner just in time for me to witness enemy sniper fire from a second-story window in a nearby building hit one of my platoon leaders. The way the lieutenant fell made it clear he would not be getting back up.

The enraged members of the lieutenant's platoon charged the building as one man, concentrating all their fire on that single target. The charge and the volume of fire took the starch out of the several NKPA soldiers in the building, who clambered down the steps and stood wavering in the doorway, their hands raised in surrender.

The platoon had lost their leader, and the men did not cease firing. Colonel Hennig was with me, and he protested violently at this development. "You can't kill enemy soldiers who are surrendering," he yelled. "I won't work with the Korean army if it fights like this!"

It is natural to spare men with their hands upraised, as the Korean aphorism suggests: "Kill not he who surrenders." I was with Hennig on this one. I instantly ordered the men to stop shooting. They stopped, but they were not happy. Their faces fairly glowed with rage and frustration. "But, sir," one objected. "Those bastards killed the lieutenant!" Fear had drained the faces of the enemy soldiers, leaving them starkly pallid.

There is a fine line in combat. One is often praised for crushing the enemy, yet it takes only a minor misjudgment for a combat situation to degenerate into barbarity. Moreover, subterfuge and deception are tactics commonly encountered in combat, often making it difficult to distinguish friend from foe. We observed many cases during the war when misidentification led our forces to inflict casualties on friendly units, sometimes by ground fire and sometimes by air attack.

Courts and judges do not accompany infantrymen in combat. My view was that crucible of combat can strip reason from men, if only momentarily. But commanders don't operate in a vacuum, and if a unit inflicts unnecessary deaths and injuries on the enemy, the fact cannot be concealed forever. On this occasion, I took the opportunity to press home the need for control. I ordered the men who had lost their leader to "never, never shoot enemy soldiers who have thrown away their weapons and are surrendering."

I received my very first visitors during a lull as we completed the mop-up of Pyongyang. A group of U.S. officers wearing the Indian Head patch of the 2d Division sought me out. Their leader, a Lieutenant Colonel Foster, showed me a letter of reference and explained that the group was on temporary loan from MacArthur's headquarters as a "document collection team." Foster requested that I authorize them to enter Pyongyang. I complied, and the seventy members of the team immediately began seeking out every official building in the city. They combed these buildings for official documents, finding great quantities, which they evacuated to MacArthur's headquarters in Tokyo. The surprisingly large quantity of valuable documents the team discovered suggested the haste with which the enemy had abandoned Pyongyang.

As I reflected on how quickly the Americans had put a noncombatant, document-collection team into Pyongyang, I linked this amazing fact to another I had always regarded with equal wonder. The U.S. Army assigned officers whose sole duty it was to record combat history to units all the way down to regimental level. The American army managed to record a day-by-day chronology of events even during intense combat, and they had printing facilities permanently assigned at the corps level. Their printing presses literally accompanied them into the combat zone, and American commanders periodically printed and distributed various documents to their men in the field.

I'm afraid that I must contrast this with the ROK Army, where our records are sparse and where we must rely on the memory of participants for descriptions of many facets of the Korean War. This leaves us in a position where we have little evidence to refute charges that we exaggerated a victory or concealed a defeat.

On Sunday morning, October 20, 1950, from somewhere in downtown Pyongyang—the heart of the still-unliberated Korean capital of communism—came the pellucid tones of a church bell, pealing boldly. You could have knocked me over with a feather.

Pyongyang had been a center of Christianity before the communist regime came to power in 1945, but the church bells had remained silent for five years. Now the clear tones of a single bell pealed over the city. It was if the silent bell had found its tongue to announce to the world that Pyongyang was free at last. I cried shamelessly.

I learned the full story behind that bell later. My division had been fighting in East Pyongyang the previous evening, October 19, and I wanted to get intelligence on the situation in downtown Pyongyang. We also needed to locate American and Korean prisoners of war as well as prominent South Koreans who had been kidnapped when the communists occupied cities in the Republic of Korea. I selected two young officers to execute the intelligence mission, 1st Lt. Nam Sung In and Capt. Chun Ku Baek of the division G-3 section. I sent the two men into downtown Pyongyang, getting them across the Taedong River on a ferryboat.

They spent the night checking out key buildings in the downtown area, and with the dawn they ducked inside a Christian church to hide out during the day. Once inside, however, they were carried away by the high drama of the moment and couldn't resist ringing the church bell. It was the miracle of this bell that touched me so much that morning. As I had listened to its clear tones, I didn't realize that I knew only a small part of the miracle.

As they continued ringing the bell, my young officers fully expected to be confronted by angry enemy soldiers. Quite the contrary, the church began to fill with local believers, a lot of them. A minister materialized and conducted an ad hoc worship service right there in the midst of the partially liberated city. The minister even insisted that the two ROK 1st Division officers stand and introduce themselves during the service.

As the two young men described it to me later, most of the congregation were older people, but many were dressed in impeccable Western-style suits, while their wives wore Korean traditional-style dresses. The two officers who unexpectedly triggered this touching scene have claimed proudly ever since that they were personally responsible for "liberating Christianity" in Pyongyang.

As soon as the mop-up operations in Pyongyang concluded, I hurried over to visit the nearby hamlet of Sin-ri. I had lived there before fleeing North Korea five years before. My married older sister was the sole member of my family to remain in Pyongyang, and I was very concerned about her well-being. I found a number of people in the village whom I had known before and learned from them that my sister was safe, having fled the city to avoid the fighting. The villagers also shared with me their stories of privation and suffering under the communist regime.

I dropped by to inspect Pyongyang Prison and witnessed a hellish scene. The enemy had murdered the inmates, throwing their bodies into every well on the compound in an attempt to hide the deed. By the time they finished, bodies lay in numberless profusion throughout the compound. Evidence indicated that many had been sealed in cells and suffocated. Before they fled, the enemy forces butchered every single person they had kidnapped from South Korea as well as those the regime characterized as "reactionary elements." The entire prison was pervaded with an odor so foul it took my breath away. The silent, wretched prison seemed to serve as a mausoleum for the spirits of the men and women who had died so unjustly within its confines. My party and I trembled in anger as we viewed with our own eyes the inhumane consequences of the true communist character.

I found that Pyongyang hadn't changed much in the five years I had been gone. The city suffered much less damage than I feared, and all the cultural properties remained intact. After communist Chinese forces took Pyongyang later, however, the city was generally destroyed by UN air attacks.

I saw no evidence that the communist North Korean regime had constructed a single building or significant facility during the five years I had been away from the city. I drew the conclusion that the communist regime had prepared so single-mindedly for war that it had completely ignored civil construction.

To my surprise a majority of Pyongyang residents were comparatively well informed about the progress of the war, thanks, I learned, to their monitoring of "Voice of the UN" and South Korean radio broadcasts. I found that Pyongyang residents shared a particular dread of the U.S. Air Force, a natural outcome of the fact that the Americans had established and exploited air superiority early in the war.

Pyongyang, of course, is located in Pyongan Province, and I discovered that the city's residents had developed an intense antipathy toward the massive influx of Hamgyong Province natives who moved into the capital to wield real power under the Kim Il Sung regime. Men and women with ties to "Arasa," as they called the Soviet Union, rose quickly to the top in the party, the puppet government, and the military. As it happens, Hamgyong Province is the only Korean territory to share a border with the Soviet Union, so many Hamgyong citizens had traveled or lived in the Soviet Union. These men and women gained such power in the communist regime that Pyongyang natives no longer controlled their own city.

The currency of the Republic of Korea became very popular in the liberated areas of North Korea, including Pyongyang. The unit value of North Korean currency—"red paper" as it was called—had been several times higher than southern tender, but the North Korean people believed that the communist currency would soon be useless, so they were willing to exchange it on a one-for-one basis. The division, as a result, was able to acquire materiel very cheaply. I recall that as we advanced north we could procure a cow as a supplementary food item for 100 won in the rural areas we passed through. This ridiculously cheap price could not even be imagined except under chaotic wartime conditions.

Now that we had liberated the enemy capital, we believed we had completely won the war. We felt we had achieved the complete unification of the Korean peninsula, although more than a hundred miles of North Korea lay between Pyongyang and the Yalu River, all of it in enemy hands.

For the first time in a very long time I felt I had shaken off the dust of combat. I was caught up completely in the emotion of a triumphant homecoming.

I was born on November 23, 1920, on the eleventh sun of the tenth moon by the lunar calendar of that year, in Tokhung, Kangso County, South Pyongan Province, a hamlet located on the way to Chinnampo about seventeen miles southeast of Pyongyang. Tokhung served as the seat of the Kangso County government and was therefore sometimes called Kangso City.

Western culture and institutions and Christianity found their way into Kangso County at an early date, and the citizens of the area were imbued with a particularly high fervor for education. Men of national prominence like An Chang Ho and Cho Man Sik were Kangso County natives.

My mother moved into Pyongyang with my brother, sister, and myself when I was five. We were very poor, existing in a single room measuring six feet by six feet, and many days we didn't have money for food. About a year after we moved into Pyongyang, our circumstances reached such a serious pass that my mother took the three of us children to the Taedong River bridge, intending to jump with us to our deaths, for she saw no other way out. Family suicide has a long tradition in Asia.

I was only six, but I shall never forget what happened at the bridge. My sister was eleven, and she quickly understood what we were doing. She looked up at Mom and appealed to her with wisdom outstripping her tender years. "It takes a tree three years to put down solid roots, and we've been here for only a year," she sobbed. "Let's wait two more years, and if we don't make it, then we can go through with this." Our little family turned about and headed back to our tiny room.

My mother and sister both got jobs at the same rubber factory not long after the bridge incident, and our financial situation began to improve. I was able to attend primary school, although I was a year behind the others. Of course, Korea didn't have free education at any level in those years. I attended Mansu Primary School for four years before transferring to Yaksong Primary School. After graduation, I entered Pyongyang Normal School. Normal school was a five-year training course for teachers in the school system of that era, when we didn't have high schools, per se.

Mom's meager wages wouldn't cover the tuition costs at Pyongyang Normal, although normal schools were less expensive than the other types of secondary education then available. My supervising instructor in primary school, the venerable Kim Kap Rin, visited Pyongyang Normal and talked the school into reducing my tuition by explaining that my widowed mother was our family's sole means of support.

When I was a senior I got to know a number of cadets from the Manchurian Military Academy, including Lee Sang Yol, who was to reach the rank of captain in the navy, and the famous pilot Park Sung Hwan. These men urged me to take up the profession of arms. I had never really regarded myself as cut out to be a teacher, and I wanted to be a soldier very badly.

I discussed the matter with my mother. Mom's father had served the Chosun dynasty as the Royal Army's chief logistician in Pyongan Province, and Mother understood my feelings. She gave her permission. "Take whatever path you want to take, Son."

I completed the Manchurian Military academy at Mukden and was commissioned in the spring of 1942. I served one year with the Jamusu Unit before transferring into the Korean Unit of the Kando Special Force, a battalion-sized unit where I served for three years, until the end of World War II.

I spent many of those months engaged in combat with the communist Chinese Eighth Route Army, both at Jehe near the Great Wall and outside Beijing. The Kando Special Force served as a training ground for a number of Koreans besides myself who soldiered with the unit and who later made major contributions to the Republic of Korea Army, men like Kim Paik Il; Song Sok Ha, who retired as a major general; Kim Suk Bum, who served as Marine Corps commandant; Shin Hyun Jun, who served as the first commandant of the Marine Corps; Lee Yong, who retired as a major general; Im Chung Sik, who retired as a full general and served as minister of defense; Yun Chun Kun, who retired as a major general; and Park Chang Am, who rose to the rank of brigadier general.

The Soviet Army plunged across the border between the Soviet Union and Manchuria in the final days of World War II and thrust into the heart of Manchuria. The Soviets disarmed my unit on August 9, 1945, at Mingyuehkou, near a trail that leads up the Chinese side of Mount Paektu, Korea's most famous mountain.

I had asked a Korean interpreter attached to the Soviet Army what he thought about the future of Chosun. Chosun had been Korea's name for five hundred years under the most recent dynasty, the Japanese had kept the name during the forty years of their occupation, and Koreans universally used that term for Korea in 1945. It was incorporated into the official title of North Korea—the People's Republic of Chosun—but dropped in the South. North Koreans continue to use the term *Chosun* to this day. "Chosun will soon become independent," the interpreter had said. "We'll call the new country the People's Republic of Tongjin. If you're here then, you'll be arrested and exiled in Siberia. Get back to your home as fast as you can go."

I had bolted as soon as my unit was disbanded. I walked through Yongjong, crossed the Tumen River, and set out for Pyongyang, passing through numberless towns and cities on the way. I walked hundreds of miles without a break, reaching Pyongyang one month after I started.

Arriving in Pyongyang, I learned that the Soviet Army already had occupied the Korean peninsula north of the 38th parallel. The Soviet puppet Kim Il Sung had emerged from nowhere and was rising rapidly in power.

In the governmental vacuum that resulted when the occupying Japanese surrendered, Cho Man Sik had established a provisional provincial government. Cho's title was chairman of the South Pyongan Province People's Political Committee. Although this name smacks of communist jargon today, Cho's politics were, in fact, right wing. As it happened, one of my relatives, Song Ho Kyong, was employed as Cho's chief secretary, and I, too, found work in the office of the chief secretariat through Song's kind assistance. Luckily, the job put me in day-to-day contact with people very knowledgeable about the Communist party's activities, placing me in an ideal position to track the movements and intentions of the communists.

Even Kim Il Sung occasionally visited Master Cho Man Sik, already a famous political figure. Kim had established an office in a building in downtown Pyongyang, which he called the "Northern Branch Bureau of the Chosun Communist party." Outside the office hung a red cloth banner on which white characters spelled out "The Discipline of the Communist party Is as Hard as Steel." I could not have imagined then that this insignificant man would go on to rule North Korea for more than forty-five years.

The organization of the communist Chosun Workers' party gained strength by the day, as did its auxiliary organs, the Korean People's Army, the Kangdong Political Academy, the Military Academy, and the Democratic Youth League. We were astounded at its growth.

Discipline among the occupying Soviet troops was lax, meanwhile, imposing a tortuous burden on the Korean people. The Soviet Army established the Red Guards, which by early October 1945 were already maneuvering to disband Master Cho Man Sik's Security Force, the private military arm of Cho's provisional government that, not incidentally, was commanded by my younger brother, Paik In Yup. The communists incarcerated Cho Man Sik in the Koryo Hotel in early December.

Events unfolded at a breakneck pace, and before he was incarcerated, I took an opportunity to deliver a warning to Master Cho. "So long as Kim Il Sung continues to gain power," I insisted, "the North will inevitably go communist. Why don't you consider fleeing to South Korea?"

Master Cho's answer was short but compelling. "I can't just run away and abandon the people in the North to their fate." I tried again to persuade him to join the exodus to the Republic of Korea, but he refused.

Chung Il Kwon, Park Ki Byong, and Won Yong Duk, who rose to the rank of brigadier general in the ROK Army and served as national defense provost marshal general, approached me separately during this period to inquire about where the political situation was going and to ask my advice about what they should do. I advised every one of them to flee to the South, and in early December 1945 Chung Il Kwon and my brother Paik In Yup did so. A few days later, Kim Paik Il, Choi Nam Kun, and I left Pyongyang and fled south, crossing the 38th parallel on December 27, 1945.

The Chinese Trap

After liberating Pyongyang, the ROK 1st Division stood down to await orders to return to the attack, setting up division headquarters in a building that had been the capital of South Pyongan Province before the communist regime took it over to serve as the official home of the Supreme People's Committee. Kim Il Sung's office was in the building. I dropped by to take a look and was confronted by a huge photograph of Stalin on the wall. The furniture in the office was practical and sturdy. The office was intact, and I couldn't resist the temptation to sit in Kim Il Sung's own chair.

Both my 1st Division and the U.S. 1st Cav Division were withdrawn to the outskirts of Pyongyang, leaving the city center to the small document-gathering unit of the U.S. 2d Division, which still pursued its mission doggedly. Armed soldiers must be stationed in urban areas only for the briefest of periods, both because a city has a way of "chewing up and spitting out" soldiers and also to avoid unnecessary contact between soldiers and civilians. Thus, I spent only two days in Pyongyang, two days in a maze of personal memories. We now faced a march northward 105 miles straight through to the Yalu River, which formed Korea's border with China.

While we had been busy mopping up Pyongyang, General MacArthur's United Nations Command Headquarters was preparing to cut the routes of retreat used by fleeing NKPA units and obliterate them. A huge airborne operation was planned to rescue prisoners of war held north of Pyongyang. The U.S. 187th Airborne Regiment, expanded into a combat team, was to parachute into Sukchon, thirty-five miles north of Pyongyang, and into Sunchon, thirty-seven miles north of the former communist capital. This operation would sever the roads leading from these locations to Sinuiju and Manpojin on the banks of the Yalu.

Airdropped units that do not link up swiftly with friendly ground forces are in great danger of being surrounded and cut off deep in enemy territory. Thus, the British 27th Brigade and my 1st Division were selected to conduct the ground link-up operation with the airborne troops. The 27th Brigade was ordered to attack toward Sukchon, while we were ordered to attack toward Sunchon, the other airborne drop site.

Elements of the parachute combat team took off at noon from the Kimpo airbase outside Seoul in C-47s and C-119s, the large transport aircraft that ferried the men to the jump zones. The first sky soldiers hit the silk over their targets two hours later. More than four thousand paratroopers were to float down through the North Korean skies during the next two days.

The paratroopers brought plenty of equipment with them, including jeeps, half-ton trucks, communications equipment, 90mm antitank guns, and even seventeen 105mm howitzers and one thousand rounds of shells for the big guns. This was the first time in the history of warfare that 105mm howitzers were dropped from the air. All together, about six hundred tons of equipment and supplies were inserted by parachute

As we charged north for Sunchon and a rendezvous with the paratroopers, our usual team of tanks and infantry led the division. The armor was commanded by Lieutenant Colonel Growden, while Maj. Park Chin Suk, my assistant G-3, commanded the infantry, a battalion of our 12th Regiment.

We could have saved ourselves the trouble. The NKPA forces we expected to encounter weren't there. The U.S. airborne unit parachuted safely onto targets free of the enemy, and we smartly executed our end of the link-up operation, but our net closed on very little of military interest. The entire operation rescued a few American prisoners, to be sure, uncovered dozens of American prisoners murdered by the NKPA, and made short work of an NKPA regiment near Sukchon.

On October 21, 1950, General MacArthur and Lt. Gen. George Stratemeyer, commander of the U.S. 5th Air Force, inspected the operation by air and then landed at Pyongyang Airport. In a speech he delivered there, General MacArthur predicted that "half of the remaining 300,000 North Korean troops—150,000 men—would fall victim to the massive double envelopment, pounded on one flank by the U.S. 187th Airborne Regiment and the ROK 1st Division and hit on the other flank by the U.S. 1st Cav Division. The war will soon be over."

At the airport, General MacArthur inspected Company F of the 1st Cav Division's 5th Cavalry Regiment, which had led the 1st Cav into Pyongyang. Toward the end of the ceremonies, General MacArthur said, "Those of you who landed in Pusan three months ago with Company F please take one step forward." Of the more than two hundred troops in the formation, only five stepped forward, a testament to the tough combat of the early period of the Korean War.

Needless to say, General MacArthur's prediction about the war missed the bull's-eye by a mile. The commander in chief initially established the "MacArthur line" running from Chongju to Hamhung as the northern limit of the UN Command's advance. Subsequently, however, he moved the original line farther north, to a trace running from Sunchon through to Sungjin. This second line amounted to a de facto removal of limits on the UN Command's offensive.

We had been worried that communist Chinese forces would intervene in the war ever since the moment UN forces broke through the 38th parallel and headed north. But at this late date we were so focused on winning total, unreserved victory that we had put thoughts of the Chinese out of our minds. No one knew that the communist Chinese Army had crossed the Yalu River into the Korean peninsula by the middle of October 1950 and now lay in ambush in every nook and cranny of the rugged Jongyuryong Mountain Range.

After we linked up with the U.S. airborne force, the ROK 1st Division charged north without missing a beat. On October 22 and 23, the 1st crossed the bridge leading north out of Kunu over the Chongchon River. The next day we drove on through Yongbyon and reached Unsan.

During our dash from Pyongyang to the Chongchon River, we encountered large numbers of NKPA stragglers who surged around us from both sides of the road, heedless of our condemning stares. They had discarded their uniforms and now wore civilian clothing, and I saw no reason to harm them. All I wanted was for them to return to their homes and live in peace.

I set up division headquarters at the Yongbyon Agricultural School and issued my final operations order, the one I expected to end the war on the western front. My order directed the ROK 1st Division to advance northwest out of Unsan, thrust to the Supung Dam, and dash from there to the Yalu.

Meanwhile, the larger plan for the rest of the UN forces on the western front was straightforward. The U.S. 24th Division was to advance toward Uiju; the British 27th Brigade was to attack through Chongju and continue toward Sinuiju; the ROK 7th Division, which had just been assigned as U.S. I Corps reserve, was to pass through the 24th Division and the 27th Brigade just before these units reached the Yalu River. The ROK 7th was to conduct the actual assault on the Yalu, the border between the Korean peninsula and China's Manchuria. The 1st Cav, meanwhile, was to remain in Pyongyang to mop up in the capital and the area extending from Pyongyang to Chinnampo.

That was the plan. Maj. Gen. Yu Jae Hung's II Corps was advancing to the right of U.S. I Corps. As my ROK 1st Division was closing on Unsan, the ROK II Corps's 6th division under Brig. Gen. Kim Chong O already had pushed north until it was a scant twelve miles from the Yalu. The ROK 8th Division had reached Kujang and was closing quickly on the Yalu. Across the peninsula on the eastern front, meanwhile, ROK I Corps under Maj. Gen. Kim Paik Il continued to attack up the east coast, taking Iwon virtually unopposed.

As we in the 1st Division were about to cross the Chongchon River, we felt a sudden sense of isolation. We couldn't put a finger on it, but the atmosphere had changed. Then I noticed something concrete. So far the roads leading north had been filled with NKPA stragglers and refugees, but north of the Chongchon River the road was empty. The mercury plunged suddenly, and we didn't have winter uniforms. The men began to suffer constantly from the cold. The sharp peaks surrounded us down in the valley like so many Oriental screen paintings.

Despite our vague feelings of uneasiness, the division was not gripped by widespread apprehension. We had marched from one victory to the next and were still completely absorbed in the business of dashing to the Yalu, winning back every last inch of our divided nation. "On to the Yalu," the men yelled in high spirits. "On to the Yalu!"

We pushed on. We discovered hardly a soul in Unsan, although the town had a fairly large population and was famous for its gold mines. My 15th Regiment under Col. Cho Jae Mi was leading the division as we passed through Unsan and headed north. We had been charging northward virtually without resistance for many days, but on October 25, 1950, we ran full tilt into a brick wall. The ROK 1st Division smashed into a huge military force, and we didn't even know what it was.

The 15th regiments's advance ground to a sudden halt under a withering barrage of mortar fire. My 12th Regiment under Col. Kim Chum Kon was at division left, and Kim suddenly came under sharp attack from his left flank. My mind was still trying to deal with the terrible implications of this intelligence when I was startled by a report that our U.S. 6th Tank Battalion had suffered tank losses to heavy direct-fire weapons.

The next report floored me. My 11th Regiment under Col. Kim Dong

Bin was in reserve at division rear but reported being hit by an attack from an unknown enemy in the flank and—to my amazement—from the rear as well. The enemy had surrounded the entire division!

In a reflexive move that was to save us, we didn't try to press home our attack but fell back immediately to Unsan and established a defensive perimeter in and around the town. Our situation resembled nothing so much as a scene from an American Western movie, where a caravan of Conestoga wagons is suddenly attacked by Indians and forms a defensive circle.

Although we didn't know it then, the ROK 1st Division had triggered an ambush set by the communist Chinese Army. The Chinese waited for us to advance into the Unsan Valley and then hit us from all sides. This was our first contact with the Chinese Army, and it very well could have been our last. Chinese stagehands had raised the curtain on the Battle of Unsan, and a bitter battle it proved to be.

On that first day of combat, my 15th Regiment captured a communist Chinese soldier. I had the prisoner brought to division headquarters, where I interrogated him myself. The man was about thirty-five and wore a thick, quilted winter uniform that was khaki on the outside and white on the inside and manufactured in such a fashion that a soldier could wear it with either color showing, a simple but effective method to facilitate camouflage in snowy terrain. The prisoner's thick winter cap was equipped with integrated ear muffs, and he wore rubber sneakers.

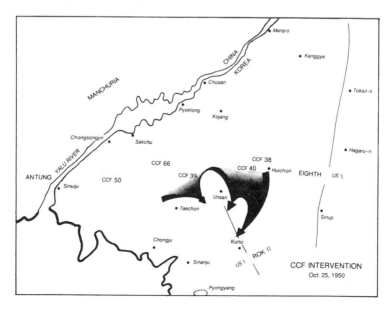

My interrogation revealed that the prisoner hailed from China's Kwangtung Province and that he was a regular soldier in communist China's conventional army. In a flat, matter-of-fact tone, the Chinese prisoner told me the most shocking news I had heard since the war began. Tens of thousands of communist Chinese soldiers swarmed in the mountains around the ROK 1st Division, trapping us in the Unsan Valley.

I lost no time in contacting my corps commander, Major General Milburn, and asked him to meet me at Yongbyon Agricultural School. I interpreted for General Milburn as he put questions directly to the POW and determined for himself that the communist Chinese Army had entered the war in Korea. Milburn's questions and the prisoner's answers ran generally this way.

"Where were you born?"

"I'm from south China."

"What's your unit?"

"The thirty-ninth Army."

"What fighting have you done?"

"I fought in the Hainan Island battle."

"Are you a Korean resident of China?"

"No. I'm Chinese."

General Milburn reported these facts through Eighth Army to Charles Willoughby, General MacArthur's deputy chief of staff for intelligence.

At that time, however, General MacArthur's headquarters held an extremely optimistic view of the war and decided the interrogation of the Chinese POW represented an anomaly. Their evaluation was that at worst the prisoner was a Korean resident of China who had volunteered to fight in his homeland.

I had no other Chinese Army POW I could trot out to challenge the conclusion of the UN Command, but I realized that a terrible breach had opened in the U.S. Army's intelligence information bank.

U.S. President Harry S Truman and General of the Army MacArthur were extremely concerned about Chinese intervention when we crossed the 38th parallel and advanced northward, but at their meeting on Wake Island on October 14, 1950, they reached the conclusion that the Chinese would not intervene. Later, when confronted with evidence that contradicted this conclusion, MacArthur dismissed it. This misjudgment among the top echelon of the war's leaders was to prevail for close to a month and was responsible in large measure for the grave losses that both Korean and UN forces were to suffer.

On October 23, 1950—at this most critical moment in the war—I suddenly received orders to assume command of ROK II Corps. My assistant division commander, Brig. Gen. Choi Young Hi, was to take command of the 1st, while I was to proceed to II Corps Headquarters at Kunu in Kaechon County and assume command of II Corps from Maj.

Gen. Yu Jae Hung. General Yu was appointed to be army deputy chief of staff and departed for Seoul to take up his new position. I was honored to be appointed a corps commander, but II Corps had been thrown unceremoniously into a state of crisis. Indeed, the situation at the front was so bad that I didn't even have time to make the traditional rounds to say hello to division commanders and other key corps leaders. The chief of staff of II Corps was Brig. Gen. Lee Han Lim, and the G-3 was Col. Lee Ju Il. ROK II Corps Headquarters had received numerous, urgent reports from its field elements that huge formations of the communist Chinese Army had appeared along the front.

The chief U.S. Army adviser to II Corps was Colonel Gillet. I had known him from the days when we both served in Pusan. I was the senior officer of the 5th Regiment when that unit was being created at Pusan in 1946, and Gillet served as military governor of South Kyongsang Province under the U.S. Army military government. I had a talk with Gillet now on the issue of acquiring clothing and provisions.

During our discussion, I found that Colonel Gillet was extremely worried about the situation ROK II Corps faced on the battlefield. I decided to see for myself just what that situation was. I undertook an inspection tour of the subordinate divisions of my new command. First I would inspect the 6th Division and then proceed to 8th Division. The 6th Division under Brig. Gen. Kim Chong O had established its headquarters near Tongyong Cave, site of one of the world's most famous collections of stalactites. Kim had been wounded and at this crucial moment of the war was recuperating at a private home. As it happened, I was unable to meet Kim at all. After inspecting an underground enemy armory discovered near Tongyong Cave, the jeep in which I was riding was involved in an accident in which I seriously injured my jaw.

The ROK 6th Division had earned an enviable combat record, having fought well and hard both at Chunchon when the NKPA first invaded South Korea and again in the area around Umsong when we had withdrawn to the Naktong River.

Faithful to its reputation, the 6th was far out front of the rest of II Corps in its drive to reach the Yalu. Its 7th Regiment under Col. Lim Bu Taek had advanced as far as Kojang, hardly more than a stone's throw from the river. Indeed, the 7th Regiments's Reconnaissance Company under Capt. Lee Dae Yong actually reached the Yalu at Chosan, the first friendly unit to do so. The 6th Division's 2d Regiment under Col. Ham Byong Son had done almost as well, advancing as far north as Onjong. Unfortunately, these fine regiments were now paying in blood for their prowess. Both were surrounded in mountains by the communist Chinese Army, and both were fighting desperately for survival.

Their situation was the more desperate because the two regiments had competed to see which could reach the Yalu first. In their headlong rush, they had ignored the principle of unit cohesion; as a result, the two regiments were scattered over an immense area measuring some sixty miles across and thirty miles deep. The new enemy had severed their lines of withdrawal.

The scattered units of the two regiments maintained a flood of radio requests for resupply. The messages from the 7th regimental commander Lim Bu Taek, whose unit had advanced farther north than any other ROK Army unit, were particularly worrisome. "We're out of ammo and supplies," came his chilling plea. "Please send by emergency airlift." Of the ROK 6th Division's regiments, only the 19th was not in mortal danger. The 19th had slowed farther south to cover the advance of the follow-on ROK 8th Division.

Brig. Gen. Lee Sung Ga's 8th Division, meanwhile, was frightened. The ROK 8th had yet to encounter the new enemy, but General Lee told me, "My men have heard that the Chinese are in the war, and the bottom has dropped out of their morale."

I returned to corps headquarters at Kunu and convened a conference of key members of the corps staff and Colonel Gillet. We tried to find some way to get air resupply to the 7th Regiment. But the situation had deteriorated so badly that there simply was no way to do it. We could do nothing more than agonize for them.

As the conference was ending, former II Corps commander Maj. Gen. Yu Jae Hung suddenly burst into the room, having flown in on an L-5 light aircraft from Seoul. "Hey, dey say all gedon back," General Yu yelled at me. Yu had been born and raised in Japan, and his Korean was so heavily accented that it was all but impossible for me to understand. I finally realized he was saying that he had been ordered to revert to his position as commander of II Corps and that all recent high-level personnel shifts had been rescinded until we could solve the terrible new challenge confronting us. I was once again commander of the ROK 1st Division.

On October 27, as I crossed the pontoon bridge over the Chongchon River in my jeep heading back to division headquarters, I mulled the war over. In my absence, the 1st had been engaged in continuous, day-and-night combat with the Chinese Army. My stint as corps commander, however truncated, had allowed me to see the war from a much broader perspective, and this experience was to prove invaluable in subsequent operations.

Our enemy was now the Chinese Army. An enemy dozens of divisions in size had waited patiently as our own momentum carried us deep into its mountain ambush, had cut off our routes of retreat, and now sought to annihilate us. We were in a completely new war. I realized that morale would play a vital role in our survival, and I promised myself that from that moment on I would work to alleviate the tightening sense of tension that gripped us all.

I got back to division headquarters, bellowed a confident hello to my staff, and immediately set out again to see exactly what it was that faced the ROK 1st Division. My aide Captain Kim drove the jeep, and I took the division G-3 Mun Hyong Tae along with me. I always had a trailer attached to the jeep in which I kept a tent, blankets, and other items that might prove handy in an emergency.

We careened through Yongsan-dong, and on an S-curve near Camel's Head Pass just south of Unsan, we suddenly came upon a group of Chinese Army troops manning a roadblock about three hundred yards away. Absorbed in driving, Captain Kim didn't see the roadblock. When I yelled for him to stop, he finally looked up, saw the problem, and brought the jeep to a shuddering halt. Now the problem was turning around on the narrow mountain road. Turning a jeep with an attached trailer on a narrow road is no mean trick. To do so under fire is just short of miraculous. We managed to detach the trailer, turn the jeep, and reattach the trailer faster than humans have ever before accomplished these tasks—way, way under a minute—but it seemed like an eternity. We got away unscathed and only later blanched at the foolishness of bothering to rehook the trailer. We returned to Yongsan-dong and found a narrow, winding track along a bank of a stream. We used this faint road to get to Unsan safely.

The men of the ROK 1st were exhausted from nonstop combat and suffering acutely because we couldn't keep our supply routes open. They weren't getting any resupply and especially needed winter uniforms. The men had every reason to be dispirited, and indeed their morale hit bottom out of intense fear at the nightly Chinese Army tactic of blowing bugles, striking gongs, and attacking in human waves. Lieutenant Colonel Growden's tank battalion was unable to face night combat. The tanks had run out of both ammo and gasoline but managed to get back into the fight after we received an air drop of these crucial supplies.

The men of the ROK 1st Division had been frightened by the sound of the Soviet T-34 tanks during the fighting at the Imjin River in the early days of the war. Once again it was sound that frightened them, this time the sound of Chinese bugles and gongs. How to deal with this fear placed an additional worry on my already overburdened mind. I must say that if ever any combination of manmade sounds qualified as diabolical, the eerie strains of bugles, the wildly manic clanging of gongs, and of course, the jabbered oaths of the Chinese language itself qualified fully.

The impetus of the Chinese attack seemed to have tailed off for the moment, but no matter how much I racked my mind I could not come up with a scheme to resolve the terrible turn the war had taken. The ROK 1st Division was stuck.

Our Last Hours in Unsan:
The Bloody Autumn Night

The ROK 1st Division's attack toward the Yalu River had stalled at Unsan. U.S. I Corps Commander, Gen. Frank W. Milburn, ordered the

U.S. 1st Cav Division's 8th Cav Regiment to bypass us and continue on to the original objective at Supung. I Corps also issued orders for the British 27th Brigade—which had been pushing for Sinuiju on the Yalu River—to swap combat missions with the U.S. 24th Division, since the British had asked for relief for rest and refitting. The intent of the latter order was to grant relief to a unit that had remained at the vanguard of the attack for a considerable period, replacing it with a well-rested unit from corps reserve.

General Milburn at U.S. I Corps and the big boys above him in the chain of command still only half-believed that China's conventional ground forces had entered the Korean War, despite mounting evidence to the contrary. Although we were now capturing a succession of Chinese prisoners who unequivocally identified their units as part of the conventional Chinese Army, the Americans continued to fool themselves because the Chinese had yet to challenge a U.S. Army division directly, and because to the American eye, the Koreans and Chinese looked and sounded very much alike. To us, of course, the differences were vast. The Americans clung to the view that at worst we were facing small numbers of Chinese volunteers who had joined defeated NKPA units. And then, too, was it not true that there was no trouble on the eastern front, over in Hamgyong Province?

Chinese soldiers fought well, but once captured, their docility knew no bounds. Prisoners even volunteered answers to questions our interrogators hadn't put to them. The enemy we faced were members of the Thirty-ninth Army, subordinate to the 13th Army Group under Huang Yung-sheng, which was itself subordinate to the Fourth Field Army. The Thirty-ninth Army had been stationed north of Hong Kong in Kwangtung Province until early September 1950, when most of the unit boarded trains and headed for Manchuria. The Thirty-ninth crossed the Yalu River into Korea in mid-October. The Chinese moved only at night and went to extraordinary efforts to leave no telltale sign of their passage to be picked up by U.S. Air Force reconnaissance.

The situation worsened. On October 31, 1950, I went up to Unsan for the second time. At night the hamlet was completely cut off and under attack from every direction, but in the daytime our artillery and armor established fire superiority. With close air support we found it possible to advance, although our gains were measured in inches rather than miles. The U.S. 8th Cavalry Regiment, which was to bypass us and attack northward toward our original objective, had not yet made an appearance.

Forest fires had broken out at a number of places in the mountains surrounding Unsan, and the smoke and haze from the fires severely restricted our vision. The Chinese had deliberately set the fires to establish a smoke screen that reduced the effectiveness of friendly artillery fire and air attacks during daylight.

My first act upon arriving in Unsan was to drive to the primary school that served as the headquarters of division artillery. I wanted to discuss the situation with Colonel Hennig first.

My old comrade surprised me. "The Chinese keep infiltrating through our seams," Colonel Hennig warned. "It will be difficult for us to last the day. Our situation is desperate."

I retorted without thinking. "Where's your fighting spirit, Colonel?"

Hennig grew even more solemn. "Okay, sir," he said firmly. "Then I'll give it to you straight. If we don't withdraw, they'll destroy us before the day is over." My warrior comrade Colonel Hennig had always managed to maintain his composure, but now strain furrowed his face.

I visited each of my three regiments in the order they were arrayed around the outskirts of the hamlet. I talked with each regimental commander and took a firsthand look at the situation. The 15th Regiment, which had led the division as we tried to advance north from Unsan, had sustained the most serious losses, while the 11th and 12th regiments were in enormous and imminent peril.

The situation worsened noticeably even during the time I was conducting my inspection. The valleys in the mountains around the town filled to the brim with communist Chinese Army soldiers in assault formation. One could palpably sense the sheer enormity of the menace that surrounded the ROK 1st Division in the smoke-enshrouded mountains.

"The enemy fire's not all that bad," my tank battalion commander Lieutenant Colonel Growden assured me. "But they're damn good at night attacks and infiltration." Growden's assessment tracked with what my regimental commanders had told me. The division faced a serious crisis.

After touring the front, I went back for another talk with Colonel Hennig. This time the American officer recommended that the two of us personally go see I Corps commander General Milburn and recommend withdrawal.

The Chinese Army had been attacking the ROK 1st Division from every direction for six straight days, inflicting serious losses. In my judgment it was crystal clear that my ten thousand officers and men, artillery, tanks, and other heavy equipment could not hold the massive enemy at bay much longer. We had reached the breaking point.

I had to make the decision, but I was in agony over it. A decision to withdraw would run directly counter to the overall flow of the war. United Nations forces were on the offensive. All my superiors—Generals Milburn, Walker, and MacArthur—remained flushed with our victories and pressed with a single voice for a return to the assault. A commander who bucks the flow in a situation like this and chooses to recommend withdrawal risks his career even if his superiors acquiesce. But if they reject the recommendation, the commander's career will probably end on the spot.

I asked Hennig how much artillery ammunition we had left. He said

we had a bit more than thirteen thousand rounds. With that information, I worked out a plan of withdrawal under which Hennig would fire
every last artillery shell to cover the withdrawal of all three regiments.
I jumped into my jeep, barreled out of Unsan, and drove straight to
U.S. I Corps Headquarters in Sinanju, two hours down the road.

I had called ahead, and when I arrived, Major General Gay, commander of the U.S. 1st Cav Division, and Major General John Church,
commander of the U.S. 24th Division, had also been called to headquarters and were awaiting my arrival. It was already growing dark. The
bugles would start soon.

I explained to the small group of commanders the urgent situation I
had witnesses in Unsan and recommended outright that the ROK 1st
Division withdraw to a line along the Chongchon River. By this time no
friendly units remained on the ROK 1st Division's right flank. The ROK
II Corps—the 6th, 7th, and 8th divisions—had been hit hard by the Chinese and had not been able to maintain the line. They had flooded south
to Piho Mountain, some twelve miles southeast of Unsan, and seemed
unequal to the task of holding the line even there.

Four months after war broke out, we were back to a situation that bore
all too much resemblance to the early fighting at the Imjin River. By
chance, then and now, units on my right flank were under the command of General Yu Jae Hung, and then as now, irresistible enemy pressure had fallen first on the ROK Army units on my right.

The ROK 1st Division had suffered terrible losses in the initial days of
the war because we were ordered to defend to the death, an order that
had never been lifted. The chief difference this time was that the chain
of command remained intact, and I was sitting down and talking to a
commander who found it possible to issue an order to withdraw. Withdrawal is never an attractive alternative, and the faces of General Milburn and the two American division commanders were masks of gravity
as I spoke.

General Milburn heard me out. When I was finished, he abruptly
picked up the telephone and called General Walker at Eighth Army
Headquarters, explained the situation to him, and after a long conversation finally put the handset down. He asked me if it would be possible
for the ROK 1st Division to conduct a night withdrawal right now. I
explained the withdrawal plan I had worked out with Hennig, and Milburn made a decision. "The ROK 1st Division," he said, "will withdraw
to a line between Ipsok and Yongbyon. Confer with the U.S. 1st Cav
about cover for the withdrawal. The U.S. 24th will cease its attack where
it is and await further orders." I immediately contacted my regiments
in Unsan, gave the order to withdraw, and accompanied General Gay
to his 1st Cav headquarters at Yongsan-dong.

About this same time Col. Raymond Palmer's 8th Cavalry Regiment—
subordinate to the U.S. 1st Cav Division—passed through Yongsan-

dong on its way to Unsan. Two roads lead from Yongsan-dong to Unsan, and the two are separated by a narrow string of mountains. Colonel Palmer's 8th Cav Regiment advanced along the route on the west of the mountains while my ROK 1st Division withdrew south along the road to the east. On this fateful night, the mountains separating the two roads made the difference between life and death for the two units.

It was almost midnight by the time the conference at I Corps Headquarters ended and General Gay and I arrived at 1st Cav Headquarters. By that time, 1st Cav Headquarters personnel were already absorbed in a tense drama playing out in minute-by-minute radio reports of a tremendous fight involving the 8th Cav Regiment. Even the terse radio style could not conceal the anguish.

"Enemy troops are in the perimeter!"

"Enemy soldiers are climbing up on our tanks!"

The breathless words were punctuated by explosions and the sounds of gunfire. We understood immediately that the unit had been hit by surprise and was now caught up in a horrendous melee of combat and death. I monitored the radio just long enough to be certain the shocking situation was really happening and then took off for ROK 1st Division Headquarters at Yongbyon, ignoring the danger of traveling at night. Bouncing along in the jeep, I fought to control my anxiety and impatience. Would the 1st be able to get out?

My concern for the ROK 1st Division suddenly paled to insignificance as it suddenly dawned on me that if the Chinese broke through us, nothing could stop them before they crossed the Chongchon. Once the Chinese were south of the Chongchon, they could readily contain and cut off all forces north of the river. I whistled in disbelief as I realized that the entire U.S. I Corps was in clear and present danger of encirclement by the Chinese Army.

U.S. I Corps represented fully half of the total combat force of the UN Command, and the crucial half at that.

As my jeep drew closer to the fighting, I began to suspect that this bloody autumn night would not witness the destruction of the 1st Division. My confidence stemmed from the guns. The closer I drew to the front, the more clearly I could hear the rumble of friendly artillery fire coming from the mountains to my north. I felt sure that a unit that could maintain its artillery fire was a unit that could preserve its integrity.

Throughout the long months of the war the booming of friendly artillery always boosted my courage. I was right this time. During the night, the ROK 1st Division successfully managed to execute a six-mile withdrawal from Unsan to Ipsok.

The men of Colonel Hennig's 10th Antiaircraft Artillery Group fired all the weapons they had as fast as they would fire at the Chinese lines all through the night. In those brief hours Hennig fired the prodigious number of thirteen thousand rounds of artillery ammo. Under the cover of this bombardment, the entire ROK 1st Division, all three of my regiments, were able to escape from the Unsan Valley with only minor casualties. Our only serious equipment loss was four or five of the 4.2-inch mortars of the U.S. 2d Heavy Mortar Battalion.

The withdrawal of my division presented the Chinese Army with six miles of golden opportunity to attack, but the enemy could not capitalize on this opportunity because of our absolute fire superiority.

If the news was good for the ROK 1st Division, however, it could not have been worse for the U.S. 8th Cavalry Regiment, advancing to cover our withdrawal. The 8th Cav was given an order to withdraw immediately, but by the time the unit received the order, the Chinese had cut its withdrawal route and surrounded it in a valley. The Chinese forces engaging the 8th Cav Regiment were so lightly equipped that a single cavalry unit of some one hundred Mongolian ponies could transport its equipment. Yet this same unit had so many organic infantrymen that it was able to maul a U.S. Army regiment armed with tanks and heavy artillery.

The fate of the 3d Battalion of the 8th Cavalry Regiment was especially painful. The battalion was completely surrounded during the night, and by dawn all communications with the unit had been lost. Moving without delay, 1st Cav commander Gen. Hobart Gay sent his 5th Cav Regiment out to rescue the battalion. Although it was then daylight, the smoke from the forest fires hid the Chinese in their deep trenches in the mountains. The Chinese not only escaped U.S. artillery fire and close air support missions unscathed, but inflicted serious losses on the 5th Cavalry as well.

On November 2, General Gay had no choice but to make the bitter decision to abandon further efforts to rescue the 3d Battalion. This choice was forced upon him as the crisis in our sector increased to the point where the front itself was in danger of collapsing, forcing the would-be rescuers to withdraw. I was told that this was the first time in the history of American arms that efforts to rescue a surrounded unit were abandoned. This single fact should suggest the urgency of the situation in the western sector. "A soldier accumulates many sad memories over his lifetime," General Gay was to reminisce. "But I have never before or since made a decision that was more sad or more lonely."

In the battle that came to be called the "tragedy of Unsan," six hundred of the eight hundred men of the 8th Cavalry's 3d Battalion were either killed or missing in action. The battalion lost most of its heavy equipment, including seventeen tanks and thirteen 105mm howitzers.

The 3d Battalion had occupied Hill 303 on my division's left flank in the Tabu-dong perimeter along the Naktong River east of Waegwan when the battalion joined the war. The battalion conducted joint operations with us on that left flank, and its commander, Lt. Col. Harold Johnson—who was to serve as U.S. Army chief of staff during the Vietnam War era—was reassigned as U.S. I Corps G-3 just one week before the tragic battle at Unsan. During the Unsan battle, the battalion was commanded by its new leader, Lt. Col. Robert Ormond. Colonel Johnson himself was thrown into inconsolable grief at the time, and when next I met him he told me, "The shock was indescribable."

As word of the tragedy at Unsan spread, the U.S. press picked up the story and reported erroneously that the "U.S. 8th Cavalry Regiment and the ROK 1st Division were destroyed." When I was serving as Korean ambassador to Canada, I met with Colonel Hennig's wife at Colorado Springs in 1968, and she told me she had heard the erroneous radio report saying that the ROK 1st Division had been destroyed. "I heard the news on the radio and cried all night," she said.

The unvarnished truth is that the U.S. 8th Cavalry Regiment had been on a mission to cover the withdrawal of my division when it encountered so much misery. The regret I feel on that account shall be with me so long as I live.

The ROK 1st Division withdrew again on the night of November 2, 1950, this time to Yongbyon, and managed to hold Chinese forces advancing southward along the right flank of U.S. I Corps. The next day the ROK 1st Division turned this mission over, on order, to the U.S. 1st Cav, crossed the Chongchon, marched south to Sinanju, and went into corps reserve.

The Chinese offensive that began on October 25 entered a temporary lull during the night of November 5. Those first days of the Chinese attack are called the "Chinese First Offensive." During the eleven days of the Chinese First Offensive, the ROK 1st Division lost about 530 men killed or missing in action, not an inconsiderable number. The 15th Regiment under Col. Cho Jae Mi had absorbed the heaviest blows because Cho had been at division point.

The defeat of the U.S. and Korean armies in this first great clash with the Chinese Army provided many lessons to those who research the history of warfare, and I understand that it is still studied today. In my judgment, the first reason for our defeat was our failure to prepare for a surprise attack. Victorious armies commonly suffer from inflated morale, so that the faster they advance the more likely they are to stumble, even over a small obstacle. The foreign news media at the time had reported repeatedly that the Chinese Army had crossed from Manchuria into Korea. Yet the UN Command and the ROK Army continued to rush toward the Yalu as if competing in a hundred-yard dash.

The second reason for our defeat, in my view, was that we were ignorant of the enemy. No modern soldier can be unaware of Sun-Tzu's famous injunction that "If you know yourself and you know your enemy, then you will win one hundred victories in one hundred battles." The UN Command overlooked this basic principle of warfare and consistently underestimated the Chinese. The Chinese Army established communism in China only after successfully conducting a very long war of resistance against the Japanese and winning a civil war against Kuomintang forces. The Chinese understood combat tactics thoroughly, and unlike the UN Command, the Chinese Army knew its enemy well. Its knowledge of U.S. and ROK forces was generally very accurate.

A Chinese POW later gave me a copy of the "Military Lessons Bulletin" published on November 20, 1950, by the Chinese Army's Sixty-sixth Army Headquarters. The bulletin's subject was "Results of the Battle at Unsan." The article was written by the deputy commander of Chinese Army forces, Teng Hua, who the next year was to be my counterpart at the cease-fire talks held at Kaesong.

In his article, Teng noted that

> the U.S. Army relies for its main power in combat on the shock effect of coordinated armor and artillery . . . and their air-to-ground attack capability is exceptional. But their infantry is weak. Their men are afraid to die, and will neither press home a bold attack nor defend to the death. . . . Their habit is to be active only during daylight hours. They are very weak at attacking or approaching an enemy at night. . . . If their source of supply is cut, their fighting spirit suffers, and if you interdict their rear, they withdraw on their own.

In the article, Teng said of the ROK Army, "The Korean Army is deficient in all pertinent aspects. Their training is absolutely insufficient. Three Korean divisions do not equal one American division when it comes to firepower and overall combat strength. But the Koreans do have a measure of fighting spirit." I can't contain an ironic chuckle when I read these words because the Chinese seemed to suffer from the mistaken impression that the ROK 1st Division with its U.S. armor and artillery was a U.S. Army unit.

4

DASHED HOPES

Rest and Recuperation

The communist Chinese Army struck like a tidal wave, but about midnight on November 5, 1950, its offensive subsided. We found the sudden withdrawal as incomprehensible as it was welcome. The U.S. Army's top leaders recovered from their shock and immediately and variously characterized the Chinese offensive as "an armed demonstration designed to protect their industrial facilities in Manchuria" and "merely providing pro forma support to North Korea."

We need to examine these assumptions in the light of the communist Chinese Army's own documents. A number of Chinese Army publications make the Chinese intentions and combat situation clear. These include the memoirs of Peng Teh-huai, the Chinese general who was the commander in chief of Chinese forces during the war, published in the 1970s; "A Collection of Combat Experiences," published during the war by the Chinese 13th Army Group; and "Results of the Battle at Unsan," the document published by the Chinese Sixty-sixth Army that I mentioned earlier.

Under Peng's overall command, Lin Piao's Fourth Field Army began moving from the Chinese continent proper toward Manchuria, using the success of the amphibious landing at Inchon as both motivation and excuse.

The final decision to enter the war in Korea was taken on October 4 and 5, 1950, in Beijing during a session of the Chinese Communist party's Central Committee. Mao Tse-tung defended the decision in these words:

The United States has occupied Korea, crossed the Yalu River, and is threatening our northeast territory. Moreover, the Americans control Taiwan and are threatening Shanghai and Nanking. If the United States intends to start a war of aggression against China, they are in a position to do so at any time and will find plenty of excuses for doing so.

Waving the flag of duty, Mao decided to dispatch Chinese troops. "There can be no excuse," he said, "for looking idly on when a neighbor's house is imperiled."

In evaluating the relative military prowess of China and the United States, the communist Chinese Army concluded that the U.S. Army was superior in conventional warfare and in swift, mechanized operations, but that the Chinese Army was superior in guerrilla operations and at protracted warfare. "Considering that we will receive Soviet aid," the leaders estimated, "we will be in a much better position than we were in our war against the Japanese."

Advance elements of the Chinese Army crossed the Yalu River and entered Korea during the night of October 13, 1950. About 150,000 men in eighteen Chinese Army divisions under six armies subordinate to the 13th Army Group crossed the Yalu, advanced southward, and participated in the first attack.

Chinese Supreme Commander Peng himself crossed the Yalu with a leading unit on October 18, 1950. the Thirty-eighth Army under Sung Shuang-ken and the Forty-second Army under Wu Juei-lin passed through Chihan, crossed the Yalu, and continued to Manpo before they went their separate ways. The Thirty-eighth Army advanced to Huichon, and the Forty-second Army deployed around the Changjin Reservoir (also known as the Chosin Reservoir). Crossing the Yalu at Sinuiju, the Thirty-ninth Army marched toward Unsan, while the Fortieth Army passed through Onjong and attacked toward Kunu. The Fiftieth Army under Huei Tse-sheng and the Sixty-sixth Army under Hsiao Hsin-huai also crossed the Yalu at Sinuiju, and their plan was to bypass Kusong and surround the U.S. 24th Division, but the two Chinese armies were running behind schedule and arrived too late to participate in the attack.

The two Chinese regiments that launched a surprise attack on my own ROK 1st Division at Unsan on October 25 were the first units of the Thirty-ninth Army to enter Korea and the first Chinese Army units to participate in combat. The communist Chinese Army celebrates October 25 as the anniversary of its participation in the Korean War, commemorating this initial combat. The rest of the Thirty-ninth Army caught up with its advance regiments by October 31, cut our line of withdrawal southwest of Unsan, and attacked the ROK 1st Division in Unsan from every side.

From Ipsok to Yongbyon, the Chinese Army found the ROK 1st Division to be unexpectedly powerful and our artillery mortally dangerous. When the battle ended, the Chinese withdrew to a line extending from Taechon to Kujangdong, where the Chinese units prepared for their next offensive. Chinese sources later claimed that they "killed or captured fifteen thousand United Nations Command men and officers" during the first offensive.

Pilots of the U.S. Air Force had not spotted the huge influx of Chinese Army forces during their reconnaissance runs, and this was not accidental. To prevent discovery, the Chinese commanders strictly forbade daytime movement, and a soldier caught violating this order was shot on the spot. The Chinese Army observed strict radio silence and marched eight hours a night, from 7:00 P.M. to 3:00 A.M. hours. Chinese units carefully policed up even minor traces of their passage. These simple methods allowed large units to enter Korea and maneuver undiscovered into positions from which to launch the Chinese First Offensive. Indeed six hundred thousand soldiers of the Chinese Army had entered North Korea by the end of November.

Chinese Army tactics were as simple and repetitive as they were successful. They attacked by surprise and infiltrated significant forces through and around the unit under attack so as to cut withdrawal routes and encircle the objective. Chinese unit commanders then pressed home a withering attack from all sides. They simply repeated it all at the next engagement. These tactics required Chinese units to march fast, operate at night, and trek through tough mountainous terrain. Chinese soldiers proved more than equal to these tasks and could easily march fifteen to twenty miles a night.

The Chinese Army used bugles, whistles, and gongs during night combat, partly to exercise tactical control but also for their psychological effect on the enemy. Friendly soldiers sometimes revealed their night positions when the Chinese cacophony startles our men into firing individual weapons. The Chinese Army launched attacks with large numbers of concentrated infantry armed with small arms and hand grenades, seemingly without the slightest regard for the staggering human cost imposed by such human-wave attacks.

Peng Teh-huai himself tells us why the Chinese Army tidal wave ebbed, why he didn't follow up his initial attack on the UN Command:

Our Army had annihilated only six or seven ROK Army battalions and small units of the U.S. Army. We had not yet been able to smash the enemy's main force. Our strategy was simple. We made it appear that our combat power was much weaker than it was, enticing our arrogant enemy into ever deeper penetrations. We positioned our main force east and west of Pukjin, where we had secretly prepared positions about 20 miles from the enemy's line of departure.

The communist Chinese Army's expressed perceptions of the armies of the United States and the Republic of Korea above should not be taken at face value because Chinese documents were published for Chinese Army officers and men and naturally overstated enemy weaknesses. For one thing, U.S. Army officers at that time were very much superior to counterparts from all nations involved in the war. You could see that, and you could feel it as well. U.S. officers were easily the best in the world when it came to tactics and to instilling a sense of responsibility in their troops.

I heard a number of American officers express concern about their men, however. Brigadier General Williams, assistant division commander of the U.S. 25th Division, whom I met in combat, was candid about it. "We're in big trouble with these green soldiers," he said. Aside from the new recruits, many of the American enlisted men who fought in Korea had served in World War II. It was unreasonable to expect them to fight their best in an alien land after they had enjoyed five years of peace and family life only to be recalled suddenly and sent to a war in distant Korea. For our part, the officers and men of the Republic of Korea Army were so short on combat experience that our difficulties were infinitely greater than those of the U.S. forces.

The first Chinese offensive affected me individually. I became busier than I can ever remember being in my life. Indeed, all I remember is a long blur of activity. I can't remember times, days, or dates for that period at all. We had been charging north rapidly and had run into a wall. While we were still reeling from the shock, I found myself suddenly in command of II Corps, only to be reassigned to the helm of ROK 1st Division three days later. In the midst of everything else, I had to leave the fighting and travel down to Pyongyang on two separate occasions.

President Syngman Rhee was scheduled to attend a rally to commemorate the liberation of Pyongyang on October 25, and I had to make my way back to prepare the rally and provide presidential security. Because President Rhee couldn't come, Home Minister Cho Byong Ok did the honors, and I returned to the front. They decided to hold the ceremony again on October 29, when the president was available, so I had to hasten back to Pyongyang for the rescheduled presidential visit.

President Rhee's keynote speech was excellent. He appealed for unity, speaking from a rostrum at Pyongyang City Hall plaza. The plaza was packed with North Korean citizens who gave the president a wildly enthusiastic welcome. President Rhee returned the emotion, plunging into the crowd as his speech ended to shake hands with the people. Those of us responsible for the president's personal safety nearly suffered heart attacks.

I had attended Kim Il Sung's maiden speech at a mass meeting held on the campus of Pyongyang's First Middle School on October 14, 1945.

After hearing President Rhee's address, I was one of very few people who personally heard speeches delivered in the same city by the leaders of both North and South Korea, even if the speeches were separated by five years and a chunk of downtown Pyongyang real estate. I'm not sure any useful purpose can be served by comparing the two speeches at this late moment, but in point of fact, I can't deny that the experienced politician Syngman Rhee's dignity and popularity enthralled the crowd, contrasting starkly with the youthful Kim Il Sung, who barely managed to stir his audience. President Rhee was fond of saying, ''A leader is honored by his people to the same degree that he devotes himself to the people.'' On this occasion in Pyongyang, President Rhee received a popular welcome worthy of any president.

The ROK 1st Division was pulled off the line and permitted our first rest and recuperation since the war began, four months before. We assembled south of Sinanju near the airport in Ipsok, a different place from the Ipsok near Yongbyon mentioned above. I was swamped with work and found our time off the line neither restful nor relaxing. Replacements and new equipment flooded in, and I had to accommodate them even as I made other adjustments in the division as well, overseeing tactical training and inspecting the various units composing the division.

At that time the airport at Ipsok was almost as big as those at Youido or Kimpo outside of Seoul, at least before these were expanded, and American transport planes landed and took off from the field all day long, ferrying in supplies in a stream so dense that each aircraft seemed to be biting the tail of the one preceding it. Our rear-area location afforded us an enlightening view of combined operations in war.

As I caught on to how things worked in the rear, I realized why resupply had been so difficult during the fighting along the Chongchon River. The railway system throughout North Korea had been knocked out by air strikes, and the lengthy process of repair was still under way. In the meantime, we had to rely solely on trucks to bring war materiel and supplies all the way north to Pyongyang. Given the abysmal state of the road net and our shortage of drivers, this was a nightmare to the logisticians.

Once the airfield at Ipsok had been secured, large, dual-engined U.S. Air Force transport planes airlifted in provisions, clothing, POL (petrol, oil, and lubricants), ammunition, and other materials, yet even this barely kept the supply line open. The airfield at Ipsok bustled with aircraft, trucks, and personnel from morning to night. Rail service from Seoul to the Taedong River was not restored until November 12, and telephone service remained inoperative until November 21.

Sinanju was situated on the vast Anju Plain, North Korea's most productive rice-farming area. During ROK 1st Division's period of rest and recuperation (R and R) in the vicinity, the rice had just been harvested, and our cooks treated the men to delicious rice cakes made from the newly harvested grain.

The division's Troop Education and Information Office's entertainment section managed to arrange entertainment for the troops. I was pleased that the division's fighters, who had been in combat for so long, were able to enjoy a few good laughs, even if the respite was only momentary. The comedian Kim Hi Gap visited us during this period and performed with dancing girls on a field stage we put together with blankets and straw bags. The girls valiantly tried to dance, but of course we were outside, and they trembled and shook in the terrible cold.

I shall not soon forget the delicious flavor of the cold buckwheat noodles and sweet sliced radish kimchi in water I enjoyed at a civilian house during our R and R period at Ipsok. After four months of army field cooking, I found that even the home-cooked soup tasted like ambrosia. I felt like Simsin in the "The Sandfish," a famous Korean story with a starving protagonist, enjoying my food the more because I was so exhausted and hungry.

The officers and men of the division got away from the heavy pressure of combat and recharged their batteries for about ten days. We weren't all that worried about the Chinese. Even at this late moment, we believed that the unexpected Chinese onslaught had served to block our northward course temporarily. No one understood that the course of the war had been irretrievably reversed.

The Christmas Offensive: Blind March to Disaster

Our R and R period over, the ROK 1st Division returned to the front. It was the middle of November 1950.

U.S. I Corps assigned my ROK 1st Division to the center, flanked by two U.S. divisions, and we advanced toward the Yalu, some fifty miles distant. We crossed the Chongchon River again and concentrated for battle at Pakchon, standing by for orders to launch the assault.

The UN Command actually controlled two distinct fronts in the North Korean fighting. The Eighth Army's western front ran east from the Yellow Sea to the Nangnim Mountains, while the eastern front under U.S. X Corps extended east from these rough, interior mountains to the Sea of Japan. We were really fighting two distinct wars, Eighth Army on one front, X Corps on the other.

At that juncture of the war, Eighth Army's order of battle consisted of U.S. I Corps (composed of the U.S. 1st Cavalry Division, the U.S. 24th Division, the ROK 1st Division, and the British 27th Brigade), the ROK II Corps (composed of the 6th, 7th, and 8th divisions) and the U.S. IX Corps.

U.S. IX Corps under Maj. Gen. John Coulter being assigned to the western front required a readjustment of the line. IX Corps's constituent units included the U.S. 2d Division, the U.S. 25th Division, and the Turkish Brigade.

On the west, the Chinese First Offensive had hit Eighth Army like a sledgehammer, inflicting considerable losses and causing serious resupply problems in the bargain. On the east, X Corps continued to push north, unimpeded. To be sure, Maj. Gen. O. P. Smith's 1st U.S. Marine Division had run into Chinese forces near the Changjin Reservoir, but the rest of X Corps swept smoothly northward. The Capital Division under Maj. Gen. Song Yo Chan advanced to Chongjin; the 3d Division under Brig. Gen. Choi Suk advanced to Hamsu, where his soldiers literally could see the Tumen River boundary with China; and the U.S. 7th Division under Maj. Gen. David Barr charged all the way to Hyesanjin on the Yalu River, within sight of Mount Paektu. The peninsula's highest mountain, Paektu is the mystical home of the ancient Korean people and straddles our boundary with China. The three X Corps divisions advanced so far north as to suggest to senior commanders along the chain of authority that they had accomplished their assigned missions. Any observer would believe that North Korea was ours, certainly on the eastern front.

American officers at U.S. I Corps Headquarters, however, made no secret of their concern that X Corps had not been placed under Eighth Army command. Indeed, common sense alone would dictate that a single general officer should command the ground forces deployed in a single theater of war, but in Korea, two men commanded the ground forces, and cooperation between the two left much to be desired.

Keeping his own counsel, General of the Army MacArthur, commander in chief of the UN Command, decided to divide his Korean theater into two commands, selecting the Nangnim Mountains as the boundary between the two. Ultimately, operations in both sectors failed, and tacticians have criticized MacArthur ever since for not establishing unity of command.

In an eerie turn of affairs, the situation in 1950 closely resembled that which prevailed in a Japanese army that had invaded Korea under Hideyoshi in 1592. In both cases a supreme commander headquartered in Japan commanded two field generals in Korea. In the sixteenth century, Toyotomi Hideyosi commanded Konishi Yukinaga and Kato Kiyomasa. Konishi crossed from Nagoya in Japan and marched on Pyongyang, while Kato crossed the Sea of Japan and advanced up the east coast. Some 350 years later General MacArthur's Supreme Headquarters in Tokyo's Daiichi Life Insurance building commanded the Eighth Army under Gen. Walton H. Walker as it advanced on Pyongyang and X Corps under Maj. Gen. Edward M. Almond as it drove up the east coast.

In each case, the two field generals found themselves in competition. Both in 1592 and in 1950, a frigid formality characterized relations between the two field commanders. General Walker wanted the eastern and western fronts to push northward in concert, even if this slowed the tempo of the attack. For his part, General Almond prodded his divisions far forward of those on the western front in an effort to satisfy MacArthur's expectations. Naturally, this caused MacArthur to favor Almond over Walker. Almond took advantage of MacArthur's regard to gain the upper hand for X Corps both in operational matters and in the distribution of supplies, stepping on General Walker's toes in the process, although Walker outranked him.

MacArthur plainly was dissatisfied. Why couldn't Eighth Army charge north like X Corps? Tokyo hatched a hasty plan called the "Home by Christmas Offensive," choosing not to resolve the disharmony in the field caused by the disunity of the command. The name of the operation reflected the desire of the UN Command officers and their men to end the war quickly and return to their homes by Christmas.

On November 8, 1950, the U.S. Air Force conducted a fierce bombing campaign to keep pressure on the enemy once the Chinese withdrew from the front. The U.S. Air Force sortied six hundred aircraft on a single, mammoth bombing raid on Sinuiju, virtually razing the city. Indeed, the air force bombed every town and city north of the Chongchon River.

As the time to launch the Christmas Offensive neared, I sent my division reconnaissance unit out to conduct a deep reconnaissance in force to our front. We found no sign of the enemy. Orders came down establishing the Christmas offensive H-hour at 10:00 A.M. on November 24, 1950, the day after Thanksgiving.

The UN Command managed to provide turkey and all the trimmings to every front-line unit, and the men enjoyed the festive meal together. Signs of our defeat the previous month were completely gone, and no one now considered those clashes of any consequence. The officers and men of the UN Command turned their hearts and minds homeward. The UN Command had maintained airtight secrecy about the landing at Inchon, but this time it was different. General MacArthur publicly announced a Christmas offensive and assured the world of our victory.

At H-hour on November 24, 1950, the entire front surged forward in a massive assault. All five corps arrayed along the eastern and western fronts—three UN corps and two ROK Army corps—jumped off at the same time. My ROK 1st Division bolted out of its assigned assembly point at Pakchon, crossed the Taeryong River, and charged forward, encountering only light enemy resistance. At sunset on the first day, I felt sure the ROK 1st Division would have little trouble pushing all the way to the Yalu.

It was not to be. On the second morning of the Christmas Offensive, the Chinese Army launched a fierce counterattack, and we quickly found ourselves locked in a furious struggle in the rugged mountains south of Taechon. I felt confident, that second day, that we could break through the enemy resistance easily. In the two days of the Christmas Offensive we had advanced more than six miles, occupying the ridges overlooking the hamlet of Taechon.

I directed our attack from a forward command post we had set up on a high point southeast of Taechon. Our air-ground liaison officer, 1st Lt. William Mathis, was standing beside me in the command post talking on the radio to pilots flying tactical ground strikes in support of our attack. Suddenly, an enemy bullet whistled in from our front and caught the American officer full in the chest. He fell, bleeding profusely.

I had Mathis evacuated immediately in my jeep to the Mobile Army Surgical Hospital (MASH) at Sinanju. The wound was serious, but miraculously he made a full recovery. Years later Mathis was promoted to full general and served as chief of staff of the U.S. Air Force. I was reunited with him in 1978, when, as a U.S. Air Force lieutenant general, he was installed as deputy commander of the U.S. Tactical Air Force Headquarters at Langley Air Force Base in Virginia.

I digress, but I heard an interesting anecdote about General Mathis. When he learned in America in 1961 that a Major General Park had staged a coup d'état and taken control of the Korean government, he thought I was the perpetrator. Mathis asked friends assigned at Osan U.S. Air Force Base in Korea to determine if I had been involved. Of course, I was not. The coup was executed on May 16, 1961, by Maj. Gen. Park Chung Hee, but to Americans "Park" and "Paik" can sound very much alike.

As we charged forward on the first day of the Christmas Offensive, the ROK 1st Division captured a Chinese soldier. Or so we thought. To our amazement, we discovered that he was in fact Japanese. The man had fought originally with the Japanese Army but was captured during action in China. The Chinese eventually allowed him to join their army. Here was a rare breed indeed, a Japanese serving in the Chinese Army fighting South Koreans in North Korea. The soldier was a member of a cavalry unit, where his assignment was to guard the horses.

The Chinese's counterattack against the ROK 1st Division, indeed the whole of the U.S. I Corps, did not appear to represent their main effort. The Chinese directed their main energy to our east against Eighth Army's extreme right wing where it abutted the Myohyang Mountain Range. Eighth Army's line began to rupture at that point. The ROK 1st Division was frustrated. Before we could even manage to engage the enemy decisively, the collapse of units to our east began to render our own position untenable.

On November 25 as the ROK 1st Division was fighting a seesaw battle with Chinese units south of Taechon, attacking and defending, attacking and defending, the enemy surrounded the ROK 7th Division at Tokjon, and the ROK 8th Division at Yongwon. Chinese forces then proceeded to destroy the two ROK divisions. A mere one day into the Christmas Offensive, the ROK 7th and 8th Divisions had disintegrated in the mountains and for practical purposes ceased to be combat capable.

This disaster threatened the integrity of the adjacent U.S. IX Corps. Having penetrated Eighth Army's eastern flank, Chinese Army forces pinned IX Corps in place with a frontal attack, while other Chinese units launched telling attacks on the unit's exposed flank. In a favorite tactic, still other forces rushed through the hole in our lines to block the withdrawal routes available to IX Corps. The plan worked. Friendly units fell one after the other, starting on the extreme right flank. The Americans called it "the Chongchon River dominoes."

The mission of U.S. IX Corps had been to attack north along the Chongchon River to Huichon, but Eighth Army issued new orders on November 27. The corps was to abandon the attack, switch to defensive operations, and extend its area of operations to include the sector previously assigned to ROK II Corps. These changes proved to be too little and too late. On November 28 the situation deteriorated sharply across the entire front, including the U.S. X Corps sector on the east. Eighth Army ordered a general withdrawal along the entire front before the day was out. Before this order could be issued, however, both Walker and Almond had to fly to Tokyo and explain the seriousness of the situation to MacArthur.

The IX Corps massed its indirect fire weapons to cover the collapsed right wing, providing my ROK 1st Division and the U.S. 24th Division an opportunity to withdraw unchallenged. We crossed the Chongchon River heading south on November 28, 1950. It was snowing.

Most of my officers and men were bewildered that the mighty ROK 1st Division was withdrawing without a single slugfest worthy of the name. We marched without incident to Yongyu, fifteen miles north of Pyongyang. Two days later, the U.S. Army struggled through an unforgettable day of hell.

Unable to resist the massive pressure applied by the Chinese Army, the UN Command began a general withdrawal from a line extending from Sunchon to Yangdok. We were to defend at a new line running from Pyongyang straight across the entire peninsula to Wonsan on the Sea of Japan. The U.S. 2d and 25th divisions of IX Corps had propped up the unraveling line until the very last minute, but now they had to abandon Kunu and withdraw hastily toward Sunchon.

Two roads lead from Kunu to Sunchon, a direct eastern route and a circuitous western route that detours through Anju. The western route was much safer but was packed with withdrawing Eighth Army units and could accommodate no more. A single American division typically required an entire day to pass a given point on the narrow, unpaved roads common to Korea in that period. If Maj. Gen. Laurence Keiser's 2d Division was to get out at all, it had to deploy down the eastern road. That route wound through a valley of sorrow. The God of Death himself hovered with heavy, beating wings over that road.

The main body of the U.S. 2d Division, complete with its tanks, artillery, and vehicles entered a valley about nine miles long. The entire stretch of road was bordered closely by mountains on both sides. As the 2d neared Yangpyon, Chinese Army forces lying in ambush in the hills suddenly opened volley fire and pressed home a merciless attack from both flanks. The narrow road was so clogged with vehicles that those which survived the initial barrages were unable to pull free from the wreckage around them. The British Commonwealth Brigade occupied positions at the southern tip of the valley, but the British could do nothing to relieve the situation. They could see what was happening, however, and quite literally stamped their feet in frustration.

In the brief span of half a morning the 2d Division lost three thousand killed and wounded. The 2d Division effectively lost its main punch. The Americans themselves called this disaster the gauntlet. When American Indians wished to punish a prisoner or a criminal, they sometimes formed their warriors into two lines and forced the unlucky victim to dash between the rows as the braves rained blows on him. Victims who managed to exit the gauntlet were allowed to survive.

The U.S. 2d Division ran the gauntlet on November 30, 1950. Its defeat was the worst recorded for the U.S. Army during the Korean War. The decimation of the 2d Division sent a terrible shock wave rolling through the UN Command.

The plan was for the ROK 1st Division, the U.S. 1st Cav Division, the U.S. 25th Division, and the British Commonwealth 29th Brigade to form a defense line north of Pyongyang. The U.S. 2d Division and other units withdrawing later were to extend this line to the east. The mission was to contain the Chinese Army north of this so-called Pyongyang-Wonsan line. But the line was thin on the east, too thin.

On December 3, MacArthur's headquarters decided on a general southward withdrawal to the 38th parallel of all forces in action in North Korea. The parallel had served as the prewar border between North and South Korea. MacArthur's order betokened the UN Command's abandonment of its objective to seize North Korea. For us in the ROK Army, December 3, 1950, lives as the day when our dream of national unification by force was dashed forever. MacArthur's Christmas Offensive had run full tilt into Peng's Second Offensive and collapsed completely.

Tacticians have heaped scathing criticism on the UN Command's Christmas Offensive, calling it a "drastic miscalculation" on a "blind march to disaster." The UN Command undertook the offensive because it estimated that Chinese forces in North Korea numbered between

30,000 and 70,000. Because 110,000 troops served under the UN Command banner, the commander judged that he had sufficient strength to defeat the Chinese Army deployed in North Korea.

That was the UN Command estimate. In fact at that time, the Twentieth, Twenty-sixth, and Twenty-seventh armies of the 9th Army Group under Sung Shih-lun, subordinate to the Third Field Army under Chien I, had infiltrated the eastern front, their numbers reaching the breathtaking total of six hundred thousand troops. These forces watched the roads and bided their time, poised to deliver a massive counterblow to the pending offensive that an excess of confidence prompted MacArthur himself to announce.

Eighth Army's operations plan has also been criticized. For one thing, Eighth Army had done nothing to rebuild the 6th, 7th, and 8th divisions of ROK Army II Corps after they had been badly mauled in the Chinese First Offensive. Despite a significant decrease in the combat capability of these units, Eighth Army assigned them to its most vulnerable sector, the rugged, mountainous area on Eighth Army's extreme right wing. Past masters at mountain warfare, the Chinese Army outmatched the weakened ROK divisions.

Rather than provide a detailed description of the fate of these three ROK divisions in II Corps, I'll quote instead the testimony of KMAG's Robert Cameron.

> The ROK Army divisions were only lightly equipped. A mere fraction of their units were supplied with the customary number of mortars and machine guns, and each division had only a single 105mm light artillery battalion. ROK II Corps itself had neither its own tanks or artillery nor any supporting U.S. Army armor or artillery units.

Nonetheless, two of the three division commanders were held responsible for the failures and remanded to court martial, where they were sentenced to death. Both were pardoned and reinstated later. The incident revealed the underlying intensity of President Syngman Rhee's repeated calls for unification by force; he was even willing to reinstate convicted generals if that would help him achieve unification.

Major General Keiser, commanding general of the U.S. 2d Division, was also relieved of command. The fate of a few flag officers, however, was inconsequential when contrasted with the general psychological blow the Chinese offensive dealt to friendly forces. The morale of officers and men of both UN and ROK forces plummeted.

Every unit in the war was caught up in a maelstrom of psychological collapse, fed by the shock of the heartbreaking defeats, the frustration felt by foreign troops who had believed they would be home by Christmas, and the disheartening reversal in the tide of the war. This reversal was so total and so swift that soldiers couldn't deal with it. An officer who has not experienced commanding a unit sunk in panic and despair cannot fathom the pain. When morale sinks to such depths, units simply ignore orders and directives. The commander can't even determine what is happening in his subordinate units. Soldiers are obligated to obey the orders of their commanders unquestionably, of course. But at the practical level, soldiers place great store in the views of combat veterans in their units, and they act in accord with the instinct for self-preservation rather than in accord with the imperatives of the mission.

We had been knocked to our knees. Who could pull us to our feet? And how?

The Wretched Withdrawal of January 4, 1951

My division withdrew through Pyongyang on December 5, through Sariwon on December 11, and reached the Imjin River, where the war had begun for us on June 25. Tears clouded many an eye during that bitter trek.

The sun had just dipped below the horizon as we passed through East Pyongyang during the withdrawal. Geysers of flame from fires around the city lighted the darkening sky. Despite the bitter cold, large numbers of refugees poured onto the roads from everywhere, heading south with us.

Pyongyang's fires proved to be funeral pyres for U.S. Army supply storage points. After the railroad link with South Korea had been restored, veritable mountains of U.S. supplies had appeared in Pyongyang. General Walker had ordered that these be destroyed to prevent them from falling into enemy hands.

As we passed through the city, the light from the flames treated us to terrible spectacles. Numbers of Pyongyang's destitute citizens approached the pyres and risked blazing death to retrieve clothing and food from the flames, even as American guards fired warning shots over their heads. Some of my own soldiers salvaged items of clothing from the flames and draped them over their bodies against the sting of the cold.

At the Taedong River railroad station, I saw eighteen tanks on flatcars surrounded by oceans of flame. The tanks had crossed the broad Pacific Ocean to support our battle, but now at the end of their long journey they were being destroyed before they had fired a single shot.

Military engineers blew the temporary pontoon bridge over the Taedong River, stranding huge crowds of refugees. But that didn't stop the people. Desperate to escape, hundreds died fording the chest-high water in the freezing weather. No pen can describe the grief that engulfed me as I watched helplessly. The dream of uniting the fatherland was gone, and I had no reason to believe that I would ever see my home again.

I suffered an attack of malaria as we passed through Sariwon, and my health deteriorated beyond the point where I could hold body and mind together by force of will alone. When it rains, it pours. In the midst of these troubles, our next shock came in the form of a rumor that the Americans intended to abandon Korea and withdraw all the way to Japan. This rumor was so strong that I felt obliged to ask General Milburn, the I Corps commander, what the U.S. Army planned to do. "We are soldiers," he answered. "We will fight to the last even if it means surrendering our lives." He refused to explicate.

I ran into Colonel Michaelis in Sariwon and ran the rumors by him. "There is no possibility the U.S. Army will withdraw to Japan," Michaelis fairly screamed. "But we're going to have to fight our very best. Don't be so pessimistic!"

The ROK 1st Division alternated with U.S. divisions covering the rear during the withdrawal. But the Chinese Army's pursuit was sluggish, and we had no contact with the enemy during our withdrawal to the Imjin River. That suggests, I suppose, the speed of our withdrawal.

Four ROK Army divisions participated in the fighting on the western front, but the ROK 1st Division was the only one that emerged with its organization intact.

ROK II Corps Headquarters disbanded. The situation was so bad that after we reached Korangpo on the Imjin River, General Walker gave me a personal order. "General Paik," he said. "You are to be responsible for processing withdrawing ROK Army officers and men and act as their overall commander."

The ROK 1st Division underwent some personnel changes during this period. Assistant division commander Brig. Gen. Choi Young Hi was transferred out to serve as an adviser to the newly founded Citizens Defense Force and then was immediately reassigned to replace Brig. Gen. Lee Sung Ga as commanding general of the 8th Division. Colonel Yu Hung Su who commanded my newly organized 13th Regiment was appointed to be my new assistant division commander. Commander of the 11th Regiment, Col. Kim Dong Bin, was designated division chief of staff, while Lt. Col. Mun Hyong Tae assumed command of the 11th Regiment, and Maj. Park Chin Suk was appointed division G-3.

Also during this period, Colonel Hennig, who had fought shoulder-to-shoulder with me as commander of the U.S. 10th Antiaircraft Artillery Group, and Lieutenant Colonel Growden, the commander of our tank battalion, were both recalled to their original American units. I felt like the ROK 1st Division's firepower had shrunk to nothing after they left.

As we completed our withdrawal to the 38th parallel, the UN Command's order of battle was as follows. The U.S. I Corps defended north

of the Imjin River; the U.S. IX Corps defended north of Uijongbu; Maj.
Gen. Lee Hyung Koon's III Corps defended north of Chunchon, and
the ROK I Corps abutted the Sea of Japan on the extreme right wing of
the entire line. U.S. I Corps was composed of the U.S. 25th Division,
the ROK 1st Division, and the Turkish Brigade; IX Corps was composed
of the U.S. 2d Division and the ROK 6th Division; the divisions assigned
to the newly organized ROK III Corps were the ROK 2d, 5th, and 8th;
and the ROK I Corps consisted of the 3d and Capital divisions.

Before Eighth Army withdrew on the west, Chinese Army forces surrounded the elite U.S. 1st Marine Division in the vicinity of the Changjin Reservoir in northeastern North Korea. The marines withdrew under
fire in a desperate battle all the way to the port city of Hungnam on the
Sea of Japan and were evacuated by sea to Pusan.

The ROK 3d and Capital divisions were taken out by sea, as well.
They disembarked at the port of Samchok and deployed once again
along the eastern coast.

As the UN Command and ROK Army forces withdrew from North
Korea on both the eastern and western sectors of the front, huge numbers of North Korean refugees took to the roads and streamed south in
the midst of one of the snowiest, most bitter winters in memory. The
vicissitudes of war and the difficulty of the trek hopelessly split apart
thousands of refugee families. Most remain separated to this day, living
out lives stained by bitter resentment at the loss of their loved ones.

By December 15, 1950, the ROK 1st Division occupied defensive positions stretching along the Imjin River from Changpa on the west to the
salient of land where the Hantan River joins the Imjin on the east. Put
another way, we occupied the whole of Choksong Township.

The U.S. 25th Division was located on our left flank, directly north of
Munsan. Our right flank marked the eastern boundary of I Corps. The
ROK 6th Division, attached to U.S. IX Corps and commanded by Brig.
Gen. Chang Do Young, was stationed immediately to our right, defend-
ing the approach to Tongduchon.

In December 1950, the ROK 1st Division occupied generally the same
area in Korangpo we had defended when the North Koreans invaded
in June 1950, although we were a bit farther to the east than we had
been then with narrow frontages ranging about 20 miles. This was familiar ground to me and the other officers and men of the division who
had survived the intervening months of combat.

Two things were very different, however. In June the division had
been assigned an impossibly wide sector, and we had been able to use
the Imjin River as a barrier to slow the enemy. Now the bitter winter
cold had frozen the Imjin to such a depth that it presented no obstacle
to our new enemy. We could not expect to exploit the usual advantages
of a waterway in conducting a defense.

The Americans supplied us with barbed wire and mines, and we used

Brig. Gen. Paik Sun Yup, twenty-nine-year-old commander of the
1st ROK Division, with a USAF forward observer near Pyongyang,
October 19, 1950. *U.S. Army*

In Pyongyang with Maj. Gen. Frank "Shrimp" Milburn, I Corps
commander, October 19, 1950. *U.S. Army*

Paik at his Shihung command post greeting Gen. Matthew
B. Ridgway, February 1951. *U.S. Army*

Gen. Douglas MacArthur leaves the 1st ROK Division's command post following the recapture of Seoul in March 1951. *U.S. Army*

Rear Adm. Arleigh Burke welcomes Paik aboard the USS *Los Angeles* off the east coast of Korea, May 1951. *U.S. Army*

Maj. Gen. Paik Sun Yup, commander of ROK I Corps, May 1951. *ROK Army*

Gen. Omar N. Bradley visiting Paik's ROK I Corps Headquarters, summer of 1951. *ROK Army*

En route to the first session of the Kaesong armistice talks, July 1951. To Paik's right is Vice Adm. C. Turner Joy, senior UN delegate. *UN Command*

The UN delegation at Kaesong. From left: Maj. Gen. L. C. Craigie, USAF; Paik; Vice Adm. C. Turner Joy, USN; Maj. Gen. Henry Hodes, USA; and Rear Adm. Arleigh Burke, USN. *U.S. Army*

South Korean president Syngman Rhee; Gen. James A. Van Fleet, USA, commander of the Eighth U.S. Army; and Lt. Gen. Paik, ROK Army chief of staff, at a ceremony honoring Van Fleet in Seoul, January 26, 1953. *U.S. Army*

From left: Brig. Gen. An Dong Sun, Gen. Paik, Gen. Matthew B. Ridgway, Gen. John Hull, and Gen. Maxwell Taylor, in Pusan during October 1953. *ROK Army*

Paik visiting Douglas MacArthur at his Waldorf-Astoria suite, New York, May 1958. *U.S. Army*

Gen. Paik Sun Yup, ROKA (Ret.).

them to build barriers across the key approach routes leading into the division's sector. We put prodigious efforts into improving the defenses, partly because that was a military necessity and partly because it served as a ready means to divert the men from negative thinking. They worked feverishly to dig trenches and defensive positions in the frozen earth.

The lull ended soon enough. Communist Chinese forces advanced swiftly south and began to apply pressure on us around December 20. Tension soared, but the Chinese didn't keep us in suspense very long. They soon launched a major attack at the middle of the western sector, near Chunchon. Two ROK divisions absorbed the brunt of the attack: the 8th Division under my former regimental commander Brig. Gen. Choi Young Hi and the 9th Division under Brig. Gen. Oh Duk Jun. Brig. Gen. Kim Chong Kap assumed command of 9th Division on December 31.

As the Chinese attack began, I received word of the sudden death of Eighth Army commander, Lt. Gen. Walton H. Walker. On the morning of December 23, 1950, General Walker visited the U.S. 24th Division and spoke with his son, Capt. Sam Walker, who had been awarded the Silver Star for gallantry the previous day. General Walker then left to visit the British Commonwealth Brigade near Uijongbu, where he wanted to inspect preparations for a visit by Republic of Korea President Rhee. General Walker had a reputation as a speed demon, and his jeep was flying when it plowed headlong into a ROK 6th Division truck speeding from the opposite direction. I was told that General Walton H. Walker breathed his last before he could be evacuated to hospital.

Like his mentor General Patton, General Walker died in a traffic accident. And I saw another parallel as well. For the second time now, a supreme commander of ROK forces had been killed. Immediately after our defeat at the 38th parallel in June 1950, Army Chief of Staff General Chae Byong Duk was killed in the Naktong River line. Now, at another crucial moment in the war, immediately after our defeat by the Chinese at the Chongchon River, another top commander was removed from the scene.

I had met General Walker four times during the war. I met him for the first time at Yongchon on the Naktong River line when he awarded me the U.S. Legion of Merit, and again when he accompanied U.S. Army Chief of Staff Gen. J. Lawton Collins in a visit to ROK 1st Division Headquarters in the Tabu-dong lines. I met General Walker a third time near the Tongchon Airport outside Taegu when he dropped by to urge me to more vigorous efforts after we had been unable to crush the enemy and move to the offensive. I saw him for the last time north of the Chongchon River when the division was conducting a road movement.

General Walker was assigned to Korea on July 13, 1950, at the darkest hour of the war, and led UN Command forces to victory in the battle to defend the Pusan Perimeter. General Walker achieved many brilliant military exploits, leading the UN Command forces northward, opening the door into North Korea, and capturing Pyongyang.

General Walker's leadership was pivotal in shoring up our stubborn defense at the Naktong River line. The amphibious landing at Inchon that reversed the direction of the war could not have been launched had the Naktong River line collapsed. Indeed, the nation itself would have collapsed, and the Republic of Korea would not exist today.

General Walker boasted a bulldog face and always wore his helmet, which rode too high on his head. He was a most active commander and a bold soldier, and he conveyed that impression to all who met him. As a gesture of respect to General Walker, the U.S. Army nicknamed its light, M-41 reconnaissance tank the "Walker Bulldog."

President Syngman Rhee relied greatly on General Walker in directing the war, but apparently President Rhee did not find Walker entirely agreeable. Even after General Walker's death, President Rhee was known to have commented occasionally that "my friend Walker, he was a bit ill mannered." I think the president drew this impression because General Walker always complained that the ROK Army didn't fight well enough. Then, too, General Walker's manner was not particularly docile, and I think he stepped on old President Rhee's pride some.

Lt. Gen. Matthew B. Ridgway was appointed the new Eighth Army commander. Ridgway had been serving as deputy chief of staff for operations at the Pentagon. He had commanded the U.S. 82nd Airborne Division in operations in Sicily and in the Normandy invasion during World War II. Ridgway was an energetic soldier who earlier in his career had served in the Philippines and at Tienchin in China.

General Ridgway visited us at ROK 1st Division Headquarters at a primary school in the vicinity of Pobwon on December 29, 1950. He always wore a grenade and a first-aid pouch pinned to web gear on his chest. As his predecessor General Walker's symbol had been the high helmet, so Ridgway's symbol was the grenade. The general asked me many questions, including what I thought about our enemy, where I thought it was possible for the Chinese to cross the Imjin, and the state of the morale of my officers and men. After twenty minutes, he left me with a simple, "Good luck." Ridgway's biggest problem was how to overcome the contagion of defeatism that had taken such deep root in the UN Command and the ROK Army.

With that problem foremost in his mind, General Ridgway set out on an inspection trip of every front-line unit as soon as he was appointed. He wanted to familiarize himself with the terrain, make judgments about the capability of his commanders, survey morale, and develop a grasp for the actual situation he faced. Ridgway recorded his impressions in his memoirs. "MacArthur told me that my mission was to defend Korea with present forces assigned on a line as far north as possible. . . . After meeting all ranks of officers and men, it was my impression that they were deficient in vigor, bravery, and fighting spirit.''

The Chinese Third Offensive hit the ROK 1st Division on December 31, 1950, just ten days after we had once again deployed into defensive positions along the 38th parallel. Everything seemed perfectly normal right up until noon on the day of the attack. Indeed, that morning we distributed traditional New Year's rice cake to all division units as a special New Year's treat, hoping the familiar holiday food would help assuage the sorrows that had beset us and our country in that terrible year. A civilian delegation from Seoul visited the division that morning.

In the afternoon, Chinese Army units facing the ROK 1st Division began laying down a fierce barrage of fire from mortars and machine guns to prepare for an attack. The assault followed shortly, as a veritable flood of Chinese soldiers hurtled into my 12th Regiment on the division's right wing.

As clever as ever, the Chinese chose to concentrate their attack on a point east of Yulpo that served not only as the sector boundary between my ROK 1st Division and the adjacent ROK 6th Division but also as the boundary between U.S. I Corps and U.S. IX Corps. Chinese forces deeply penetrated the line at this crucial point, not with their wailing bugles or clanging gongs but with their human-wave tactics.

The Chinese Army first interspersed soldiers clad in civilian clothes among the refugees flowing into the front. When these infiltrators closed our lines, the main units followed with a murderous attack. Col. Kim Chum Kon's 12th Regiment could not hold for long, and the Chinese broke through.

I was quickly informed of the situation at my headquarters and immediately ordered the 15th Regiment in division reserve under Col. Cho Jae Mi to move his men into a line of reserve fighting positions we had prepared. There wasn't much else I could do. I monitored the situation on a minute-to-minute basis. Once darkness settled on the battlefield, our situation worsened with every passing hour. The situation soon deteriorated to the point where I could not even maintain communications with my regiments.

In desperation, I organized an assault battalion from the engineers, communications types, and others around division headquarters and rushed them into the breach. They proved insufficient to restore our line. On my left wing, Lt. Col. Mun Hyong Tae's 11th Regiment was doing fine, but my two rightmost regiments faced a hopeless situation.

I found the shock of defeat unbearable. I fell into a state of deep apathy that turned the world to darkness. I couldn't believe how I reacted. The enemy had broken through the 1st Division, the seasoned, accomplished ROK 1st Division. The 1st Division was collapsing for no purpose. It was a nightmare. So great was my anger, so deep my shame, that I had difficulty controlling my mental faculties. After hours of soul-searching, I finally had to issue the order for the entire division to withdraw and set up another defensive line around Koyang. I sent division headquarters itself to Nokbon, on Seoul's northwestern outskirts.

I remained at the primary school where division headquarters had originally been to monitor the withdrawal process but sent virtually all my staff officers and the U.S. KMAG advisers on to the new division headquarters. Two or three members of my staff insisted on remaining with me and worked desperately to maintain communications with my units. Virtually alone, I felt like I had lost half my soul.

I had been lucky. I'd made no serious mistakes as a commander up until then and actually believed that I could deal adequately with this difficult war. The Chinese Army mercilessly popped my bubble. I grew so apathetic that I lost even the physical energy to leave my increasingly exposed perch. Division communications officer Lieutenant Colonel Yun Hyuk Pyo stayed with me that night and later described my actions.

Yun said my face had a tragic, resigned cast to it, as if I had abandoned the will to live. The atmosphere was such, he said, that he hadn't dared utter a single word. Occasionally Yun was able to get through to one of our subordinate units. He said I would get on the radio and talk to the commander of the unit in a normal way, but when the conversation ended I would just let the receiver drop into its cradle, while I sat and talked to myself about the commands I had just issued. Yun said that although it was clear the enemy would soon reach the building we occupied, my frozen features revealed no suggestion that I intended to evacuate the premises. Yun said he had resigned himself to dying with me where we stood.

In the end I endured the embarrassment of having an American adviser, Captain May, charge into the room and doggedly and with apparent ease wrap me in his arms, carry me out to a jeep, and rush me to our new headquarters at Nokbon. Captain May tried to console me all the way. "In war," he kept saying, "sometimes you lose, right?" May insisted that everything would be all right if we lived to fight another day.

The Chinese offensive across the 38th parallel hurt the ROK 1st Division. My 12th Regiment had been hit hard. The U.S. 9th Artillery Battalion supporting us from the frozen, high mountain road west of Mount Kamak lost three 155mm howitzers. As the sun rose on the first day of 1951, the 1st Division faced the outset of another wretched year, licking our wounds at the base of Pukhan Mountain, virtually in Seoul.

The Chinese Third Offensive sent the ROK 1st Division reeling, but we weren't the only ones. The Chinese attack struck with irresistible force along the entire front, sending friendly units surging to the rear. Every single ROK Army division along the 38th parallel was penetrated and withdrew, some with heavy losses, some with light. Those divisions unlucky enough to be holding the line in the central front around Hong-chon were particularly hard hit.

The ROK 1st Division abandoned Seoul once again on January 2, 1951, and executed a UN Command operations order directing that friendly forces establish a defense line along the south bank of the Han River. We deployed along a line extending from Yongdungpo to Tongjak Subward, where the National Cemetery is located today.

I was overwhelmed with feelings of guilt and responsibility as I watched tens of thousands of Seoul's citizens fleeing south again, pouring across pontoon bridges or braving the frozen surface of the river itself. The Chinese outnumbered us badly, but had we been able to make a better fight of it, we might not have had to endure the ignominy of losing our country's capital city for a second time, and perhaps we could have spared Seoul's citizens the tragic experiences of the wartime refugee, especially in the deadly cold of winter.

The UN Command soon rescinded the order to defend on the south bank of the Han. The worsening situation on the central front obliged UN Command and ROK Army forces to withdraw farther south, to the 37th parallel, a line running east across the peninsula from Pyongtaek to Samchok on the Sea of Japan. The military leaders' basic concern was that Chinese forces that had broken through the Central front would flank a Han River defense line from the east. A second element in the decision was the conviction that extra space and time would allow Eighth Army divisions to recover from their intense exhaustion, regain their self-confidence, rebuild their morale, and boost their fighting spirit, all steps we had to take before we could mount a counterattack.

Meanwhile, I was racking my brain to determine why my division had fared so badly. The primary responsibility was my own. My health was bad, thanks to the effects of a malaria attack, and I found that when my physical energy was impaired, I flared quickly into anger and easily became nervous and peevish. If a commander allows himself to become testy, his subordinate commanders waste precious time and energy trying to read his mood and lose the edge they need to perform crisply in combat.

Another factor was the attitude of my officers and men toward the Chinese. The division seemed to regard the communist Chinese Army with unreasoning terror. I must acknowledge that a pernicious aspect of this fear was widespread defeatism. My men seemed to be psychologically defeated even before the battle began. I received reports that in the last days of 1950 some of my troops had forced their way into civilian houses, others had gotten drunk, and still others had been negligent on guard duty. Other reports informed me that 1st Division troops had refused to fire at Chinese soldiers approaching our lines while using Korean refugees as cover.

My anger soared to new heights when I discovered that when I committed the reserve 15th Regiment during our fight at the 38th parallel some of its troops had not only failed to deploy into the reserve defense line we had prepared, but had simply withdrawn. Plainly put, these men had run away rather than face the enemy. Even assuming that the regiment had been in a position where it had no choice but withdraw, the rule is that units must maintain contact with the enemy, must deliver the strongest possible blows to the enemy's formations, must impede the enemy's advance, and must be ready at any moment to revert to the counterattack. That is the nature of withdrawal, which militarily is exceptionally difficult to execute and which differs as night does day from "running away" or "fleeing."

The ROK 1st Division drew a new assignment. We were to deploy into a new defense line at Ansong. No sooner had I established division headquarters at Imjang than I firmly began working on restoring discipline in the 1st. I had to renew the officers' and men's determination, resolve, and self-respect if they were to reacquire the positive mental attitude necessary to deal with a tough enemy.

I assigned Col. Yu Hung Su, my new assistant division commander, the task of determining which commanders had abdicated their responsibilities in the face of the enemy and of renewing discipline in every unit in the division. Our efforts resulted in remanding a ROK 1st Division battalion commander and company commander to court-martial. Both were sentenced to death and executed. Flight in the face of the enemy can never be countenanced because the fate of the nation depends on the integrity with which soldiers perform in combat. Moreover, no individual soldier is above sacrifice of self. Millions died or underwent extreme privation during the Korean War, and no single soldier had the right to save himself at the expense of his mission.

Army Chief of Staff General Chung Il Kwon reacted to this problem in the ROK Army at the time by delegating to all commanders the "right of summary trial." This discretionary, wartime authority to punish without resort to the usual court-martial process devolved not only on me as a divisional commander but also on commanders in the chain of authority down to the level of squad leader. I personally did not exercise this discretion a single time during the war, but I was very lucky to command that long without resorting to it. In the severe environment of war, however, some subordinates inevitably deport themselves in ways a commander cannot condone.

My command style was to exercise patience on top of patience. In cases where it was unavoidable, however, I remanded soldiers to court-martial, and I swiftly executed the sentence handed down by the court-martial board. One commander of a 1st Division unit who was court-martialed and given a heavy sentence petitioned for a retrial in 1976, twenty-five years later. A new court-martial convened and cleansed him of dishonor, however tardily. I was pleased to sign the petition requesting that a new court-martial board convene to rehear his case. I remember the courts-martial of those bitter days now only because this officer sought me out so long after the war ended to explain the full, exculpatory particulars of his case.

Seesaw Battles on the Central Front

The Korean people and the Korean Army now endured the most anguished and depressing period of the entire war, extending from the first days of 1951 until well into the spring of that benighted year.

We were unsure, for example, whether the UN Command would withdraw from the Korean peninsula or launch a new counterattack as the situation at the front deteriorated. We lost Seoul again, and I couldn't throw off nagging concerns as the 1st Division withdrew to the 37th parallel. If the UN Command lost the will to fight, my country would collapse as surely as the tides.

Suddenly, the title *Chonggamnok* flitted through my mind. I had learned someplace that the *Chonggamnok* was a book of prophecy by a Yi dynasty prophet about Korea's future. I called in my aide. "Find me somebody who is familiar with the *Chonggamnok*," I ordered Captain Kim. "Let's see if the prophet tells us how far south the Manchurian barbarians advance."

Captain Kim was a bright lad. He was back with a report posthaste. "I checked it out, sir," he said. "The prophet said that the Manchurian barbarians don't get farther south than Ansong." I was quite sure that Captain Kim saw what I was about and brought me an answer cut from whole cloth; but I had reached the point where I would clutch at any straw, and I drew great comfort from the prophesy.

Meanwhile, neither my division nor the rest of U.S. I Corps had seen hide nor hair of the Chinese for a long time. The Chinese Army gave every indication that it had abandoned the chase after advancing southward to a line above Osan, at today's Yongin. Whatever the reason for the respite, I made good use of it. I sent out reconnaissance patrols to keep informed of any enemy activity, but I devoted all my efforts to training and rehabilitating my division. The only way we could turn the tide of war in our favor was to beat the communist Chinese Army on two measures: combat power and morale.

Discipline is the military's heart and soul. An army that suffers from lax discipline is nothing more than a mirage. I tried to be sure my approach to discipline reflected an old Korean saying, "Always reward merit, and always punish offense." Meanwhile, I emphasized unit readiness even as replacements and new equipment poured into the ROK 1st Division. I noticed that the men's shadowy faces began to brighten.

Almost two hundred trucks reached us at division headquarters, greatly expanding our mobility. The trucks were all Japanese-made Nissans, Toyotas, and Isuzus. In fact, we began to see many Japanese-made items in the resupply flow. By this time what the Japanese called the "special Korean demand" had created trade opportunities in neighboring Japan, serving as the engine for that country's recovery from the economic ruin of World War II.

Something else had changed, too. High-ranking government officials had rarely visited the division before, but now they came in a steady flow to offer encouragement to officers and men alike and to urge us to greater exertions. President Syngman Rhee himself visited, as did Prime Minister Chang Myon and Defense Minister Shin Sung Mo, and their visits inspired the men, bolstering our patriotic instincts.

Defense Minister Shin was known as "Minister Tear Drop" from his reputed habit of crying around President Rhee. And sure enough, the minister's eyes brimmed with tears during the president's exhortative speech to the men and officers of the ROK 1st Division. But the effect was startling. The fact was that the officers and men of the division were touched by his tears and either cried along with him or at least suffered serious cases of blurry vision. His speech went a long, long way toward helping the ROK 1st Division team regain its fighting spirit, pull ourselves together, and get on with the war.

I give a measure of credit for this reversal to the ranking government officials who visited us and also to growing awareness of imminent Chinese attack at the time. But I can't give them all the credit, because newly appointed Gen. Matthew B. Ridgway, for his part, had expressed strong dissatisfaction about the performance of the Korean Army directly to President Rhee.

When Ridgway was informed by urgent message of the Chinese Third Offensive in early January 1951, he rushed immediately to the front at Uijongbu. He witnessed for himself the shocking, distressful rout of troops from the ROK Army 6th Division and the U.S. 25th Division. General Ridgway immediately went to President Rhee and put it bluntly. "We will abandon our support of the Korean Army if you do not display the leadership necessary to inspire your army." Ridgway then accompanied President Rhee on a tour of all the ROK Army divisions deployed on the central front, obliging President Rhee to encourage his commanders in person. But like Walker before him, Ridgway tended to blame the ROK Army for the bad and credit the U.S. Army with the good.

Having established and hardened a defense line along the 37th parallel, the UN Command turned its attention in two directions. The command began to prepare for the possibility of further withdrawal, inspecting and maintaining defense lines from the previous summer that had been erased from our memories—the Charyong Mountain Range, the Naktong River, and the Davidson line. But the UN Command also started to plan for a counterattack.

Had the Chinese Army been able to sustain its drive at this juncture, chances are good that the UN Command would have continued to withdraw. I say that not because I think the UN Command could not have emerged victorious from further fighting at the existing line, but because it was clear to me that the command simply did not possess the will to accept serious personnel losses to defend the front. Luckily, however, the Chinese Army was dilatory in unleashing its attack. The Chinese gave the UN Command and the ROK Army enough time to revive our fighting spirits and to restore an offensive mind-set, to rekindle our desire to mount a counterstroke.

The Chinese Army had appeared to us to be highly successful in combat, but in fact the reliance of Chinese commanders on human-wave tactics had inflicted horrendous personnel losses on their units. And as we withdrew farther south, their supply lines attenuated, so that lack of supplies now imposed harsh difficulties on Chinese units.

My 15th Regiment commander, Col. Cho Jae Mi, was transferred out of the division at this point, to be replaced by Col. Kim An Il, who became a Christian minister after the war. Colonel Kim immediately came to me with an extraordinary idea.

Kim had served previously as my division G-2 and done a magnificent job there. He now suggested that if we were to beat the Chinese Army what we needed were some Chinese. Kim undertook some inquiries and soon located and drafted into the division about fifty young Chinese men who were permanent residents of Korea. Kim organized these men into a reconnaissance platoon to gather intelligence about the Chinese Army and to capture prisoners. The unit outperformed our expectations by a wide margin, gathering volumes of useful intelligence.

As we interrogated our newly captured Chinese prisoners, we discovered that they were utterly exhausted. To a man they complained of abject fatigue and starvation, and many suffered from frostbite or disease as well. Water soaked through their cotton uniforms, their hands and feet suffered from frostbite, and typhoid was widespread. It required no genius to discover numerous vulnerabilities in the Chinese fighting units now that we saw the actual state to which individual Chinese soldiers had sunk. We had regarded the Chinese as mysterious supermen. Now we knew better. Our prisoners told us that their typical pattern was to fight for three days, during which time they received rations, and then to rest for three days, during which time they received nothing to eat. They told us that of all their afflictions, attacks mounted by UN Command air forces proved most galling.

The Chinese prisoners we took at Kumyangjang—which the Americans called Kingtown because they found the Korean impossible to pronounce—belonged to the Thirty-eighth Army's 113th Division. The 113th commander, Wang Chia-shan, had served as a major general in Japan's Manchurian Army, and his name sounded very familiar to me. The prisoner's regimental commander was Hu Ren-hua, who was a former captain in Japan's Manchurian Army and had been one of my instructors at the Manchurian Military Academy at Mukden. I concluded from the identities of these commanders that Manchurian Army members had surrendered to the Soviet or Chinese Nationalist armies at the end of World War II, switched their politics, and joined the communist Chinese Army en masse after the latter won mastery of continental China in 1949.

The UN Command launched its first counterattack at dawn on January 15, 1951. A tank battalion and three artillery battalions were added to Col. John Michaelis's 27th Regiment, U.S. 25th Division, to form a regimental combat team that conducted a very strong reconnaissance in force toward Suwon, supported by engineers and close air-support sorties from the air force. Ridgway began to assign code names to operations large and small at this time, and this first operation was dubbed "Wolfhound," after the 27th Regiment's nickname.

The 27th Regimental Combat Team advanced from Osan to Suwon. The Chinese Army responded with nothing more than a weak counterattack, attempting to sever the roadway between Osan and Suwon and leaving us with the impression that it wanted to avoid contact as it took cover in mountains near Yoju.

Friendly commanders held their collective breaths in suspense as the 27th Regimental Combat Team began its lonely mission into enemy territory. We were rewarded with success. This was the first time we had seen the Chinese Army run away. Maj. Gen. William B. Kean, commander of the U.S. 25th Division, was especially effusive as he explained the outcome of the Wolfhounds' expedition to me. Unable to contain his excitement, Kean said, "I think this operation will become a model for future combat." The next day Col. Kim An Il's 15th Regiment was attached to the U.S. 25th Division to provide cover to the U.S. division's right wing and thus participated in Operation Wolfhound, working side-by-side with a most intrepid Turkish battalion.

Using Operation Wolfhound as a model, U.S. IX Corps to the east of U.S. I Corps assembled Task Force Johnson around Colonel Johnson's 8th Cavalry Regiment of the U.S. 1st Cav Division. Task Force Johnson jumped off on January 22, 1951, and soon took Yongin and Ichon. Once again, the Chinese Army found itself unable to mount an effective counterattack.

Reviewing the success of these two operations, Ridgway at last issued an order for a general counterattack. The objective Ridgway assigned to "Operation Thunderbolt" was to seize and occupy a line just south of the Han River. U.S. I Corps, composed of the U.S. 3d Division, the U.S.

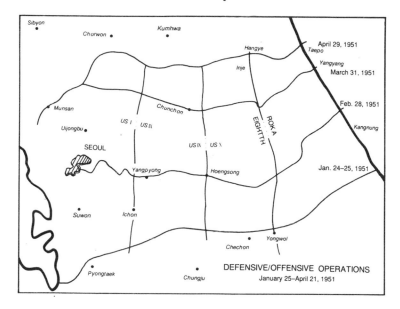

Sibyon

Chorwon

Kumhwa

Hangye

Taepo April 29, 1951

Inje

Yangyang
March 31, 1951

Munsan

Chunchon

Feb. 28, 1951

US I   US IX

Uijongbu

ROK A
EIGHTH

Kangnung

SEOUL

US IX   US X

Yangpyong

Hoengsong

Jan. 24–25, 1951

Suwon

Ichon

Chechon

Yongwol

DEFENSIVE/OFFENSIVE OPERATIONS
January 25–April 21, 1951

Pyongtaek

Chungju

25th Division, and my 1st Division, was directed to advance toward
Kimpo, Yongdungpo, and Inchon. The U.S. IX Corps, composed of the
U.S. 1st Cavalry Division, the U.S. 24th Division, and the ROK Army
6th Division, was directed to assault toward Ichon and Yoju.

Ridgway's operational style differed markedly from Walker's. Walker
relied upon shock and penetration, deploying armored units in the vanguard. Ridgway emphasized a deliberate, step-by-step advance with
units in extended lateral deployment. He ceaselessly pounded home the
need to remain closely linked with adjacent units. Ridgway had developed his tactics with the Chinese Army's strong points—bypass and encirclement—well in mind. Thus, our motto after Operation Thunderbolt
was "hand-in-hand," or "shoulder-to-shoulder," not unlike the slogan
of 1988's Seoul Olympics.

My 15th Regiment remained attached to the U.S. 25th Division during
Operation Thunderbolt, participating directly in the attack, while the
ROK 1st Division's other two regiments were held in reserve and as-
signed to guard the key supply route running from Suwon through to
Taejon.

Thunderbolt seemed painfully slow, but the front advanced inexorably northward. We retook Suwon on January 26, Anyang on February
7, and the vanguard of the corps reached the south bank of the Han
River on February 10. Eighth Army's cautious advance was based on the

supposition that the Chinese would shortly mount yet another massive offensive.

Our assault units formed what was essentially a scrum line and moved forward with utmost caution in an effort to locate the main body of the communist Chinese Army. Our offensive encountered strong enemy resistance east of Suwon, near Anyang, in the Mount Kwanak area, and around Panwol. We smashed the Chinese in firefights at each of these locations, but only after severe fighting. Chinese main-force units simply disappeared from the western front after these battles.

Composed of the U.S. 2d and 7th divisions, the U.S. X Corps on our east launched a companion offensive on February 5, kicking off "Operation Roundup" from Wonju. Using the Nanham River as its axis, U.S. X Corps advanced toward Chunchon.

Major General Almond had not been under General Walker's command during our advance into North Korea. He came under Ridgway's command from here on out, however, and Eighth Army finally enjoyed a unified command structure.

As he advanced toward Hongchon, Almond deployed two attached ROK divisions to the corps's vanguard, the 8th Division under Brig. Gen. Choi Young Hi on the left and the 5th Division under Min Ki Sik on the right. Almond positioned his two U.S. divisions in supporting roles behind the two Korean divisions. The U.S. 2d Division under Maj. Gen. Clark Ruffner trailed the ROK 8th Division, and the U.S. 7th Division under Maj. Gen. Claude Ferenbaugh trailed the ROK 5th.

In this arrangement, Col. Paul Freeman's 23d Regiment, which had fought with me at Tabu-dong, advanced as the eastwardmost unit of X Corps, tying down the extreme right wing of X Corps where it abutted the Chung Ang Sun (Central Railroad Line).

Chinese Army commanders know a prize when they see one, and they saw one in X Corps. Chinese strategists concluded that they stood little chance of opposing the U.S. I Corps attack in the relatively flat terrain on the western front. They chose to respond decisively to the X Corps offensive in the central front, where the mountainous terrain favored the Chinese style of fighting.

U.S. Army intelligence was getting better. The UN Command knew that the Chinese were going to hit in the east, and it went as far as to estimate the date of the Chinese counterattack, setting it for February 15, 1951. They were off by four days. The Chinese Army launched a massive counteroffensive on February 11, achieving nearly total tactical surprise.

Four Chinese divisions surrounded the ROK 8th Division northwest of Hoengsong and destroyed it. The reorganized and refitted NKPA II and V corps and the Chinese Army troops supporting them also dealt severe blows to the ROK 3d and 5th divisions, which had been advancing in support of Operation Roundup.

According to the command report of the U.S. X Corps for 1951, the ROK 8th Division lost 323 officers and 7,142 enlisted men, while the ROK 3d and 5th divisions lost 3,000 men each. These were horrifying casualties.

After dealing massive blows to the three ROK divisions and the U.S. 2d Division at Hoengsong, the Chinese Army directed the main thrust of its attack against the U.S. 23d Regiment on February 13, isolating and surrounding the unit at Chipyongri. Enemy units advanced ineluctably, intent on annihilating the hapless U.S. unit.

Colonel Freeman and Lt. Col. Ralph Monclar, who commanded the French Battalion attached to the 23d Regiment, hunkered down with many seriously wounded men inside a circular defensive position and commanded a desperate, life-or-death fight that continued for five days and nights until the arrival of Colonel Crombez's U.S. 5th Cavalry Regiment, which had been sent to relieve them. In the end, the 23d Regiment repulsed the entire Chinese force. These two superbly brave and competent commanders administered the first defeat to the communist Chinese Army during the Chinese Fourth Offensive.

Freeman went on to wear the four stars of a full general. Monclar was a veteran soldier who had fought in both world wars, risen to the rank of lieutenant general and been reduced in rank to lieutenant colonel to allow him to command the French Battalion, the sole tactical unit France sent to the Korean War. I happened to be the Republic of Korea's ambassador to France in 1963 when General Monclar passed away. His funeral was held at Les Invalides, a former hospital that now serves as a military museum. French President Charles de Gaulle himself attended the impressive, solemn ceremony.

On the negative side, the severe losses suffered by Almond's ROK Army divisions in the Chinese Fourth Offensive raised a question about his ability to command. Why did he position Korean units at the vanguard of the attack when this was not done elsewhere?

As I have described, on the western front U.S. regimental combat teams, reinforced by tanks, artillery, and engineer units, took the point in the assault, and ROK Army divisions were not deployed to face the enemy alone. Almond, however, chose to place Korean divisions at the vanguard despite their relatively light complement of weapons and equipment. I have been told, in fact, that Almond directly refused to switch the ROK units to a supporting role.

One cannot help but wonder whether Almond implemented his otherwise inexplicable strategy solely to allow the Korean units to absorb the initial force of the expected Chinese attack. I cannot rule out this possibility.

One of the division commanders, Brig. Gen. Choi Young Hi, had commanded one of my regiments for most of the war up to that time. Choi lost many men in the Chinese Fourth Offensive, and he told me that he believed Almond's motives were as I have outlined. Choi anticipated that he would be held unfairly responsible for the appalling combat losses his division suffered, so he went to see Minister of National Defense Shin Sung Mo to proffer an apology. Minister Shin allowed Choi to come to his headquarters but refused to grant him an audience once he arrived, ordering Choi back to his command.

Choi refused to let the matter drop. He went to Almond and demanded to be punished. Almond seemed surprised. "What are you talking about?" he said. "I can't punish a valuable officer with your service record!" Indeed, Almond went on to decorate him with the Silver Star. Almond invited Minister Shin to the award ceremony to forestall any future consequences to Choi from the Korean side, acting, I am told, from an admirable sense of solicitude.

Given the details of the situation, General Choi believed that General Almond needed to determine the location of the enemy's main attack and chose to do so by deploying the ROK 5th and 8th divisions at the front of his corps to act, essentially, as a huge reconnaissance patrol. Almond was then able to repulse the Chinese attack as a result of the sacrifices made by the two Korean divisions.

Even if we assume that Almond had such a plan in mind when he deployed the two ROK divisions forward, no one can dispute the fact that it was perfectly allowable for Korean units to operate in the vanguard and be called upon to sacrifice themselves in the defense of their own country. That said, however, many in the ROK Army cannot repress the feeling that had Almond planned more wisely, he could have reaped the same victory while minimizing the terrible Korean casualties.

The U.S. Army called the area northwest of Hoengsong "Massacre Valley" because so many ROK and U.S. officers and men were killed in action there. I have been told that at the time the U.S. Army had no choice but to censor reports of the battle to avoid severe damage both to the morale of the troops in Korea and to public opinion in the nations participating in the war.

As an aside, I should point out that statistics compiled by the Americans on Korean losses invariably were inflated because the Americans failed to allow for the fact that many Korean officers and men "missing" in action were merely scattered in battle and would find their way back to their units. That is not to say that we were proud of this phenomenon, for it is a characteristic of units that have yet to reach full maturity.

Let us see how the Chinese themselves evaluated the Third Offensive (December 31, 1950 to January 10, 1951) and Fourth Offensive (February 11, 1951, to February 18, 1951) that caused us so much anguish.

Writing in his memoirs about these two offensives, Peng Teh-huai's flourishes fail to obscure the fact that they were not successful. In the two "campaigns, our units were acutely exhausted," Peng noted, "And our supply lines had been severely attenuated, hurting resupply efforts badly. The drop in levels of non-combatants and combat soldiers alike had left our units at half strength." Regarding the Fourth Offensive, he wrote, "we assembled five armies and launched an operation to counter the enemy's counterattack. . . . A swift victory will not be possible in this war."

Supreme Commander Peng Teh-huai traveled to Beijing at the end of February 1951 and stayed for a week. He later described a meeting he had with Mao Tse-tung in the words, "I received clear directions for pursuing the war." Analysts believe that in fact Mao reprimanded him sharply.

5

BACK TO THE 38TH PARALLEL

Spring Breezes Blow on the Han River

Having repulsed the great communist Chinese Army offensive, Eighth Army immediately launched a counterattack. We could not allow the enemy time to rest and reorganize.

The western front had survived relatively unscathed, while on the central front the Chinese Army had pushed our lines southward. Eighth Army Headquarters placed considerable importance on restoring these lines; this emphasis took concrete form as "Operation Killer," launched on February 21, 1950.

U.S. I Corps operated on the far western sector of the front; the U.S. 25th Division occupied the rightmost, or eastern, position in the corps. The 25th captured Namhan Fortress, just southeast of Seoul, while U.S. IX and X corps in the central front advanced to a line running from Paldang to Hoengsong.

The U.S. 1st Marine Division participated in Operation Killer, returning to combat for the first time since its withdrawal by sea from North Korea. The 1st Marine Division was to lead Eighth Army's attack on Wonju. The operation also marked the first time since the dispersement of U.S. units during the Christmas Offensive that all major U.S. units were deployed simultaneously at the forward edge of the battle area.

Operation Killer succeeded easily. My division reached the Han River, where we deployed into defensive positions along the south bank of the river, our line stretching all the way from the Kimpo Peninsula on the Yellow Sea to Seoul's Tongjak Subward. We were to occupy this line for three long weeks, and while we marked time, the Eighth Army units to the east pushed the front forward until they drew even with our right flank.

Sadly, Maj. Gen. Bryant Moore, commanding general of U.S. IX Corps, later died of a heart attack he suffered during Operation Killer when his helicopter crashed into the Han River near Yoju. He was replaced by Maj. Gen. William Hoge, the main figure in the World War II film *The Bridge at Remagen,* a movie that had played in Korea before the war. Hoge was the commander who actually seized the famous bridge.

At least four ranking commanders were killed in accidents involving wheeled vehicles or aircraft during the war. In addition to General Moore, Eighth Army Commander Lt. Gen. Walton H. Walker, ROK I Corps Commander Maj. Gen. Kim Paik Il, and Brig. Gen. Lee Yong Mun also died. I was involved in a vehicle accident myself at this juncture of the war and operated at half throttle for about a month.

Minister of Defense Shin Sung Mo and I were riding over to U.S. I Corps Headquarters in Suwon when my driver swerved to avoid an oncoming U.S. Army truck. Our jeep tipped over. Neither Minister Shin nor Col. Robert T. Hazlett, the chief KMAG adviser to the ROK 1st Division, was hurt, but I twisted my back and cut my face badly and was taken to the MASH unit at Suwon.

General Ridgway heard about the accident and very kindly rushed over to visit me in hospital. The medical officers said they wanted to continue their examination but believed they would have to evacuate me. Ridgway adamantly opposed evacuation. "This is a time when we've got to have division commanders like General Paik." I saw no way I could absent myself from the division in the midst of a tactical operation, so I simply left the hospital after a day. I was troubled by constant pain, however. Someone noted this and brought me some bear gall. I don't know if the bear gall did it, but I was completely recovered within a month.

Vehicle accidents probably should have killed more of us. My jeep turned completely over after we skidded in mud on the partially thawed bank of a river near Yongsan-dong as we advanced into North Korea. My life was saved on that occasion only because the post on which the machine gun was mounted kept the jeep off my body.

During my recuperation, the ROK 1st was deployed along the Han River, exchanging fire with the enemy on the opposite bank and awaiting the order to cross and retake Seoul. It wasn't a good time to be hurt, but at least the reduced mobility of the division coincided with my own impaired movements.

I think I can say without fear of contradiction that Ridgway's greatest contribution to the war was helping his army overcome its loser psychology. Ridgway was a brave commander, but he also was a prudent man. He would appraise a unit's morale simply by jumping in a jeep and threading his way through the unit, watching to see whether the men saluted him. He would ask ordinary soldiers he encountered during these forays very detailed questions, hoping to uncover problems that had not come to his attention. Ridgway would ask the men whether they were receiving all the gloves and socks they needed, or whether they were getting hot meals, or even whether they had paper on which to write letters home.

Ridgway sent Eighth Army Headquarters all the way back to Taegu, but he himself followed closely on the heels of the frontline units, living in a tent. His forward command post was pitched on the river's edge at Yoju at this time. Ridgway held it as an inviolate principle of leadership that when the fighting was going badly, a commander had to remain very near the front. I believe that Ridgway's reputation as the best of Eighth Army's Korean War commanders originated from this habit.

Once the rest of Eighth Army had slugged its way north to a line roughly paralleling our positions along the Han River, the UN Command naturally set its sights on pushing back to the 38th parallel. "Operation Ripper" was designed to do just that, and we jumped off on March 7, 1951. The ice on the Han River had melted, and spring breezes were in the air.

The success or failure of Ripper—in which no fewer than 150,000 friendly troops participated—depended on the success or failure of a single operation by a single division. Maj. Gen. Joseph Bradley's 25th Division had to execute a river-crossing operation at Kumgok into the very face of the enemy.

Friendly artillery laid down terrible curtains of fire on the far bank of the Han, ripping it into stubble. The 25th crossed the river with no trouble and led the way in an assault on Pochon. Immediately to our east, or right, the U.S. 3d Division crossed the Han and made straight for Uijongbu.

Ridgway put the entire front in forward motion for Operation Ripper—except my ROK 1st on the far west of the line. We sat across the river from our capital city in sheer frustration. Our role in Ripper was to conduct a simple feint, to pretend that we were going to cross the Han and liberate Seoul. Ridgway's intent was to avoid costly street fighting in Seoul. He calculated that if Eighth Army advanced as well as he hoped on the east, Seoul would be flanked, and the enemy would be forced to flee Seoul without a fight. First Division's deceptive operations pinned major enemy units in Seoul and prevented the enemy high command from deploying these units elsewhere.

The ROK 1st was not alone in trying to mislead the enemy. The UN Command naval forces in the Yellow Sea were set on a similar mission. I was told at this time that naval vessels approached North Korea's Chinnampo and began clearing mines from the maritime approaches to the city, leading the enemy to believe that friendly forces would conduct an amphibious landing there.

The deputy commander of U.S. I Corps, Brig. Gen. Thomas Harrold, who was soon to win command of the U.S. 1st Cavalry Division, came to see me at this juncture and accompanied me to the northernmost tip of the Kimpo Peninsula to get a better view of the enemy situation. As our file of jeeps topped the crest of a hill, massed enemy fire was apparent almost as far as the eye could see along the opposite bank. We had no further doubt over the enemy's presence. The Chinese were deployed all along the Han, and in depth.

Harrold asked me whether I had experience at combined infantry-armor operations and at airborne link-up operations. I explained that the ROK 1st was the only ROK Army unit with such experience. He didn't say more, but his question suggested that such operations were in the offing.

Eighth Army, in fact, never did order me to conduct deception operations. What the Americans had done, starting on March 10, was to start supplying the ROK 1st with river-crossing equipment, although at a glacial pace. Naturally we began to prepare to cross the Han with our new equipment. I learned only much later myself that Eighth Army intended these preparations to deceive the enemy.

The ROK 1st received a battalion of amphibious vehicles and rubber boats and other river-crossing equipment, and we trained smartly for both river-crossing and street warfare. At the same time we successfully infiltrated a small reconnaissance unit into Seoul and continued to track the enemy situation closely.

On the night of March 14, our reconnaissance unit reported that enemy forces were withdrawing from Seoul. Only hours earlier, U.S. units on the central front had cut the main railroad line connecting Seoul to Chunchon and points north and had recaptured Hongchon. We had flanked the enemy in Seoul. I immediately reported to my corps commander, General Milburn, that the enemy was withdrawing from Seoul and recommended that we launch an attack to seize the city. Milburn didn't hesitate for a second. "Go ahead!" His permission was short and to the point, suggesting that he was only waiting for me to say when the time was right.

The ROK 1st Division was champing at the bit. For three full weeks we had been obliged to stand by, watching as the enemy moved about freely in our capital city. At last, on the morning of March 15, 1951, we crossed the frigid waters of the Han River, moving from Youido Island to Mapo on the north bank of the river and then into Seoul proper. Once my lead unit, the 15th Regiment, successfully established a beachhead on the north bank, the entire division followed without serious incident.

Ridgway, Milburn, and ROK Defense Minister Shin Sung Mo came down to the river bank to watch the crossing. Nothing if not consistent, Minister Shin gave me a big hug and tears flowed down his cheeks as we shared the deep emotion of liberating the nation's capital.

Enemy resistance in the city was trifling, and my troops fought only a few scattered battles in Seoul's streets before the city was ours. We found the huge numbers of land mines to be a much greater obstacle than firefights with the enemy.

The city lay in ruins. Artillery fire and air attacks had inflicted unimaginable damage. Not a single building remained unscathed in a city where only ten months before one-and-a-half million people had worked and played in peace. Power lines and street-car cables were down everywhere, forming great snarls of wire and creating the impression that the city of Seoul was entangled in spider webs up and down its entire length and breadth. The city's greatest landmark, the ancient, ornate Great South Gate, had been damaged badly and was almost destroyed.

Only about two hundred thousand people remained in the ancient city, and virtually all of these were the young, the old, the handicapped, or the sick. These unfortunate people had lived with war too long, and no emotion, no expression crossed their blank, haunted faces. When we had liberated Republic of Korea territory on previous occasions, we always had been met by crowds of grateful citizens frantically waving Korean national flags and welcoming us with warm, happy faces. Not this time. Not only were the residents of Seoul psychologically crushed, but they also teetered on the brink of physical death. Their limbs were swollen, and their skins were stained a deep yellow from starvation, sickness, and the terrible winter cold they had faced with little or no heat. They looked like starving beggars. The 1st Division had not liberated a city. We had opened a grave.

A full week later when we held a ceremony to commemorate the retaking of Seoul, we deliberately kept it simple, holding it indoors, in the mayor's office with only a few government officials in attendance. It was an unpretentious ceremony in which we simply handed Seoul over to its mayor, Lee Ki Poong.

Ridgway's Operation Ripper was an unqualified success. As he had calculated, the push north in the central front had gone smoothly, and we had recovered Seoul very easily. Ridgway himself called it "the best operation of my life." Ripper succeeded so well because Ridgway had thought like a soldier, putting the recapture of Korea's capital city at the bottom of his priority list. The political impact of losing Seoul or of taking Seoul meant nothing to Ridgway.

On the other hand, Ridgway's replacement—Gen. James A. Van Fleet—chose to defend Seoul to the death during the communist Chinese Army's spring offensive in April 1951, treating the city as if it were

Paris or Athens. Whatever the methods, we had liberated Seoul, and we would not lose it again.

War Rations, Courtesy of General MacArthur

I set up division headquarters in a primary school in Seoul's West Gate area, and to my surprise, Gen. Douglas MacArthur himself dropped by to pass the time of day. His jeep appeared at our headquarters with the supreme commander in the front seat and Ridgway and a Major General Markett, chief of MacArthur's Economic and Scientific Section, riding in the back seat. MacArthur remained seated in the jeep as I briefed him on our situation. When I was finished, he instantly asked, "How're the rations lately?"

"We're having no trouble getting rice," I responded. "But we're not getting enough vegetables, and we desperately need some sugar or something sweet."

MacArthur turned to Markett and said, "Take care of that right away." Then they drove off.

The division's chief KMAG adviser had witnessed this exchange and voiced a complaint. "There is no need to mention detailed ration problems to the supreme commander," he said. "And isn't that the responsibility of the Korean government anyway?"

"Are you telling me," I shot back, "that I should have lied to the supreme commander? It was my impression that the United States entered this war to lend a hand to the Republic of Korea and its army." The colonel let it drop.

About a week later a number of ration trucks pulled up at division headquarters. Soon we had boxes of combat rations stacked as high as the Himalayas, and they included seaweed, squid, and other delicacies designed to appeal to the Korean palate.

In May of 1953 I visited the United States as chief of staff of the Korean army and dropped by New York's Waldorf-Astoria Hotel to pay a courtesy call on General MacArthur. I was able to express my personal, if belated, thanks for the rations during that visit.

As an aside, our messing and ration situation during the war worked out something like this. Steamed rice is the basic dish served at every Korean meal. In the stringent conditions prevailing during the war, of course, we seldom had enough rice, so we usually had to mix it with other grains, although this is not as palatable to the Korean soldier. Barley was usually available, so we mixed our rice with barley much of the time. The trouble with barley, however, is that it requires more time to steam than rice; during periods of intense activity in the field, we seldom had time to prepare the barley.

ROK Army units received soybean paste and red pepper paste as items of central supply, because these condiments are crucial to our rice-centered meals. We had to make and transport our own kimchi, however, which meant that we seldom had much since it was cured in salt, difficult to prepare, and bulky to transport. The men missed kimchi very much.

Our soldiers ate very little meat, although the division did purchase the odd pig or cow from farmers near our encampments. Koreans in those years ate a lot of fish, and central supply provided us with appreciable quantities of salted fish. Even so, we ate a lot of soup made solely from boiled vegetables or bean sprouts without a fish or meat base. At a time when the Korean people themselves seldom were blessed with three meals a day, we felt very lucky to have this much.

The U.S. Army consumed three grades of rations: A, B, and C. The A rations were top-of-the-line Western food, including steak; B rations were simpler foods, like sausage, that could be heated and eaten by an individual or prepared for a unit. The famous C rations were field rations, canned and easily carried in the field.

Meanwhile, across the battlefield from us, the Chinese soldiers subsisted on *shaoping*, a hard, unleavened bread. Each mainland soldier carried his own measure of a concoction of sorghum, millet, lima beans, and wheat flour from which he prepared *shaoping*, eating while on the move. The Chinese soldier had little opportunity to enjoy hot food because our air superiority and continual air reconnaissance obliged Chinese units to avoid building fires. The steady, unvaried diet of cold food caused large numbers of Chinese soldiers to suffer diseases of the digestive tract.

Departing the 1st Division

No sooner had we taken Seoul again than we launched into "Operation Tomahawk," an airborne operation targeted at Munsan. Ridgway had commanded both an airborne division and an airborne corps earlier in his career. He drew on his airborne experience to develop Operation Tomahawk, by which Ridgway intended not only to retrieve our lost Imjin River positions at a single stroke but also to cut off a pocket of the enemy we could then destroy systematically.

Brig. Gen. Frank Bowen's U.S. 187th Airborne Regimental Combat Team lifted off from the airfield at Taegu on March 23, 1951, his paratroopers poised to drop over Munsan. Earlier in the day, my division jumped off from Independence Arch on Seoul's western outskirts and charged up the road for Munsan, timing our attack so that it coincided with Bowen's parachute drop. A battalion of U.S. tanks had been attached to the division, and once again they roared along at our vanguard. Kim Chum Kon's 12th Regiment led because the 12th had rich experience in link-up operations and at coordinating with armor.

The 3,447 troopers of the 187th Airborne Regimental Combat Team jumped into the skies over Munsan from 135 transport aircraft at 9:00 A.M. on March 23. In the following four days, the U.S. military parachuted a total of 220 tons of supplies and equipment to this force, including 105mm howitzers.

The ROK 1st Division advanced rapidly, and I had a field conference with Bowen as soon as we closed on Munsan. He told me his intent was to lead his paratroopers in an advance from Munsan to Uijongbu to link up with the U.S. 3d Division and close the net on the enemy trapped between the two forces.

It was not to be. One of Tomahawk's objectives was to cut off and destroy some six thousand men of the newly organized NKPA I Corps who were located within the net. The North Koreans withdrew rapidly, however, and made good their escape. We had to be content with mopping up a single NKPA regiment. Nonetheless, Tomahawk was a success. In a single, lightning operation we had retrieved the area along the 38th parallel we had lost three months earlier when we withdrew January 4. For the fourth time in the war I stood on the banks of the Imjin River.

The ROK 1st Division deployed once again along the Imjin River, a line that had served us well in our resistance when the North Korean blitzkrieg erupted June 25, 1950. As I oversaw the move of my division command post to Kwansan, I resolved that my division would never again be shouldered out of this line. So many of our buddies had toiled in sweat here, died in blood here, that the rest of us had our backs up. We would not withdraw from the Imjin again.

The UN Command was firmly established along the 38th parallel line by March 27, 1951, when Ridgway summoned key commanders to a conference at Yoju, site of Eighth Army's forward command post. Every U.S. division and corps commander attended the meeting. Only five ROK Army officers did: Chief of Staff Chung Il Kwon, I Corps commander Kim Paik Il, III Corps commander Yu Jae Hung, and the two division commanders whose units were attached to U.S. Army corps— Chang Do Young, who commanded the 6th Division; and myself, who commanded the 1st. This was the sole instance in the Korean War when all top commanders met together in conference.

At that point of the war, every eye in Korea and virtually every eye around the world was focused once again on the 38th parallel. What exactly would Eighth Army do? Would it surge across the parallel once more? President Syngman Rhee and Supreme Commander Douglas MacArthur had both cried "on to North Korea." But President Truman in Washington and the other foreign states who had dispatched contingents to fight under the UN banner, especially Great Britain, were content merely to "destroy the invading forces remaining south of the 38th parallel."

At this sensitive point, Ridgway wanted us together so that he could clarify the principles under which he intended to pursue the conflict. On the one hand, Ridgway clearly insisted, "There is no 38th parallel." But at the same time, he described the "Kansas line" in detail and stressed that in future we would limit ourselves to pursuing an offensive defense.

The Kansas line was an operational control line running east and west some six to twelve miles north of the 38th parallel across the entire Korean peninsula, from the Imjin River on the west to Yangyang on the Sea of Japan. Although we were not to be tactically cognizant of the 38th parallel, Ridgway made it clear that we would not be advancing northward without restraints. We had reached that point in the war where the threat posed by the huge Chinese Army and the imperatives of international politics combined to cause us to limit battlefield objectives.

Right after the conference, my division jumped into the game of offensive defense. Rather than maintain a static line, we shifted to projecting influence north of our positions, planning and executing reconnaissance operations directed at the salient bulging northward from the Imjin River ferry along the national highway connecting Seoul and Kaesong.

Employing massed artillery fires to interdict the enemy's rear at the salient's northern extremity, I put a force of commandoes across the Imjin River with sterling support from our engineering people. The commandoes charged up the salient, behind enemy lines, shot the hell out of the place, and captured fifty Chinese soldiers before returning to our lines at the end of the day. Needless to say, this did wonders for the morale of the men in the lines and made it easier to maintain a high state of combat preparedness.

Then an urgent message arrived most unexpectedly. ROK I Corps commander Maj. Gen. Kim Paik Il had been killed. After the Yoju conference on March 27, General Kim was flying back to his headquarters at Kangnung on the east coast when his light aircraft crashed in bad weather in mountains around Taegwallyong Pass. His body was not recovered until May 9.

General Kim was an intimate friend. We had served together in the Kando Special Force during World War II. After liberation in 1945, we fled to Seoul from North Korea, crossing the 38th parallel together, Safely in our new homeland, we threw ourselves into the profession of arms. He was an active, spirited commander who bore on his shoulders the sole responsibility for the eastern front. He had achieved brilliant military exploits while doing so. During our drive into North Korea, Kim triumphantly liberated his own hometown, Myongchon in North Korea's North Hamgyong Province, just as I had been honored to liberate Pyongyang, my own hometown. During our general withdrawal from North Korea in December 1950, Kim was instrumental in arranging the safe evacuation of ninety thousand North Korean refugees gathered at the port of Hungnam.

I regret the lack of concern our government and even the ROK Army displayed for the Korean people, especially the refugees, during the Korean War. In the first days of the war, the bridge across the Han River was blown too soon, killing many refugees and leaving many others trapped in Seoul at the mercy of a heartless enemy. Later, on the western front in North Korea when we withdrew from the Chongchon River to the 38th parallel, the UN Command designated the main road leading from Pyongyang to Seoul a main supply road, or MSR. This designation meant that the roadway could not be used by refugees fleeing to the south.

The pitiful refugees then were obliged to struggle along the steep and tortuous mountain paths in lengthy detours to freedom. Some made for the coast at Haeju, the Ungjin Peninsula, or elsewhere and tried to find a boat to ply the Yellow Sea to the beckoning south. Either way, they stumbled along on foot in the midst of a bitterly cold winter, burdened by whatever fraction of their worldly possessions they could carry on their backs. I understand refugees suffered even more on the eastern front, where all existing roads were blocked by the military forces of one side or the other.

During the withdrawal through the port of Hungnam, U.S. X Corps initially opposed the idea of boarding refugees, saying that there was not enough space on the available ships and that North Korean spies were bound to be mingled with the refugees. ROK I Corps commander Kim Paik Il and his provost marshal were not satisfied with this rejection and continued to consult with U.S. X Corps commander, General Almond, until the general agreed. Some ninety thousand refugees stamping the docks at Sohojin and Hungnam were crammed into fishing boats, LSTs, and commercial vessels and transported to Koje Island in the south. Numbers of these refugees from North Korea's Hamgyong provinces got work at Pusan's International Market and soon rose to dominate it. Gen. Kim Paik Il's successful initiative to secure the evacuation of those freezing men, women, and children ranks as a national achievement as great as any combat victory. General Kim's death robbed the army and the Korean nation of a true giant.

The UN Command dubbed its next tactical undertaking "Operation Iron Triangle." The triangle in question can be formed by drawing a line on a map connecting Chorwon, Kumhwa, and Pyonggang. The ground within the triangle was crucial militarily because it lay at the heart of communications on the Korean peninsula. The shortest travel routes to and from key cities in North and South Korea lead through the triangle. The roads to and from Seoul, Pyongyang, Wonsan, and Chunchon all converge there. The side that controlled the triangle held the upper hand in the war itself.

The original North Korean invasion on June 25, 1950, had relied heavily on the communications advantages provided by the triangle, and the communist Chinese Army also used the Iron Triangle as a staging area, shifting forces into and out of the sector freely and assembling huge formations in the triangle to use as a base for launching major offensives.

We launched "Operation Rugged" on April 7, 1951, as the first phase of the more comprehensive Operation Iron Triangle. Operation Rugged's objective was to push the enemy back, bringing our front lines closer to the southern boundary of the triangle.

As the major command in the central front, the U.S. IX Corps headed up the main thrust of Operation Rugged, while my 1st Division was directed merely to maintain a stubborn defense of the Imjin River line. As D-day for Operation Rugged dawned, it all became academic to me. I received a communication from army headquarters informing me that I would replace my friend Maj. Gen. Kim Paik Il as commanding general of ROK I Corps and that I would be promoted to major general.

Brig. Gen. Kang Mun Bong replaced me as commander of the magnificent ROK 1st Division. Serving as G-3 at army headquarters at the time, Kang, who is now deceased, was to rise to the rank of lieutenant general. Kang arrived at the division command post at Kwansan shortly after I received notification of my transfer. Kang's reputation for integrity was as high as any officer in the ROK Army, and the army leaders held high expectations for him. Years later, however, he was imprisoned for complicity in the assassination of Kim Chang Yong, commander of the ROK Army Counterintelligence Corps (CIC).

The moment had finally arrived when I had to leave the officers and men of the 1st Division, and with precious little warning at that. I had shared the joys and sorrows and the life and death pressures of combat with these men for ten long months, and we had grown as close as brothers. The blood we shed in combat built within us a love and affection shared only by comrades who have served in the crucible of combat. I see them vividly yet in my mind's eye, crying as they bade me farewell.

I rode over to Uijongbu to pay my respects to my own boss, U.S. I Corps commander, Gen. Frank Milburn. The American general expressed genuine congratulations and real affection for me, insisting he could not do without me at the ROK 1st Division. Since I had to report to distant Pusan, Milburn had his pilot fly me down in his L-17. (I have learned that General Milburn played the key role in reversing my first appointment to command ROK II Corps, requesting ROK Army to return me to command of the ROK 1st Division in order to help deal with the growing Chinese threat at Unsan at that time.)

General Milburn's trust and support had been instrumental in helping the 1st Division deliver a good account of itself so many times in combat. His kind assistance also helped us avoid the lapses that stalked other ROK Army outfits. General Milburn also had been the one who decided to attach U.S. armor and artillery units to the 1st Division during our lunge into North Korea, giving the division every bit as much combat power as an American division. Nor is it hyperbole to say that General Milburn was the mentor responsible for making the 1st Division into the ROK Army's outstanding example of efficiency at joint operations.

When the North Koreans invaded in June 1950, the ROK Army was composed of eight infantry divisions. We consolidated these into five divisions after our losses in the early days of the war. As I assumed my new command, however, the army had grown to ten divisions.

The war was nearly a year old now and had been characterized by intense, unrelenting combat, most of which went badly for ROK forces. ROK divisions knew too well the anguish of defeat. In some battles, not just battalions or regiments but even our divisions had been hit so hard that for practical purposes they were annihilated.

War is hell, they say, and war is nowhere more hellish than in the matter of competency for command. The ROK Army's mistakes were inevitably followed by one or more division commander being relieved, so that by the time I left the ROK 1st Division I was the only officer who had retained command of the same division since the outbreak of the war. Now it was my turn to change. I had served as a division commander for nearly two years, almost half in intense combat. I had been assigned to command the 5th Division in July 1949 and went directly from that assignment to command the 1st in April 1950. Now it was my turn to leave a division to take up command responsibility of a corps— a promotion, after nearly two years' tour of duty, almost half of which was with the ROK 1st Division in intense combat.

The ROK Army was badly mauled in the bitter fighting that followed the entrance of the Chinese Army into the Korean War. We were a fledgling outfit. Before the war, the ROK Army had never conducted a maneuver exercise higher than regimental level, yet we fought the war at division, corps, and even army level. Given this lack of training, our performance could only be shabby, especially in comparison with two of the world's premier fighting forces with which we shared the battlefield. The army of the United States of America boasted the strongest conventional war-fighting capability and the most advanced weapons systems of any ground force in the world. The Chinese Army represented the world's mightiest unconventional warfare force.

I arrived in Pusan on April 12, 1951, the very day that news reached that city that General Douglas MacArthur had been relieved of duty. Pusan was then serving as the temporary seat of government of the Republic of Korea, and President Syngman Rhee was using the South

Kyongsang Province governor's official residence as a presidential mansion. I received official notification that I was to be promoted to major general and was directed to proceed to Pusan to receive the promotion from the president at his temporary residence. As I went along Pusan's streets on my way to the mansion, I found the traffic to be ghastly, striking me as very much like a rippling explosion of rioting along the length of every street.

President Syngman Rhee personally pinned the two stars representing my new rank on my uniform, but the news about MacArthur had visibly unsettled the old gentleman. His face was completely enshrouded in deep shadows of disappointment. "MacArthur," Korea's president confided to me, "was a soldier who really understood my heart." The president said he was now concerned about the future course of the war.

General MacArthur wanted to lead another charge into North Korea, and he had not been tractable in his dealings with U.S. President Harry S Truman. Overnight, MacArthur was obliged to surrender his three major positions, supreme commander, U.S. Far East Command; commander in chief, U.S. Far East Ground Forces; and commander in chief, UN Command. MacArthur himself used the term "fired," but that is technically incorrect. An American five-star general is considered on active duty throughout his life and is furnished with an aide, a sedan, and an office until his death.

Matthew B. Ridgway was promoted to four-star rank and appointed to replace MacArthur. James A. Van Fleet was selected to take command of U.S. Eighth Army.

In Pusan, meanwhile, I was determined to be reunited with my family, whom I hadn't seen since the war began. I had had previous opportunities to see them, of course. I could have arranged to take my family with me when we withdrew across the Han River after the Munsan battle at the beginning of the war, but my conscience would not allow me to do so when I could not even guarantee the safety of my subordinates. The orders to march into North Korea in the war's second stage came so quickly that I had not had time to find my family. During the January 4, 1951, withdrawal, I simply sent an aide into Seoul to act on my behalf and put my family on the refugee road.

I found my mother, my wife, and our three-year-old daughter living in a twenty-square-foot rented room in Pusan. They had no money and eked out a wretched existence, eating barely enough to stave off starvation. My wife had contracted typhoid fever and hovered at death's door for some time. As I entered the tiny room, I barely recognized the haggard, sunken-cheeked woman lying on the mat. All she could do was cry. All I could do was cry with her. My family and relatives who remained in Seoul under enemy occupation suffered many privations, but luckily they all survived.

Withdraw or Fight to the Death

Located at Kangnung on the Sea of Japan, I Corps was responsible for the eastern front. I assumed command at a time when a number of ugly incidents involving the ROK Army had roiled the waters inside Korea and out. One of these was MacArthur's sacking. Another was the Citizens Defense Force Case—in which officials diverted army funds—and the third was the Kochang Massacre. In the fall of 1950, the 9th Regiment of the ROK 11th Division killed hundreds of civilians in Kochang that the troops mistakenly thought were communist guerrillas. As a frontline commander, however, I had no time to spare for newspapers or radio, and I took little interest in events in the rear.

The ROK Army had sole responsibility for the eastern front, and the situation there was encouraging. On March 27, the ROK Capital Division, an I Corps unit, had charged across the 38th parallel, the first friendly unit to do so. Then I Corps began pushing the line slowly northward. When I assumed command, the front ran from a point south of Sokcho to Mount Sorak and on to Sinnam.

ROK I Corps was responsible for the area bounded on the west by the long, north-south spine of the Taebaek Mountain Range and on the east by the Sea of Japan. ROK III Corps under Maj. Gen. Yu Jae Hung guarded my left flank and was responsible for the strip of real estate that lay immediately west of my command along the center of the peninsula. The Sea of Japan, of course, protected our right flank. ROK I Corps and ROK III Corps represented the only frontline ground forces under the direct command of ROK Army Headquarters. Overall operational planning, of course, was accomplished at Eighth Army Headquarters, but ROK Army exercised direct command and control of I Corps and III Corps based on these general plans.

To exercise its command and control, ROK Army Headquarters had established a frontline command post in Kangnung, and Army Chief of Staff Chung Il Kwon frequently visited this facility. The director of the forward command post, Brig. Gen. Lee Jun Sik, was stationed permanently in Kangnung.

About the time I was appointed to command I Corps, ROK Army shifted a number of its divisions, newly assigning the 11th Division to I Corps. Brig. Gen. Choi Duk Shin, who was later to head a large, indigenous Korean church, the Chondo-kyo, commanded the 11th, which had been engaged in suppressing communist guerrillas in the Chiri Mountains. I deployed the 11th Division on my right wing, adjacent to the Sea of Japan, a relatively secure position consistent with the division's lack of front-line combat experience. I positioned Brig. Gen. Song Yo Chan's seasoned Capital Division on our western flank, where the unit could provide cover from enemy attacks originating in the mountain ranges for which the area is famous.

The Capital Division had assumed the vanguard in ROK I Corps attacks on the eastern front, and the division fairly trembled with intense self-confidence. The Capital Division's three regimental commanders were officers of the highest caliber. The 1st Regiment was commanded by Col. Han Shin, who rose to four-star rank; the armor regiment was commanded by Col. Lee Yong, who rose to the rank of major general; and the 26th Regiment was commanded by Col. Suh Chong Chol. In stark contrast, the 11th Division was assigned to ROK I Corps after division elements were implicated in the Kochang Massacre.

When I took over ROK I Corps, my major staff officers included Brig. Gen. Chang Chang Kuk as deputy corps commander, Brig. Gen. Choi Hong Hi as chief of staff, Col. Kim Pyong On as G-1, Col. Shin Chae Sik as G-2, Col. Kong Kuk Chin as G-3, and Col. Kim Yong Taek as G-4. This group of select, competent officers was unmatched anywhere in the ROK Army.

My new unit was nominally a corps, but when I reviewed its composition, I found it to be something less than that. The ROK I Corps commander had neither artillery nor tank units under his direct command. Indeed, the only unit directly available to me as corps commander was the 1101st Field Engineer Group under Col. Huh Pil Eun. Each of my subordinate divisions had only a single battalion of light, 105mm howitzers. Nothing had been done to improve the divisions' combat capabilities since the outbreak of the war.

After the Tabu-dong battles in the fall of 1950, the ROK 1st Division was attached to the U.S. Army and gained experience at coordinating combined arms in combat. Frankly, the more I understood of ROK I Corps, the more I felt like a city boy who suddenly is dropped into the countryside. It was as if some mischievous goblin had wrenched the hands of the clock back decades.

In addition to ROK I Corps units, a number of other military organizations were stationed on the east coast. A Construction Engineer Group was located south of Kangnung under the command of Col. Yun Tae Il. Yun's mission was to maintain the road running along the coast from Kangnung to Pohang and to conduct rear-area security. A ROK Air Force Mustang Squadron was stationed at Kangnung Airfield.

Meanwhile, one positive element in the situation on the east coast was the deployment in the Sea of Japan of units of the U.S. Navy. These ships provided significant firepower to ROK I Corps, which was woefully short of artillery, as I have noted. The destroyers and cruisers of Cruiser Division 5 of the U.S. Navy's Seventh Fleet gave us with overwhelming naval gunfire support. Meanwhile, the aircraft of the U.S. Navy's Task Force 77, based on two aircraft carriers, provided bombing and close air support up and down the entire east coast, all the way to the Tumen River on North Korea's border with the Soviet Union.

My first act as I Corps commander was to move corps headquarters from a building housing the prosecutor general in downtown Kangnung to Chumunjin, a small hamlet much farther north up the coast. The front ran just south of Sokcho and was simply too far from Kangnung to allow effective command. Apart from that, I moved the headquarters because I believe that military units have no place in urban areas.

Even when involved in active combat, such as our various struggles into and out of Seoul and Pyongyang, I strove to keep the time my unit spent quartered in cities to an absolute minimum. When military forces are stationed in urban areas, law, order, and discipline degrade precipitously.

We pitched our tents in a grove of pine trees south of Chumunjin and set up corps headquarters there. Some of my staff officers evinced considerable dissatisfaction at the move, and I heard some grumbling from line divisions that if corps headquarters moved so far forward the division command posts would have no place to go. My months of combat experience had taught me, however, that when the fighting is tough, the good commander must be wedded to the front line. On the other hand, when things are quiet, the good commander must put some distance between himself and the front.

I found the task of corps commander to be vastly simpler than that of division commander. The corps commander's role is pretty well limited to making sure the operations and training of his subordinate divisions proceed as planned.

ROK divisions were authorized to deal directly with ROK Army Headquarters on administrative and logistical matters. That is why corps commands are characterized as "intermediate headquarters." Whenever I found any logistic deficiencies affecting combat capabilities of the divisions, I could call the attention of the army headquarters to expedite its prompt action to resolve the problems.

On a typical day as a corps commander, my staff briefed me on the situation at the front first thing every morning. Then I drove to the front to inspect areas where I knew or anticipated that battles would be fought that day. At the front, I exchanged views with regimental and divisional commanders, patiently listening to their recommendations, complaints, or problems, and if I noticed something amiss, I directed the local commander to remedy the situation. I always believed that a commander must keep in touch with his troops to read the pulse of the battlefield. Some Americans said, "General Paik's CP (Command Post) is where his hat is."

I also made myself available to provide liaison services to ROK Army Headquarters on behalf of my division commanders and coordinated fire support and close-air support with KMAG, the U.S. Navy, and both Korean and U.S. air forces. I conducted inspections throughout the corps area of operations, from the fighting positions at the very front edge of the battle area to rear-area supply points, traveling virtually all the time. Each day passed swiftly, but at the end of the day I found myself wondering whether I had accomplished very much.

Ridgway stressed that his commanders should exercise command to a level two echelons below his own. As a corps commander, then, I should exercise direct command authority down to regimental level. The division commander should do the same down to battalion level; and the regimental commander should do the same down to company level.

UN Command attacks along the front in the spring of 1951 had to be closely coordinated with units on either flank, imposing limits on the advance but forestalling the flanking attacks at which the Chinese excelled. Our position as the easternmost unit in the line, however, made ROK I Corps less encumbered by this stricture. Nor did we face the difficult terrain features that complicated the advance on the west, obstacles like the Imjin, the Han, and the Yesong rivers. As a result, ROK I Corps continued to slug away at the enemy, pushing it slowly northward.

The Chinese Army launched its Fifth Offensive, sometimes called the First Spring Offensive, on April 22, 1951, about ten days after I assumed command of ROK I Corps. The Chinese attack was aimed at the western and central fronts, not at us. The Chinese offensive was gigantic, involving 250,000 men in nine armies.

The enemy we faced wasn't Chinese at all, but troops of the North Korean People's Army. As long as the enemy remained the North Koreans, the officers and men of my new command asserted their self-confidence and fought admirably. The eastern front remained relatively untroubled.

As they had done repeatedly in the past, the Chinese commanders picked the relatively vulnerable ROK Army units as the objectives of their offensive. One prong of the Chinese assault bore down on Brig. Gen. Chang Do Young's 6th Division at Sachang.

The ROK 6th was on the right flank of U.S. IX Corps. The 6th broke and ran under the shock of the blow. The Chinese pursued hotly, forcing the front to bulge southward all the way to Kapyong, where the U.S. 1st Marine Division, the U.S. 3d Division, and the British Commonwealth 27th Brigade fought desperately for several days before they could save the situation.

Another prong of the Chinese offensive caught the British 29th Brigade attached to U.S. I Corps by surprise east of Munsan. The Chinese forces isolated Lt. Col. James Carne's Gloucester Battalion on a hill near Choksong, whereupon the British fought like wildcats for sixty straight hours to defend their perimeter, forging a Korean War legend in the process.

Some 760 of the Gloucester Battalion's complement of 800 officers and men were killed or wounded. Had it not been for the sacrifice of the

Gloucesters, the enemy surely would have won a position from which to threaten the approaches to Uijongbu. Great Britain sent two brigades to participate in the Korean War. A composite unit of one artillery, one Australian, and two U.K. battalions, the British Commonwealth 27th Brigade from Hong Kong arrived first, to be followed later by the British 29th Brigade, sailing directly from England.

Like my former ROK 1st Division, the British brigades and a Canadian brigade were attached to U.S. I Corps, so I had fought with them and observed them in combat. Discipline at lower levels in the British Army was harsh, and each soldier and officer had a clear understanding of the precise nature of his mission. The British seemed to have a built-in compulsion to accomplish in detail any responsibility assigned them and were especially strong on the defense.

Each British brigade was composed of an infantry regiment, an artillery regiment, and a battalion of Centurion tanks mounting a 90mm cannon. Neither too small nor too large, the exceptionally fast and maneuverable British brigade was always deployed to defend friendly bridgeheads. On three separate occasions, British ground forces performed formidable missions in exemplary fashion, at the Chongchon River, at the Han River during the January 4, 1951, withdrawal, and again at Choksong on the present occasion.

The British were regarded as far and away the most accurate artillerymen in the war. In the U.S. Army, artillery officers at the rank of lieutenant were assigned as artillery observers, but the British assigned the artillery battery commander himself to be the forward observer, while the next senior officer commanded the guns. The Japanese Army also used this approach.

The British were absolutely devoted to the ritual observance of teatime. They dropped everything each day at 4 P.M. to consume tea and cookies, even during combat. British artillery ceased firing for teatime and then picked up the tempo afterward

Of the forces in the British Commonwealth Brigade, I remember the Australian battalion to be the toughest fighters.

The Gloucestershire Battalion of the 29th British Brigade held at Choksong at enormous sacrifice, but now the Chinese Army switched its attack to the eastern central front, specifically against the 5th Division under Brig. Gen. Min Ki Sik and the 7th under Kim Hyong Il. The two divisions began to fall back under heavy Chinese pressure, but the U.S. 2d Division shored them up from behind and prevented a breakthrough.

The Chinese 63d Army then hurled three divisions across the Imjin River at my old friends in the ROK 1st Division on the western front. The Chinese hoped this assault would punch through the line and allow them to seize Seoul from the east. Under its new division commander, Brig. Gen. Kang Mun Bong, however, the outnumbered ROK 1st Division stood up to the onslaught and fought back bravely. New Eighth Army commander Gen. James A. Van Fleet proved unwavering in his determination that Korea's capital city would not again fall to the enemy. Eighth Army forces fought determinedly to protect Seoul, holding at the "Golden line" extending from Susaek to Wabu. The ROK 1st Division anchored the left end of the Golden line, while the U.S. 3d, 25th, and 24th divisions fought along its length to the east.

The sheer momentum of the Chinese divisions forced the ROK 1st back to a line running from Susaek to Pyokje, but after six days of bloody combat, the 1st Division contained the Chinese attack. This was an extraordinary achievement. No ROK Army division had managed to contain the Chinese Army in any of its five offensives.

General Van Fleet was very worried about the series of defeats the Chinese had inflicted on ROK Army divisions, and on this occasion he was unrestrained in his praise for the gallant defense mounted by the ROK 1st Division. Of course, I went into transports of pride when I learned of this magnificent feat by a unit I had commanded for so long and had left only days before.

In *The Forgotten War,* Clay Blair describes that battle in these terms:

> On the extreme left of the corps front the ROK 1st Division, reinforced intermittently by Hannum's 73d Tank Battalion, continued to fight skillfully and valiantly. Its fine performance in this battle would earn the youthful commander, Paik Sun Yup [sic], a promotion to ROK I Corps commander and put him on a road that would lead one day to the post of chief-of-staff of the ROK Army.

Frankly, I felt a bit ashamed to share in the battle honors earned by the 1st Division under the command of Brig. Gen. Kang Mun Bong and his three magnificent regimental commanders, Kim Chum Kon, Mun Hyong Tae, and Kim An Il.

As April became May, my I Corps remained the only friendly unit with forces deployed north of the 38th parallel. My units engaged in violent seesaw battles, first attacking and then defending, in the alpine terrain around Mount Sorak. A rare area of level ground at the entrance to Sorak-dong became the center of an out-and-out dogfight. We took the area and lost it; the enemy took it and lost it back to us. Each side planted land mines, making the fight in the area all the more bloody. The extremely rough topography interfered with communications so frequently that it was commonplace for units to lose contact with each other. Fighting in such terrain proved to be an extreme challenge to tactical commanders.

Brig. Gen. Choi Duk Shin commanded my 11th Division. Choi was the first Korean officer to attend the U.S. Infantry School at Fort Benning, Georgia. A very soldierly man, Choi nurtured a voracious appetite for reading U.S. Army field manuals. During the thick of the fighting, I received an emergency message saying that the 11th Division had lost communications with one of its regiments. I motored up to 11th Division Headquarters and, sure enough, found General Choi reading a field manual.

I asked him what was going on, and he responded almost monosyllabically, as if quoting from a field manual. He described the situation: "Communications out. I'm worried." As I recall it, I stood in silent frustration for a few moments, and then told him, "Look. Manuals are important, surely, but you've got to maintain contact with that regiment even if you have to do it on foot, with runners and liaison officers. I don't think you're going to find the answer in a U.S. Army field manual. Do you?"

It seemed to me that General Choi's mind was still unsettled by the Kochang Massacre. Not many days passed before Choi was relieved, and Brig. Gen. Oh Duk Jun arrived to command the 11th Division. General Oh was commissioned in the Japanese Army through a program similar to the U.S. ROTC and was stationed in Hiroshima when the Americans dropped the atomic bomb on that city. Oh managed to survive by a stroke of good fortune. He was indoors using the latrine when the bomb exploded. Even so, the flash from the explosion burned one entire side of his body, and six years later the scars showed no signs of fading.

I met a company commander of the Capital Division in a valley on Mount Sorak whose boldness and intelligence burned his name into my memory. It was Kim Hyong Uk, who would later serve as director of the Korean Central Intelligence Agency. Kim was an outstanding soldier, one who attracted attention even as a company grade officer.

The Collapse of III Corps

The UN Command had contained the Chinese Fifth Offensive, but the enemy had pushed our front south to a line running from Munsan on the west to Inje on the east. In early May, ROK I Corps received an order to seize the road running from the east coast to Hongchon. In the terribly rugged terrain common on the eastern front, victory or defeat was often determined by who could protect his supply lines and who couldn't.

One can hardly imagine a more Herculean task than trying to use the undeveloped road net in Korea at the time to transport great stocks of supplies and materials coming off ships at Pusan to the units fighting on the eastern front. The problem was only partially remedied by sending supplies by sea to the east coast ports of Mukho, Samchok, and Chumunjin and then transporting them by road up the formidable Taegwallyong Pass that stood sentinel just inland from the coast and on to III Corps immediately to our west. The process was complicated because we had to use secondary roads not much better than mountain trails. If we could seize the road to Hongchon, supplies could flow to III Corps in the quantities it needed.

Six ROK Army divisions, including the 5th and 7th, were to lead the operation against this crucial road. The six divisions were under three separate corps: ROK I and ROK III Corps and U.S. X Corps. Eighth Army's master plan was to stabilize the situation on the east then mount a counterattack on the western front to restore the lines to the 38th parallel.

As we prepared for our own operation, intelligence information revealed that the Chinese Army was again massing on the central front. We established that the Chinese were readying yet another of their patented offensives. Eighth Army estimated that the Chinese would aim their offensive at the western front in another attempt to take Seoul and began preparing to contain such an attack. But the Chinese fooled us again.

The Chinese Army aimed its Sixth Offensive, or Second Spring Offensive, straight at the eastern front.

Blowing flutes and pounding gongs, Chinese units crossed the upper course of the Soyang River southwest of Inje on the morning of May 16, 1951, and hurtled like a battering ram into Namjon, a hamlet that marked the boundary between the ROK 7th and 9th divisions and between U.S. X Corps and ROK III Corps. The Chinese broke through Brig. Gen. Kim Hyong Il's 7th Division at a stroke and pushed southeast during the night to occupy Omachi Pass.

One could hardly imagine a more terrible tactical situation for ROK III Corps. Literally overnight, the Chinese Army had managed to sever the road from Inje to Hajinbu. This road served as the sole supply route for the 3d Division under Brig. Gen. Kim Chong O and the 9th Division under Choi Suk. Both divisions were assigned to ROK III Corps, the unit on my immediate left flank.

Faster than you can bat your eye, ROK III Corps found itself facing a double envelopment, with the enemy poised to attack from front and rear simultaneously. Tactical situations tend to recur in war, varied only in time and place. In many respects the situation at this juncture resembled that which had prevailed during the Chinese Third Offensive at the Chongchon River in North Korea. The major geographic elements were similar on each battlefield. The Soyang River on this occasion matched the Chongchon River in the earlier battle in the north, and the Nangnim Mountain Range of the previous fight matched the Taebaek Mountain Range in the present case.

As in the earlier fighting, the enemy occupied the upper reaches of the river, while UN forces held the downriver segments. Maj. Gen. Yu

Jae Hung commanded ROK III Corps, while in one of the strange coincidences of the war, the U.S. 2d Division was once again positioned immediately to the left of Yu's imperiled corps. Finally, as in the first battle, the Chinese Army had managed to isolate the rear.

Given all these similarities, the outcome was never in doubt. Under attack from front and rear, ROK III Corps had two choices. It could throw every available man at the Chinese forces that had cut off Omachi in a desperate bid to break through the Chinese units at its rear. Or, ROK III Corps could withdraw in brutal terrain. Military units, of course, must abandon their heavy equipment when they withdraw over mountainous ground. Faced with a choice between a battle to the death or withdrawal, the two divisions chose the latter.

Discarding howitzers and trucks, they scattered and fled south on foot through the Pangdae Mountains. Reports suggest that in many instances enlisted personnel abandoned even their personal weapons, while officers stripped off their rank insignia and fled south empty-handed. ROK III Corps had made the worst choice possible. They collapsed without a fight, leaving a huge gap in the front around Hyon-ri.

After cutting off Omachi and Sangnam, on May 17 the Chinese Army set about enlarging the huge bulge it had gouged in the line. On May 18 it advanced as far as Samgo; on May 19 its lead units smashed into Soksa on the old Seoul-Kangnung Road, site of the present expressway that connects Seoul to Kangnung on the east coast.

The collapse of III Corps threatened Clark Ruffner's adjacent 2d Division, part of X Corps, more than any other single unit. The eastern flank of the U.S. 2d lay fully exposed to the enemy, a development identical to the situation that had unfolded at Kunu on the banks of North Korea's Chongchon River. Six months before, the exposure of its flank had inflicted the pains of hell itself on the U.S. 2d Division.

U.S. X Corps commander General Almond moved quickly. He directed the 2d Division to establish order among the withdrawing men of the ROK 7th Division and to protect its flank. At the same time, Almond instantly requested that Van Fleet send reinforcements.

On May 18, 1951, U.S. X Corps artillery and U.S. 2d Division artillery fired more than forty-one thousand shells at Chinese Army units on their flank, and the U.S. Air Force flew 165 close air support sorties. Even this remarkable effort barely prevented the Chinese Army from surrounding and destroying the U.S. 2d Infantry Division.

As the enemy crashed through ROK III Corps, Eighth Army directed that a new defense line be established. The "Waco line" was to run from Namae, at the halfway point between Kangnung and Yangyang, to Turobong, the central peak in the Odae Mountains, and on to Hill 1009 about six miles from Hongchon. The unexpected speed of the ROK III Corps collapse, however, made such a line impossible to establish.

ROK III Corps's distintegration had also exposed the left flank of my

I Corps, which was east of the unlucky ROK III Corps. The difference was that we had more time than the 2d Division to react, because our flank was also protected by the Taebaek Mountain Range.

I moved corps headquarters back to Kangnung and deployed the Capital Division and the 11th Division along a front running from the Odae Mountains to the coast.

Chinese forces had advanced as far south as the road connecting Seoul and Kangnung, and I was willing to bet that the Chinese commanders would not stop there. I was sure they would charge east down that road with the intent of reaching Taegwallyong Pass and taking Kangnung itself.

The ROK Air Force operated K-18 Airfield in Kangnung, its only tactical strike base, and the field was literally stacked with bombs and supplies. ROK Air Force P-51 Mustangs based at K-18 sortied as far afield as Pyongyang. A U.S. Marine Air Wing was also based at the Kangnung Airfield. Were the enemy to take Kangnung, all the supply ports on the east coast and the air force base at Kangnung would be lost to the war effort. In view of the distinctive topography of the region, if Kangnung were to fall, the enemy would have little trouble turning south to take Samchok and Pohang. I was tense, I was agitated, and I should have been.

The crisis heightened. On the morning of May 21, 1951, I received instructions from Eighth Army Headquarters to attend an operational conference at a simple III Corps airstrip at Yongpyong just west of Taegwallyong Pass.

Accompanied by the chief KMAG adviser to I Corps, Col. Glen Rogers, I flew to the rendezvous in a U.S. Army light observation aircraft. We soared up the precipitous face of Taegwallyong, which stood like a majestic sentinel dominating Kangnung and the entire coastal fringe far below. As we cleared the pass, the serenity of the scene was shattered by heavy black smoke pouring into the sky from behind distant mountains to the northwest. The sheer volume of smoke shocked even an old war-horse like myself, and for a moment I thought a chemical factory had been bombed. Then I realized where all the smoke was coming from. The U.S. Air Force was bombing and strafing the heavy equipment, ammunition, gasoline, and other supplies abandoned by ROK III Corps to prevent it from falling into enemy hands.

When we landed on the little airstrip, I found that Brig. Gen. Eugene Ridings of the U.S. 3d Division had arrived just a minute ahead of me. Ridings told me the 3d Division under Maj. Gen. Robert Soule had been ordered to deploy into the sector vacated by ROK III Corps. The U.S. 3d had been in Eighth Army reserve, deployed near Seoul to defend the capital, but had already departed its bivouac area to accomplish this new mission. It had reacted swiftly to the sudden order to move, and the division's advance elements had already reached Hongchon.

The airstrip where we were had been built by ROK III Corps, whose headquarters was located at nearby Hajinbu. I saw no one in the vicinity and decided corps headquarters had already withdrawn.

Shortly after I landed, two L-19 light aircraft appeared in the western sky. Both planes had been hit by enemy antiaircraft fire and were leaking fuel, which vaporized as it hit the air, looking like white smoke pouring from the aircraft.

Both planes managed to land safely. Gen. James A. Van Fleet deplaned from one aircraft, while Eighth Army G-3 Col. Gilman C. Mudgett clambered out of the other. I was amazed at the spectacle of the commander of Eighth Army, a four-star general, landing at a tiny airstrip high in the mountains, his aircraft perforated by enemy ground fire and fuel streaming from its fuselage.

Mudgett had no sooner hit the ground than he was unrolling an operational map and explaining the situation to us. On the map, the Chinese breakthrough appeared as a huge bulge stretching southward through our lines. As I listened to Mudgett, I realized that I had not overestimated the seriousness of the situation. We were in trouble.

Mudgett finished, and Van Fleet spoke. "I want the two of you to cooperate to clean up this mess," he said. "I Corps, you attack from the right flank. Third Division, you attack from the left." As he spoke, he pointed to the east and west sides of the bulge on the map.

He was ordering my corps to attack northwest from Taegwallyong Pass and the 3d Division to attack northeast from Hajinbu. Van Fleet repeated one phrase over and over. "I want you," he stressed, "to inflict the greatest possible punishment on the enemy."

He turned to the subject of ROK III Corps. "I ordered them to undertake a retrograde movement while continuing to resist the enemy," the general fairly hissed. "I regret that they were unable to do so."

I asked Van Fleet when we should attack. "Without delay," he replied.

The U.S. 3d was the sole division in Eighth Army reserve, and in response to X Corps commander General Almond's request for reinforcements, Eighth Army had directed the U.S. 3d Division to move out immediately. The 3d covered the amazing distance of 155 miles in a single day. Even after so many months of working with the Americans, the speed of the 3d Division's movement taught me something about the nature of the U.S. Army.

The Chinese Army, meanwhile, advanced as far as Soksa on the road leading to Taegwallyong and Kangnung and was now charging from that village in two directions. One Chinese column was pushing straight for Kangnung; the other was headed for Chongsun.

If my mission was to succeed, ROK I Corps had to beat the enemy column in a race for Taegwallyong Pass, the region's commanding terrain feature and the doorway to Kangnung. The Seoul-Kangnung road plunges to the low coastal fringe and Kangnung over Taegwallyong. We had no hope of beating the Chinese unless we could fortify the pass.

The operational conference was over in ten minutes, and I flew back to Kangnung. I used the time to work out ideas for the operation in my head. The situation did not allow a moment's delay.

Outnumbered, my corps would have to fight Chinese Army units hurtling into our western flank even as we maintained a defense line against the NKPA to the north. If the North Koreans pushed us south or if the Chinese pushed us east, Kangnung and the entire east coast would be in jeopardy. As I planned the redeployment of I Corps forces, I had the same feeling you get when you throw dice at a gambling table. Who knew the outcome?

My first move, I decided, would be to order the crack ROK Capital Division to dispatch its 1st Regiment under Col. Han Shin to Taegwallyong as fast as possible. Then I would direct the Capital Division to redeploy so that it faced west rather than north. Next I would have the ROK 11th Division extend its line west to fill the gap created by the Capital Division's shift of axis. Finally, I would assign the 1101st Engineer Group the mission of manning the extreme right, where the line ran into the Sea of Japan, defending the crucial coastal area. The rub, of course, was that neither the 11th Division nor the engineers had any combat experience worth mentioning. My plan was to coordinate with the U.S. Seventh Fleet to blunt enemy attacks by throwing walls of exploding shells between the enemy and my inexperienced troops.

As soon as my little plane touched down in Kangnung, I summoned my two division commanders and their staffs and explained the operational plan to them. I emphasized that ROK I Corps had not yet faced the Chinese Army in head-to-head combat, and I spent precious time explaining the Chinese Army to them in detail.

"The communist Chinese Army does not have the ability," I stressed, "to continue this offensive for more than three or four more days. The enemy resupply system, relying as it does on men and horses for transport, suffers severe limitations. Meanwhile, we enjoy air superiority. Base your detailed operational plans on an estimate of how far the enemy can advance in three or four more days."

I anticipated that the Capital Division's 1st Regiment could move overland to Taegwallyong in something like three hours and that three or four hours would be required for the other adjustments to our combat dispositions. If the 1st Regiment took longer than that, the enemy would probably beat us to Taegwallyong. But as the minutes ticked by, I received no report that the 1st Regiment was under way.

Finally, my G-3, Col. Kong Kuk Chin, and a few other staff officers came into my office. It was about 3 P.M. As Kong began his report I realized that he was agitated and almost out of control. Kong was to rise to the rank of brigadier general and serve as ROK Army provost marshal general, but right then, he was fit to be tied. "General Song Yo Chan will not allow the 1st Regiment to move out," Kong yelled. "This is mutiny!"

General Song, it turned out, would not obey the order to send his 1st Regiment to Taegwallyong. He did not want to lose a regiment at a moment when the enemy was threatening his area of operations.

No commander relishes loaning out his units during combat. I had felt the same way. The commanders on the eastern front were particularly susceptible to this feeling because their war was almost always confined to the narrow fringe of coast separating the high mountains on the west from the sea on the east. Moreover, eastern-front commanders had virtually no experience in joint operations. I was frustrated that I had no time to train General Song to adopt the broader perspective.

I sensed, however, that General Song's foot-dragging might be motivated by something other than his desire to maintain unit integrity. The fact was that until only a few weeks before, he and I had held equal rank and were both serving as division commanders. Moreover, Song was the toughest, most fearless commander on the eastern front. And to top it off, he and I were about the same age. General Song possessed a well-developed sense of pride. His attitude now, I surmised, would be something like, "The likes of you won't be telling me what to do." Song would find it difficult to acquiesce meekly to my orders.

As these thoughts ran through my mind, Colonel Kong continued jumping up and down all over my office, urging me to take immediate action. "Maybe General Song's division has a problem we don't know about," I said in the most soothing tone I could muster. "Let's wait a while longer." I don't know if I sounded controlled, but the fact was that rage surged and pounded in my veins. I had no intention of losing control in front of Kong and my other staff officers, however.

But Colonel Kong wouldn't let it drop, insisting that I move immediately to quell the "insubordination" and using language designed to goad me to action. "Sir, I Corps is facing its greatest crisis. Our very survival is at stake. This is not the time," he spat out, "for effeminate leadership. Sir, are you content to be a major general? Or do you want your name to go down in history as a great commander?"

The 1st Regiment still remained in place by late afternoon. I could temporize no longer. I strapped a .45-caliber pistol around my waist and jumped into my jeep, directing Colonel Kong to accompany me. We had to turn on the jeep's lights in the thickening darkness as we fairly flew down the road to the headquarters of the Capital Division. The jeep jerked to a halt after we turned sharply into division headquarters, and I buttonholed the first soldier I saw. "Where's your division commander?" The soldier pointed to General Song's tent.

I strode into Song's tent, sat down facing the division commander, and without preamble said, "Are you going to obey my order or not?"

I didn't yell, but I did raise my voice, and the chill in my voice would have cowed a stone. General Song realized instantly that my visit was no ordinary event. He jumped to attention. "Your Excellency," he said in the most effusively polite language forms. "I'm sorry. I shall obey your order." Song apologized and asked my pardon with no further prodding from me.

He then picked up his field telephone, called Col. Han Shin, and ordered the 1st Regiment to move out. Luckily, the 1st Regiment's leaders had fully prepared the regiment to redeploy. Colonel Han was aware of the conflicting orders of his division commander and corps commander, and although this knowledge put him in an agonizing position, he handled it well. He had not been dilatory in preparing to move his command, yet he properly awaited orders from his immediate superior before directing his regiment to move.

Colonel Kong told me later that he had used such grating language to me because I Corps was facing an emergency, yet my face had not revealed a flicker of emotion. Kong said he was trying to rile me up until I exploded into action. I live by the personal maxim, however, that control must be maintained as long as control is required.

At that point in the Korean War, senior army commanders were young men of about the same age, around thirty. We customarily used familiar language forms with each other, so as differences in rank and position gradually emerged among us, our former familiarity tended to blur leadership lines. If a senior officer facing such a situation could not firmly establish that he was the boss, he found that he could not establish unit discipline either.

The 1st Regiment hotfooted it for Taegwallyong. It reached the summit at about 9 P.M., May 21, 1951. We were three hours late getting there, but the Chinese Army arrived an hour after we did. It was a close thing.

The battle developed into a total victory for us because the 1st Regiment had occupied the high ground before the Chinese force arrived. For the next two days, the 1st Regiment fought off communist Chinese Army units that smashed into its positions in human waves. The Chinese lacked the firepower to break through, and after long hours of combat, the pace of the battle wore their infantry into exhaustion.

The 1st Regiment did not fight alone. As it struggled at Taegwallyong, the rest of ROK I Corps deployed in a semicircle north and west of Kangnung and engaged in battles with the North Koreans on our north and the Chinese on our west. Col. Huh Pil Eun's 1101st Field Engineer Group successfully defended a combat sector that should have been allotted to an entire infantry regiment, establishing a record unmatched in the history of warfare, a record that is not likely to be duplicated in the future either.

The enemy attack began to run out of steam on May 23, 1951, and I instantly ordered I Corps to switch to the offense. The ROK Capital Division had been deployed over an area ranging all the way from Mount Odae to Taegwallyong, and the division now threaded its way among the maze of mountains, mopping up remnants of the Chinese Army. The 1st Regiment alone had killed or wounded 1,180 of the enemy during the battle, while suffering only 12 men killed in action. We had contained the Chinese offensive and inflicted a 100 to 1 loss ratio.

I Corps then launched a counterattack northward, coordinating with the U.S. 3d Division and U.S. X Corps. We attacked from Mount Odae to Inje and on to Wontong without meeting serious resistance. The enemy's main force had already retreated, leaving the Taebaek Mountains free from large formations of the enemy. We took Chinese prisoners like plucking apples from a tree. Lt. Col. Chung Se Chin commanded the 2d Battalion of the 1st Regiment during this period, and his unit captured a number of Chinese prisoners. Chung told me about one man who bowed so low his forehead touched the ground. "I cook Chinese food very well," the POW pleaded. "If you spare my life, I'll cook for your unit and make delicious food for your soldiers."

We encountered and processed many officers and men from the luckless ROK III Corps in the final days of the operation. These soldiers had made it all the way south to the Seoul-Kangnung road, clambering over daunting Mount Pangdae and humping over thirty miles of rugged mountains. Only about 50 percent of the ones who came that way survived. Although it was now May, snow still fell in these high mountains, and the fleeing men suffered terribly from cold and from the lack of food or water. Those who made it said they survived by catching snow in their uniforms and drinking the water as the snow melted. Survivors also said they had begged seed potatoes from the "slash-and-burn" nomad farmers in the mountains to stave off starvation.

I accompanied I Corps units attacking from Inje to Wontong and found the area to be completely deserted, suggesting that here, too, the enemy had run out of steam and withdrawn rapidly. In a single step we had recaptured the territory from the east coast through Kansong and on to Kojin, a line that very closely parallels today's demilitarized zone (DMZ).

The Chinese Army conducted its two spring offensives rashly and paid a high price for it as we dealt the Chinese the hardest blows they had felt since entering the war. The Chinese units successfully broke through our front line, and blinded by the earlier success of their tactics, their commanders ordered a flank attack. Their calamitous error stemmed from greed. Rather than be content to attack the left flank of ROK I Corps or the right flank of U.S. X Corps, the Chinese Army leaders foolishly elected to attack us both. Thus, the Chinese force itself fell victim to a double envelopment west of the Taebaek Mountains. The Chinese Army took such a beating in this battle that it was unable to recover for a long time. Perhaps the broadest hint of the kind of losses the Chinese suffered in these actions is that the Chinese Army never again launched one of its mammoth offensives.

The UN Command launched a counterattack on the western front while the Chinese Army concentrated its main force on us on the east. The UN counterattack carried all the way to the 38th parallel and relieved the pressure on Seoul.

I was proud of ROK I Corps. We absorbed the brunt of the enemy's attack at Taegwallyong and crushed it, and we switched over to the offensive smoothly and without delay. The battle was still in progress when I received a message to report to Kangnung's K-18 Airfield to meet General Van Fleet. I recall that the date was May 25, 1951. As Van Fleet disembarked from his aircraft, he didn't proceed directly to the waiting room as we expected. He made a beeline for the place where Army Chief of Staff Chung Il Kwon, Army Forward Command Post Director Lee Jun Sik, and I were standing stiffly at attention. His blunt words shocked me.

"General Chung," he began. "I hereby abolish ROK Army III Corps. And ROK Army Headquarters will no longer exercise any operational control. The mission of ROK Army Headquarters shall be limited to personnel, administrative, logistic, and training matters but shall not involve operations. ROK I Corps is hereby placed under my command, and the ROK Army Forward Command Post is abolished." The debacle of ROK III Corps had dealt a final, mortal blow to the pride of the Republic of Korea Army.

Van Fleet went on to inform us that he was attaching the ROK 9th Division to U.S. X Corps and the ROK 3d Division to me at I Corps. Then the American general was gone. He spent no more than ten minutes on the ground. The three of us were overwhelmed with dejection and went our separate ways without a word.

The ROK Army, however, did not lose its operational command authority as a result of this single incident. On July 14, 1950, President Syngman Rhee sent a "Letter in Regard to Transfer of Operational Authority" to Gen. Douglas MacArthur in which Rhee said, "To effectively repulse the aggression of the communist army," the command authority of the Republic of Korea's armed forces would pass to the UN Command. MacArthur accepted this three days later, on July 17, 1950. From that day forward, operational command authority of ROK forces passed to the UN Command, or rather to the U.S. Army, which possessed command authority over the UN Command.

In point of fact, however, neither MacArthur nor Walker, who commanded the UN Command and Eighth Army at the time, nor their successors, Ridgway and Van Fleet, chose to exercise the complete command authority President Rhee had ceded to them. Instead, they pursued the war in such a way that the ROK Army always exercised independent responsibility for a portion of the front, and they chose to exercise operational command over ROK Army corps only through ROK Army Headquarters.

Seizing the opportunity afforded by the collapse of ROK III Corps, the U.S. Army executed a major transformation in May 1951, labeling it a reorganization. Every frontline ROK Army division was attached to a U.S. Army corps. The only exceptions were the three divisions assigned to me at ROK I Corps, and we were made directly subordinate to Eighth Army.

Indeed, I Corps was the only ROK Army corps allowed to exist. ROK Army Headquarters was not abolished, but it remained an army headquarters in name only, stripped of even minimal operational functions.

It dawned on me very quickly that had I Corps performed badly in the fighting against the Chinese Army, we too would have been disbanded, and ROK Army would have prosecuted the war without a single unit larger than division.

These sweeping changes triggered a round of top-level personnel shifts within the ROK Army. Chief of Staff Chung Il Kwon stepped aside on June 24, 1951, and Maj. Gen. Lee Chong Chan became army chief of staff in his stead. ROK III Corps commander Maj. Gen. Yu Jae Hung became vice chief of staff, and Brig. Gen. Lee Jun Sik was appointed to be deputy chief of staff.

Concentrated Training for the ROK Army

In June 1951, the front ran from the Imjin River on the west of the Korean peninsula through Chorwon and Kumhwa and on to Kojin on the peninsula's extreme eastern flank.

In ROK I Corps, the Capital Division under Brig. Gen. Song Yo Chan held my left, or western, flank, and the 11th Division under Brig. Gen. Oh Duk Jun was positioned on my right flank along the east coast. The I Corps units occupied the northernmost point along the entire front and continued inching northward from that salient.

Although I Corps had advanced farther north than other friendly units, this had been accomplished with the U.S. Navy exercising control of the Sea of Japan all the way to Wonsan in North Korea and with the U.S. Air Force exercising total control of the air over North Korea. One could expect, then, that there was little chance for unilateral gains on the eastern front.

I moved my corps headquarters out of Kangnung again and into a copse of pine trees along the coast point north of Sokcho and commanded a battle in the Hyangno Mountain Range from that site. I then received from Van Fleet an order to prepare for a new operation called "Amphibious Operation Kojo." An enormous undertaking, Kojo was to involve four UN Command corps. The operation was to develop as follows.

My I Corps was to attack along the east coast to Kojo, a town some nineteen miles southeast of Wonsan. As we pushed north along the coast, the U.S. 9th Division at Chorwon would attack northward along the Seoul-Wonsan road. Meanwhile, U.S. X Corps on my left flank would attack through Mundung and follow the upper course of the Puk-han River north, skirting the Diamond Mountains along their western margin, and eventually join ROK I Corps in a final assault on Kojo. Finally, the two U.S. divisions comprising XVI Corps in Japan were to embark, cross the Sea of Japan, and conduct an amphibious assault on Kojo, linking up with friendly units attacking the city from the south.

The purpose of the operation was to flank and destroy the enemy strong points at the "Punchbowl" in Yanggu County and in the Diamond Mountains and to extend the front on the east coast to the 39th parallel. We called this area the Punchbowl because it was a big valley, or crater, surrounded by high ridge lines. This area was the most critical sector at that time, as we were fighting to secure dominant terrain.

I had already received orders to prepare for the mission and found my heart racing in anticipation of the order setting H-hour. But the mission itself was never ordered. Apparently Eighth Army commander James A. Van Fleet originated the idea for this operation but was unable to win approval from the UN commander, General Ridgway. This incident sent a clear signal that while we were to remain on the offensive, we were not to mount significant operations.

The same UN Command that had abandoned a northern advance that carried friendly forces to the Tumen and Yalu rivers would now pursue a single objective, an armistice. Another attack deep into North Korean territory would not help win a truce.

The war, then, entered a new stage, degenerating into a form of trench, or static, warfare. Each side strove to seize local terrain features advantageous to its tactical position while making no effort to extend the battle beyond the existing front along the 38th parallel. The situation resembled the one that prevailed on the western front during World War I.

I can't omit from this narrative statements made by the U.S. Navy about our war on the eastern front. Cruiser Division 5 of the U.S. Seventh Fleet under Vice Adm. Harold Martin, was on station in the Sea of Japan. Rear Adm. Arleigh Burke commanded Cruiser Division 5 from his flagship, the cruiser *Los Angeles*. Two Canadian destroyers were also attached to the division, in addition to its complement of U.S. Navy cruisers and destroyers. Occasionally a battleship—the *Missouri, New Jersey,* or *Idaho*—would take a turn on station with Division 5, even providing gunfire support to I Corps with its huge guns.

I would sometimes visit the *Los Angeles* and hold conferences with

Admiral Burke about coordinating naval fire support to ROK I Corps. Admiral Burke had commanded a destroyer in the Battle of the Solomons during the war in the Pacific and was a most capable naval commander. As a result of the "admirals' revolt" of 1949, Burke was ignominiously transferred to the Far East and was still there when the Korean War broke out.

The admirals' revolt occurred when Burke and other admirals opposed then U.S. Secretary of Defense Louis Johnson's assertion that "B-36 bombers will make aircraft carriers obsolete." Admiral Burke was an expert not only in destroyers and cruisers but also in air operations as well, and he had clear-cut rules on how the navy was to provide fire support to ground forces.

Admiral Burke's caliber as an officer can be understood when one knows that as soon as the Korean War ended in 1953, President Eisenhower promoted him directly to full admiral and made him chief of naval operations of the U.S. Navy, jumping him over fifty senior admirals in the process. Admiral Burke was to serve for six full years as head of the U.S. Navy. I have heard that the U.S. Navy recently named one of its Aegis-class destroyers the *Arleigh Burke*, after the admiral. This is always a signal honor, of course, but in this case it was the first time in U.S. history that the U.S. Navy named a destroyer after a living person.

Admiral Burke always assured me only half in jest, "I'm your corps artillery officer." He responded to my every request for fire support in the most gratifying and forthcoming ways possible.

As I look back now, I realize that during the Korean War I had the great good fortune to meet and fight beside some of the most outstanding soldiers and sailors the United States ever produced.

Admiral Burke recently mentioned me in an interview he gave to the Pulitzer prize–winning author John Toland, who was writing a book on Admiral Burke. The admiral kindly sent me a copy of his remarks, asking me to correct any textual errors. I'll quote from that text.

When I was with Cruiser Division 5, I remember something interesting happened. In May of that year [1951] my old friend Major General Paik Sun Yup was in command of the ROK Army's I Corps, the major friendly ground unit in the area, and was repulsing communist forces. ROK I Corps advanced north along the Sea of Japan, and I supported them with naval gunfire directed at the shore. The guns of our vessels were the only firepower available to Paik.

My cruisers were equipped with six- and eight-inch guns, and of course we had smaller guns on the destroyers and our machine cannon as well. We packed a lot of firepower.

The problem was that we had trouble putting this firepower where it was needed because neither Paik nor I had a ground control party. So I sent a number of my staff people to Paik's headquarters and told them, "Take along a radio and report back to me what Paik wants, tell me exactly where he wants us to place the fire." I did that because Paik made only general requests of us, but every day he requested that we fire all the ammunition that we had.

Paik had no concept of ammunition. And that's why I sent my staff officers over there on a rotation basis.

Paik spoke good English, and a large number of Korean officers knew English. Even so, we encountered immense problems with the language barrier.

I dropped in on Paik often, and he sometimes came out to see me on my flagship.

One day Paik sent me a message saying he expected Eighth Army commander General James A. Van Fleet to visit ROK I Corps headquarters, and Paik invited me to come too.

I told Paik that before I met Van Fleet I wanted to experience real ground combat and asked to accompany one of his night reconnaissance patrols. Paik said, "Great. Let's go together."

"Fine with me!" I said, "We'll make one hell of a flag officer recon patrol!" So the two of us ventured out with a patrol.

I foolishly traipsed into no-man's land wearing an alarm wristwatch set for 4 A.M. Sure enough, the watch's alarm went off, and sure enough the sound alerted the enemy, who began firing tracers off in every direction. We hunched down in trenches. I remember the area was zigzagged with a web of trenches.

Despite a long night that included exchanges of small arms fire with the enemy, none of our people were hit. But Paik never again let me go out on a reconnaissance patrol with his troops.

. . . Paik presented a briefing on the situation in his sector to Van Fleet. About the time I thought he was finishing up, Paik suddenly said, "We'll next hear a briefing from our artillery commander, Arleigh Burke." Paik had not given me any kind of advance notice, but I had no choice but stand up and wing my way through a briefing of sorts.

I was told at the time that a heavy round for a naval gun cost about the same as a Cadillac, America's finest automobile. While visiting the *Los Angeles*, I heard the sailors sing out in unison, "One more Cadillac on the way!" each time the officer gave the command to fire another salvo of the big guns. We would never let our men get away with that in the army. It was easy to see that the navy had its own customs.

I learned a bit about the U.S. Navy. A division commander on station was supported by a full complement of staff officers, including staff principals for intelligence, operations, and communications. The captains of battleships and cruisers always stayed on the bridge to command their ships, never leaving even to dine. Any wireless message received by a ship was taken first to the ship's captain. Sailors ate not three but four meals a day.

Although the U.S. Navy forbade the consumption of alcoholic beverages on its ships, the Canadian Navy had a more enlightened policy.

Thus, when I visited Burke's flagship, coming and going by launch, the Canadian destroyer captain would always invite me aboard, and I was most pleased to respond to his kind hospitality.

In any event, maintaining a very close relationship with Admiral Burke enabled us to execute the war on the east coast with that comfortable self-confidence that only absolute fire superiority can bestow on fighting infantry.

When Burke heard about my malaria, he sent his medical officers over, and they were able to cure completely the disease that had caused me such distress.

At this juncture, Eighth Army requested that the 1101st Engineer Group attached to ROK I Corps be tasked to build an airstrip at Taepo. The strip was to be used for forced landings by U.S. Navy carrier pilots whose planes were either hit by enemy antiaircraft fire or had been damaged in air-to-air combat and could not make it back to their ships. After the strip was finished, carrier aircraft in trouble did indeed land there from time to time. The strip has been expanded into the Sokcho Airport today.

After the ROK III Corps was dissolved, Eighth Army attached the ROK 3d Division to me. I assigned it a location in the rear, designated it as corps reserve, and set about in a concentrated way to rebuild the unit. Brig. Gen. Paik Nam Kwon replaced Kim Chong O as division commander. The ROK 3d Division was down to about a half of its usual complement of men and had lost nearly all its equipment. I filled the division with officer and enlisted replacements from the Cheju Training Center and requisitioned weapons from army headquarters in Taegu. It required a long time to restore the division to fighting trim.

Even before the defeat of ROK III Corps at Hyon-ri, the Republic of Korea Government and U.S. Army officials had agreed that increasing the combat capabilities of ROK Army units was a priority. The two sides differed greatly, however, on how to approach the task. President Rhee wanted the army expanded to twenty divisions from the current ten, and he repeatedly asked the Americans to supply him the equipment necessary to create the additional divisions. Neither Ridgway nor Van Fleet would accede to Rhee's requests because they believed that creating ten more divisions was a waste of money when the existing divisions could not perform adequately in combat. This argument was under way when the Chinese launched their spring offensives, and the ROK Army divisions' inability to fulfill their missions lent weight to the Americans' argument. Word trickled down to me that General of the Army Omar Bradley had gone so far as to suggest that American officers command Korean units.

President Rhee, meanwhile, insisted that the Americans were dead wrong. What was needed, he said, was not more competent commanders nor more training for existing units. What Korea needed was more soldiers and more equipment. Frankly, as a Korean soldier, the president's viewpoint embarrassed me so much I wanted to go hide.

Against this backdrop, the U.S. Army developed a program called Concentrated Training for the ROK Army. General Van Fleet had served as the commander of the U.S. Military Advisory Group to Greece at the end of World War II and had been instrumental in rebuilding the Greek Army, which had gone on to perform admirably in its war against communist guerrillas. An opportunity arose for him to use this experience in Korea.

As a first step, Van Fleet established the Field Training Command in July 1951. Brig. Gen. Thomas Cross, deputy commander of U.S. IX Corps, was put in charge, and Cross brought together a cadre of 150 U.S. officers and noncommissioned officers with experience at training. A training center was hastily constructed south of Sokcho, and the ROK 3d Division was the first unit to cycle through the new center. Training lasted nine weeks and consisted of basic individual, squad, platoon, and company training. The center started from scratch, assuming nobody knew anything. Every man in a division, with the exception of its commander, was required to undergo the training, and when the training was over, a unit had to pass a test before being assigned to the front. The ROK 3d Division completed the course, passed its test, and was attached to U.S. X Corps at the front.

After the 3d Division completed its training, each Korean combat division took its turn in the training cycle. By the end of 1952, all ten ROK Army divisions had completed the training. Units that completed the course lost 50 percent fewer men and equipment in combat than did units that had not had the training. Furthermore, divisions that completed the course and returned to the front revealed an élan and confidence quite superior to what they had shown before going through the training. No one can deny that this training of virtually the entire force provided a firm foundation for today's ROK Army.

After consulting with Army Chief of Staff Lee Chong Chan, Van Fleet established a Staff School in Taegu in December 1951 and created a four-year Military Academy in Chinhae in January 1952. Korea's West Point was under way.

In late 1951 ROK Army officers were selected and sent to attend short-term, foreign officer training courses in the United States. Of these, 250 went to the U.S. Army Infantry School at Fort Benning, and 100 went to the U.S. Army Artillery School at Fort Sill. The command skills of these officers improved so dramatically that the program was repeated yearly thereafter.

Van Fleet's emphasis on training sparked the rapid maturation of the ROK Army, progress that appeared in numerous concrete ways on the battlefield. One of the most obvious of these was the steady increase in the proportion of the front line under direct control of ROK Army. By the time the armistice was signed, we controlled two-thirds of the front.

During the summer of 1951, Minister of Defense Lee Ki Poong and then President Rhee himself visited ROK I Corps to encourage the troops. During Minister Lee's visit, I noticed that he was very correct in his speech patterns when he spoke to me, assiduously avoiding any suggestion of familiar terms. I thought he was probing my attitude, because Lee was many years my senior and had no need to adhere to formal speech. "Mr. Minister," I finally told him. "Please feel free to drop the honorific forms and address me without my title."

Minister Lee looked at me with a very serious expression on his face. "General," he said, using full honorific terms of address. "If you were a child I would use honorifics to you, for you command thousands of our Korean boys." Minister Lee provided 500,000 won as a token of appreciation to each unit in the corps.

Lee Ki Poong met a tragic end as Korean college students overthrew the Syngman Rhee regime on April 19, 1960, but I remember him from the early days when he was a most humble and most considerate human being.

Life does not abandon its regular rhythms during war. Even when fighting was at its peak, for example, the fishermen of Korea's east coast continued to set out to sea to bring in the catch, sailing from the little fishing ports that dotted the coast. I was utterly amazed at their tenacity and the toughness of their life-style.

The east coast was crowded with refugees who had fled from North Korea's Hamgyong provinces and the northern areas of Kangwon Province. For many months a steady stream of small boats filled with refugees from the north found their way into east coast ports, adding even more homeless refugees to our crowded urban areas.

During that period of the war, the civilian government administered territory south of the 38th parallel, but the army administered territory north of the parallel under martial law. Thus, I was martial law commander for the area north of Yangyang on the east coast, exercising this duty through my civil affairs staff.

As the front stabilized very near where the DMZ runs today, martial law remained in force for a protracted period. This resulted in a number of cases of malfeasance, which in turn aroused public irritation. Indeed, some sarcastically referred to the area under martial law as "*So-han Min-guk.*" This pun derives from the name for Korea in our language, "*Tae-han Min-guk,*" or the "Republic of Greater Han." "Han" was the name of several ancient states located in the south-central area of the Korean peninsula. Fed up with military government, civilian residents of areas north of the 38th parallel reflected what they regarded as their second-class status by referring to the region as the "Republic of Lesser Han." I regret the errors we made.

6

WHAT WILL WE LOSE, AND WHAT WILL WE GAIN?

Representing Korea at Armistice Talks No Korean Wants

Admiral Burke came over to see me at ROK I Corps Headquarters in early July 1951. "I've received a communication ordering me to report to Japan for something important," he told me and said he had dropped over to say good-bye. Burke had been selected to be a delegate at armistice talks that were to begin soon, and one week later I would join him as a fellow delegate, but neither of us realized it as we said our farewells.

The day after Admiral Burke's visit, Eighth Army commander General Van Fleet visited the area, and I received a message directing me to meet him at Kansong, outside my corps sector. On the way to Kansong, I couldn't help wonder why Van Fleet wanted to see me and decided it must be something important to pull me out of my unit sector.

Van Fleet invited me to share the sandwiches he'd had prepared for lunch. After touching on the domestic situation and developments in the war, he said, "Have you heard that armistice talks are to get under way soon? You do speak Chinese, right?" But that was all. He seemed to have nothing else to say and soon departed.

Of course at this point in the war, we all had been hearing talk about an armistice. But as a corps commander I was primarily concerned that my troops fight up to the mark, defending the sector of the front for which I Corps was responsible. I was, therefore, not as acutely interested in talk of an armistice as others. Indeed, my sole reaction was concern that the communists would dupe an overanxious United States of America, which had grown weary of the war and wanted a truce.

The next day I received another unusual communication, this time in the form of a telephone call from Army Chief of Staff Lee Chong Chan. Lee told me that armistice talks were about to begin and that the UN Command had requested that I sit in on the talks as the representative of the Republic of Korea military. I was to continue to serve as corps commander but was to designate my deputy, Brig. Gen. Chang Chang Kuk, as acting corps commander. I was to proceed immediately to Pusan and report directly to President Syngman Rhee.

Jacob Malik, the Soviet Union's deputy foreign minister and ambassador to the United Nations, first suggested an armistice on America's CBS radio network on June 23, 1951. The precise time in Korea was 6:15 A.M. on June 24. Commander in chief of UN Command Gen. Ridgway responded to Malik on June 30, formally proposing to the communist side that armistice talks be held aboard the *Jutlandia*, a Danish hospital ship permanently berthed in the North Korean port of Wonsan. Both sides agreed to hold the first round of talks at Kaesong on July 10, 1951, after a Radio Beijing broadcast on July 1 counterproposed that city as the site for armistice talks. Kaesong was in North Korea, just north of the front line above Munsan, northwest of Seoul.

I flew to Pusan by light aircraft on July 8 and went to the temporary presidential mansion. I was ushered in to see the president and gave him a short briefing. He seemed to be in an evil humor, and my report did not cheer him up a whit. President Rhee expressed his dissatisfaction in exceptionally blunt terms. "The Americans," he said, "want an armistice. One million Chinese troops on the peninsula, and they want an armistice. It's ridiculous. Our goal is unification. If we seek an armistice now, we accede to national division. I categorically oppose a truce."

I was shocked. I was to be, then, the representative of the Republic of Korea to armistice talks that the president himself had just told me he adamantly opposed. There was only one thing I could say. "Your Excellency, I'm a soldier. The honorable chief of staff directed me to attend the armistice talks, but now that I understand your position on the matter, I will refuse to participate."

President Rhee took that in. "No," he said after a pause. "The Americans will go through with it in any case, so you've got to go along. . . . You attend the talks. I intend to cooperate with these Americans."

After meeting with President Rhee, I flew up to Taegu to discuss the armistice talks with Army Chief of Staff Lee Chong Chan before I flew on to Munsan. General Lee told me that he had assigned Col. Lee Su Yong to join me as a member of the liaison team and an assistant.

I knew Munsan only too well. I had fought repeatedly in the area with the ROK 1st Division, withdrawing twice through the city and advancing twice back through it. Now I was returning to a battlefield where large numbers of my comrades had been killed at the hands of the same men with whom I had to discuss a truce. I did not feel any too secure, either, for I was acting solely on the basis of verbal orders and, in fact, never did receive a written document of appointment.

Those involved in the armistice talks were accommodated in a tent village near a stream in an apple orchard east of Munsan. The village was called "Peace Camp."

Vice Adm. Charles Turner Joy, commander, Naval Forces, Far East, had been appointed as chief delegate from the UN Command. The other UN delegates were Maj. Gen. Henry I. Hodes, Eighth Army chief of staff; Maj. Gen. Laurence C. Craigie, vice commander, Far East Air Forces; Rear Adm. Arleigh Burke, deputy chief of staff, Naval Forces, Far East; and, of course, myself.

Apart from the official delegates, a separate liaison team was responsible for contacts with the communist side regarding practical arrangements for the talks. The team was composed of U.S. Air Force Col. Andrew Kinney, U.S. Marine Corps Col. James Murray, and Col. Lee Su Yong. English-Korean interpreting was provided by the Underwood brothers, sons of the founder of Yonsei University, who were both serving as company-grade officers in the U.S. military. English-Chinese interpreting was handled by Lieutenant Wu, a Chinese-American officer who later rose to the rank of colonel. Two men served as interpreters from the communist side, a Chinese soldier and the NKPA's Sol Chong Sik. Brig. Gen. Leven Allen, deputy commander of the U.S. 1st Cavalry Division, was assigned as public affairs officer. Along with specialists in international law and others, Peace Camp boasted a population of about one hundred souls.

The atmosphere in Peace Camp seemed relatively optimistic, perhaps reflecting the irrepressible optimism that seems to characterize the American people. I overheard Americans making remarks like, "I think we'll have the negotiations wrapped up in ten days or so." I saw no reason for such optimism but decided the Americans must believe that the negotiations would reach an early conclusion because they were to be conducted by military men, who are known for frankness and simplicity. I decided to speak out, telling one and all that I thought the talks with the communist side would prove exceptionally difficult. I noticed, however, that no one paid much attention to me.

Our delegation held a brief meeting on the morning of July 10, 1951, then boarded helicopters to travel to Kaesong, site of the talks. General Ridgway delivered a brief speech to the delegation at Peace Camp before we left. "We are a great country," he said. "Be dignified. Deal with them openly and honestly." He repeated these same points a number of times and personally saw us off. As we left Peace Camp that morning, each member of our delegation was provided a hand mirror. If an emergency arose, we were to use the mirrors to signal a standby aircraft, and a rescue team would be on the way instantly.

The liaison officer teams of both sides had held earlier contacts and after some complications had agreed on a location and date for the first formal negotiating session. We had agreed to hold the talks at Naebong-jang, a traditional Korean mansion in northeast Kaesong not far from Sonju bridge. Kaesong, of course, lay north of the front, totally within enemy territory.

A nearby facility, the Ginseng Pavilion, had been designated for use by the UN delegation as an advanced base. Our helicopters landed near this building, and we walked over to join our support group, which had come up overland; then we boarded jeeps and drove to nearby Naebongjang. In prior times, Kaesong had been the only place the king permitted the cultivating of ginseng. Naebongjang was a classical, 3,564-square-foot Korean mansion. The structure was the maximum size allowed outside the royal palace during the Yi dynasty, whose kings ruled Korea from 1392 until the Japanese annexed Korea in 1910. The once grand Naebongjang, however, had been damaged badly by bombs earlier in the war, and one could watch the clouds scurry across the sky through the holes in the ceiling of the main building.

A rectangular table was set up in the house, and the historic first meeting got under way.

The communist delegation was composed of three Koreans: Lt. Gen. Nam Il, chief delegate and NKPA general chief of staff; Maj. Gen. Lee Sang Cho; and Maj. Gen. Chang Pyong San. Two delegates represented the Chinese Army: Teng Hua, deputy commander of the Chinese Army; and Chieh Fang, chief of staff and political commissar of the Chinese Army.

Admiral Joy sat in the middle of our delegation, facing Nam Il across the table. I sat at Admiral Joy's right, confronting Lee Sang Cho. The first meeting was frigid, with neither side shaking hands or offering any form of verbal greeting. Ten people faced each other across the table, five from each delegation, but only the chief delegates spoke. The meeting proceeded with each and every statement interpreted by turns into Korean, English, and Chinese.

The first meeting addressed the issue of a future agenda for the talks. In his first statement Admiral Joy tabled a condition for our participation. "The fighting shall continue during the course of the talks," he said. The admiral then went on to suggest that agenda items include demarcating an armistice line, exchanging prisoners of war, and the manner in which the armistice itself could be executed and guaranteed. Nam Il said he wanted the withdrawal of foreign forces on the agenda as well.

The UN side promptly opposed this, saying that withdrawal of foreign troops was a political issue and thus did not fall within the purview of truce talks held between military authorities. This item, Admiral Joy said, was one that could be discussed at a distinct venue, such as separate political talks. The communist side doggedly insisted that foreign troop withdrawal be included on the agenda.

The meeting droned on for hours. I had nothing to do all that time but remain seated and stare at the man across the table from me. I had no reason to be pleased if the talks went smoothly, and I had no reason to be disappointed if they didn't. Indeed, I felt quite certain my government would be pleased if negotiations foundered.

Our delegation returned to Peace Camp without having hammered out an agreement on a single agenda item. Once again I laid out my position to the others. To do my duty as a member of the delegation, I had to confront not my enemies sitting across from me at the negotiating table but my allies sitting on the UN Command side of the table.

I believe the communists seized the initiative in the negotiations from that very first day. Enemy troops were positioned around Naebongjang to provide security and to act as guides. As a result, when we entered the negotiating site, we could not escape the intimidation one feels when entering an armed enemy camp. Moreover, the communists had their chairs made so that they were higher than ours, their flag on the table was taller than ours, and only communist journalists were allowed to cover the talks. The communist side had stage-managed the entire environment in such a way as to give the impression that they had won the war. The UN delegation would later address each of these concrete expressions of one-upsmanship, but enormous amounts of time would be wasted in the process.

On July 12, 1951, for example, negotiations broke down for four days on the issue of whether to allow Western reporters equal access to the talks. We insisted that no international talks from which freeworld journalists were barred could have any significance. Talks began again only after the communists allowed UN-side reporters to enter Kaesong.

Even before agenda items had been hammered out, the two sides began to focus on the major point of dispute: where to draw the truce line. Admiral Joy advocated that the truce line be drawn along the present battle line, but Nam Il disagreed, stubbornly insisting that his side could accept only the 38th parallel as the demarcation line for a cease-fire.

The front at that time ran from Kaesong to Chorwon to Kumhwa and on to Kojin. Except for a short segment on the western front, the line was far north of the 38th parallel. To accept the 38th parallel as the armistice line would mean we would actually have to pull back our units. Moreover, communist forces had not recovered from the heavy blows we had delivered during their abortive spring offensives, and the UN Command was quite capable, militarily, of continuing to advance even farther north.

In effect, the UN Command had chosen to trade the option of mounting our own offensive in return for the presence of the communists at the negotiating table. This was accomplished through the simple expe-

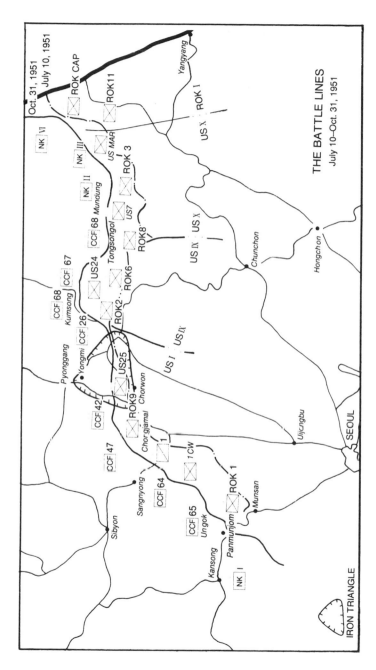

THE BATTLE LINES
July 10—Oct. 31, 1951

Oct. 31, 1951
July 10, 1951

ROK CAP
ROK 11
Yangyang
US X : ROK 1

NK VI
NK III
US MAR
ROK 3
NK II
CCF 68 Mundung
US 7
ROK 8
US 24
Tongsongol
CCF 67
ROK 6
ROK 2
CCF 68 Kumsong
CCF 26
Pyonggang
Yongmi
US 25
US IX : US X
US IX : US X
Chunchon
Hongchon
US I : US IX
ROK 9 Chorwon
US 1
CCF 42
Chorgjamal
CCF 47
1
1 CW
Sangnyong
CCF 64
Uijongbu
CCF 65 Ungok
ROK 1
SEOUL
Sibyon
Panmunjom
Munsan
Kansong
NK I

IRON TRIANGLE

169

dient of stating publicly in Korea and overseas that we would not launch another large-scale attack.

Yet the communist side demanded retreat. Nam Il became a tape recorder, repeating the following phrases over and over, ad nauseam: "The 38th parallel is recognized internationally and served as our border before the war. It is therefore appropriate that the armistice line be drawn at the 38th parallel." Each time Nam reiterated this demand, Admiral Joy rejoined with, "Don't try to recover at this table what you lost on the battlefield."

Sitting and watching the pointless discussion drag on endlessly amounted to incredibly toilsome labor for me. Moreover, I wasn't able to rid myself of the uneasy feeling that the impatient U.S. Army would accept something disadvantageous just to move the negotiations off dead center. One significant problem, I believe, was that neither delegation enjoyed the discretionary authority either to table a proposal or to react to a proposal made by the other side. The UN Command side, to be sure, communicated to the U.S. Joint Chiefs of Staff in Washington and to command headquarters in Tokyo every day, conveying details of the day's talks and receiving directions on how to proceed.

To maintain these communications, in fact, the Americans brought in the most advanced mobile communication equipment available and set it up at Peace Camp. Mounted in covered trucks, this equipment was so sophisticated that it allowed direct, two-way cable communications with both Tokyo and Washington. The communications gear at Peace Camp and in Tokyo and Washington included cathode-ray tubes on which a cable immediately appeared as it was transmitted for easy deciphering.

This equipment allowed the U.S. military negotiators to receive directions regarding the talks with very little delay. By contrast, however, each time an issue arose that the communist delegation could not handle on its own, its members would request a recess. Sometimes days would elapse before the delegation received authoritative directions and sued to reconvene the talks.

It took a full ten days to agree on the relatively few agenda items. Meanwhile, I was receiving no directions whatsoever from the Korean government. Nor was I asked to submit summaries of the talks, either to army headquarters or to the government.

The Republic of Korea government's position on the armistice talks was enunciated by Foreign Minister Pyon Yong Tae before the talks began. It consisted of the following five points.

1. The Communist Chinese Army must withdraw across the border between Manchuria and Korea, completely exiting the Korean peninsula, and this withdrawal must be executed in such a way as to bring no damage or injury to the property or lives of Korean civilians.

2. The North Korean Puppet Army must surrender its arms.

3. The United Nations must agree to prevent any third country from providing military, financial, or any other kind of aid to the communist party in North Korea.

4. An official Republic of Korea representative must attend any international conference or meeting at which the Korean issue is to be discussed, in whole or in part.

5. We will not recognize the legal force of any action or proposal which violates either the territory or the sovereignty of the Republic of Korea.

Doubtless the communists found these conditions difficult to accept. Certainly the UN side did.

On July 2, 1951, Brig. Gen. Kim Chong-myon, ROK Army Headquarters G-2, visited me at Peace Camp. Kim later brought by Defense Minister Lee Ki Poong, Army Chief of Staff Lee Chong Chan, Chief of Naval Operations Sohn Won Il, and Air Force Chief of Staff Kim Chung Yul. These men all discussed my official duties with me and invariably went out of their way to cheer me up.

I remember Chief of Staff Lee Chong Chan handed me a copy of *Korean History,* by Master Yukdang, Choi Nam Son, during his visit and suggested that I read it. I chose to interpret Lee's action as a warning that I should be cautious in the ongoing talks because Korean history already included sufficient examples of forced peace treaties, as in the Japanese invasions under Hideyoshi in 1592 and the subsequent Manchu invasion.

I was obliged to protest to my fellow UN delegates a number of times, the first in regard to my country's name. The Americans had prepared a study paper in which our country's name appeared each and every time as "South Korea." I discovered this just before the first negotiating session was to begin and requested that the document be changed to reflect our formal name, the Republic of Korea, and this change was made before the meeting began.

Two or three negotiating sessions had been held when Defense Minister Lee Ki Poong paid me a visit. "Our government's position is that the Chinese Army must withdraw from the Korean peninsula before we can agree to an armistice," he told me in no uncertain terms. "We oppose any other formula."

In view of what President Syngman Rhee had told me earlier and with Minister Lee Ki Poong's clear statement ringing in my ears, I felt I had to make my position clear to the other members of the delegation. As a first step, I sought out Admiral Burke, with whom I was well acquainted, and explained my government's views, adding that I agreed with them. "Our government," I said, "opposes these talks. As the delegate from the Korean side, it will be difficult for me to continue to attend the sessions." Admiral Burke heard me out and then advised me to discuss the matter with our chief delegate, Admiral Joy.

I immediately requested an interview with Joy. In view of the importance of the subject, I took Col. Lee Su Yong along with me to ensure accurate interpreting. My news obviously flustered the admiral. "At the present moment," he said, "not just the communist nations but the entire world is hanging on everything that happens here. We may harm our cause if we do anything that suggests that we harbor disharmony within our delegation." Turner then pointedly emphasized, "You fall under the command of General Ridgway, commander in chief of the United Nations Command." I stuck to my guns, and Admiral Joy made a final request. "Please continue to attend the sessions until I can report this matter to General Ridgway and get a response from him."

The Truce Talks Falter

Two or three days after I presented my position to Admiral Turner, Defense Minister Lee returned to Peace Camp to see me. He gave me a letter from President Rhee. Written in English, the gist of the letter was, "Although I don't want the United Nations side to make any kind of agreement that will leave Korea divided, I request that you cooperate with the United Nations side and continue to attend the sessions of the armistice talks." I could only assume that the letter had resulted from consultations between President Rhee, U.S. Ambassador John J. Muccio, and General Ridgway.

I decided that the events leading up to the letter had boosted my clout as a delegate and that I should use that clout to convey Korean government desires to the UN Command side. From then on, I did just that, and a number of such points were reflected in our negotiating position.

General Ridgway visited Peace Camp from his headquarters in Tokyo from time to time, and I spoke with him frequently. For instance, I met with the general at a point in the talks when we had set aside the agenda problem and were involved in a daily tug-of-war on the issue of where to draw the armistice line. "The communist side clings to its obstinate demand that the armistice line be drawn at the 38th parallel," I told the general. "We've got to stop insisting that we demarcate along the present front and demand instead that the line be drawn much farther north, between Pyongyang and Wonsan. That will get their attention."

I was trying to drive home to Ridgway the point that since the communists presented us with illogical, insistent demands inherently disadvantageous to our interests, we might as well adopt the same negotiating tactic. Moreover, I was certain the UN Command could launch a limited attack to the Pyongyang-Wonsan line with reasonable certainty of success.

Ridgway disagreed. "So long as we have not in fact reached such a line," he argued, "it is meaningless to demand a truce line that far north." Ridgway also said he was reluctant to authorize an assault with that line as an objective because an offensive of that magnitude would generate too many casualties. He added that he definitely did not have enough troops to launch a general attack along the entire front, nor did he have sufficient bridging materials to maintain the supply lines to support such a large-scale offensive.

I pointed out to the general that even if we chose not to push north to the Pyongyang-Wonsan line, we couldn't accept an armistice where the front now stood because it would make a "dead river" out of the Han River, which flowed, after all, through the middle of our capital city. I told Ridgway that even if I had to abandon any idea of advancing to the Pyongyang-Wonsan line, I believed strongly that we had to push on and recapture the Yesong River, which would free up the Han. He rejected this idea on the same grounds as my other idea. Unlike MacArthur, Ridgway faithfully supported his government's every position, refusing to budge a single inch from U.S. policy.

During the talks at the Peace Camp, I once got in an argument with him over the issue of Korean unification. I repeatedly argued that Korea had a long tradition as a unified country and that a basic condition for an armistice should be the preservation of national unity. I don't know where he heard it, but Ridgway's rejoinder was that Korea had not always been unified. Speaking from memory and using Japanese pronunciation, Ridgway said that Korea once had been composed of several states, and then he mentioned the ancient southern kingdoms of Mahan, Chinhan, and Pyonhan. He added that Korea had been three distinct states for centuries during the Three Kingdoms period.

Ridgway did not agree with the points I made, as I have described them above, but he did not completely ignore them either. On July 31, 1951, Ridgway issued an announcement: "In view of the existing ground, air, and naval fronts, the truce line must be demarcated somewhere in an area extending from the Yalu River to the line running between Kaesong and Pyonggang which presently marks the existing battlefront between our ground forces." Ridgway's logic was that when the UN Command's air and naval superiority were factored in, any military demarcation line would have to be drawn farther north than the existing front.

Ridgway chose to make this statement after the tenth session of the talks, held July 26, 1951, when the two sides issued the following five-point agreement.

1. Adopting the agenda.
2. Fixing a military demarcation line between both sides so as to establish

a demilitarized zone as the basic condition for cessation of hostilities in Korea.

3. Making concrete arrangements for the realization of cease-fire and armistice in Korea, including the composition, authority, and functions of a supervisory organ for carrying out the terms of cease-fire and armistice.
4. Determining arrangements relating to prisoners of war.
5. Making recommendations to the governments of the countries concerned on both sides.

Both sides yielded on points they had previously espoused in order to hammer out their agreement. In item number four, the UN side had stopped insisting on the phrase ''International Red Cross to visit prison camps,'' while the communist side abandoned the term ''38th parallel'' in item number two and set aside its demand for ''withdrawal of foreign troops.'' The agreed agenda did not include the communist side's explicit ''38th parallel'' and ''withdrawal of foreign troops'' notions, but their absence from the formal agenda in no way suggested that the communists had abandoned their dogged advocacy of these issues.

Indeed, when item two was raised in the very next negotiating session, Nam Il came out in thundering advocacy of these points, demanding them even more fervidly than before. This duplicity, in fact, caused Ridgway to choose that moment to issue his statement.

Ridgway no doubt aimed his statement not just at the communist side but at the Republic of Korea government as well. Each believed the UN Command was likely to surrender to the communist delegation's stubborn, tough, and incessant demands that the truce line be drawn at the 38th parallel.

Be this as it may, the UN Command used General Ridgway's statement to signal the end of the gentlemanly, stop-the-war-at-any-cost attitude of its negotiators. The UN Command delegates began to confront the communist side with an intensity they had not displayed before.

The Korean government, meanwhile, put out the word that I would resign from the delegation to block the UN side from giving away the farm, as we thought it was about to do. Demonstrations opposing an armistice erupted all across Korea at the same time.

The many negotiating sessions held during this period focused on the military demarcation line, yet the two sides were not able to take a single step toward agreement. The situation degenerated until the talks were recessed for an indeterminate period on August 23, 1951.

In point of fact, the communist side halted the talks unilaterally, claiming falsely that UN Command aircraft had bombed the neutral zone around Kaesong. Before this allegation, however, on August 4, 1951, the UN Command side halted the talks for six days, justifying our unilateral move on the grounds that a company-sized Chinese Army force had violated the neutral zone around the negotiating site.

I had personal knowledge that our charge was based on fact. The UN

Command delegation spent the morning of August 4 at the negotiating table, broke for lunch, and returned to the Ginseng Pavilion to dine. The entire delegation was standing at the entrance to the building when we witnessed an amazing breach of the neutrality. A communist Chinese Army unit in single file boldly marched past us at a distance of three hundred meters. The soldiers carried personal weapons, machine guns, and mortars. The communist side eventually acknowledged the incident, labeled it an anomaly, and apologized for it. Whereupon we agreed to return to the table after a six-day lapse.

The three North Korean delegates had feigned sternness since the first day of the talks, setting their faces in impassive grimaces throughout the endless hours at the table. If anything, Nam Il was worse than the others, wearing a mask of studied anger and smoking cigarettes in a steady stream. My counterpart, Lee Sang Cho, was a hard-bitten case as well. One day after an intense clash of views between the chief delegates, each asked the other only: "Doesn't your side have anything to say?" These two questions were followed by a solid hour of stubborn silence at the table. During this time, Lee Sang Cho scribbled something on a piece of paper with a red pencil and then carefully turned the paper so I could read it. He had written, "You running dogs of the imperialists are as worthless as a gutter bitch."

I was enraged. I wanted to jump up and smash the man with my fist. I couldn't believe the intense anger his craven act triggered in me. I let none of this show on my face, however, and I made no move against Lee. All I could think was that the sole path for Korea was to expand our economy and build the strength necessary to beat the North Koreans.

In stark contrast to the North Koreans, the two Chinese delegates were pleasant enough and often flashed curious smiles, which we came to call "Chinese smiles." Chieh Fang was especially careful to avoid damaging his counterpart's honor, and indeed we came to suspect that Chieh Fang was the most powerful individual on their delegation. General Craigie sat opposite Chieh and asked me to teach him how to greet the Chinese delegate in his own language.

I taught him to say *Nihaoma?* (How are you?) and *Jintien tienchi hunhao?* (How's the weather today?) Starting with the very next session, General Craigie used these Chinese terms to greet Chieh Fang at the beginning of each session. Chieh always responded with a smile. In this dreary series of talks, these two were the only participants who ever displayed the slightest civility.

Return to the Front

Once the armistice talks had fallen into a predictable pattern, the UN Command responded to insincere attitudes on the part of the communist delegates by stepping up attacks on the battlefield.

On August 18, 1951, the UN Command launched one such attack, with the Punchbowl as its objective. Immediately after the talks collapsed on August 24, I got a call at Peace Camp from Gen. James A. Van Fleet from his new headquarters in Seoul's Tongsung Subward in what had been the administration building of Seoul National University. Van Fleet directed me to report to ROK I Corps the next day.

The call caused me to worry that ROK I Corps was not pulling its weight in the attack launched the previous week at the Punchbowl, and I immediately rode down to Eighth Army Headquarters to talk with Van Fleet. Justifying my concern, the Eighth Army commander informed me that ROK I Corps was advancing at snail's pace.

We immediately jumped in a light observation aircraft at a strip in Sinsol Subward outside Seoul's East Gate at the site of a former horse-racing track. We flew to Kansong and made our way straight to the ROK 11th Division. Its headquarters were east of Chinburyong.

Van Fleet called a conference at the 11th's headquarters. Attendees included Van Fleet, myself, U.S. X Corps commander Maj. Gen. Clovis Byers, ROK I Corps deputy commander Brig. Gen. Chang Chang Kuk, ROK 11th Division commander Brig. Gen. Oh Duk Jun, and Col. Kong Kuk Chin, ROK I Corps G-3.

The situation on the front had developed as follows. A temporary lull settled over the entire front as the armistice talks got under way. But Van Fleet believed that Eighth Army had to retake the Punchbowl and other crucial terrain on the eastern front. The Punchbowl was as crucial to the eastern front as the Iron Triangle was to the central front, and capturing it would be an outstanding way to underscore our military dominance. Cognizant of the value of the terrain, the enemy had concentrated no fewer than six divisions in the area, was building strong points at an accelerated rate, and was fortifying its lines.

ROK I Corps had initiated its assigned attack on August 18, following an operational concept that was simple enough on paper. ROK I Corps was to maintain its defenses on the east coast and at the same time attack west from Hyangno Peak toward the Punchbowl. Meanwhile, U.S. X Corps was to attack north from Yanggu toward the same objective. ROK I Corps was to hold the high ground east of the objective, while U.S. X Corps polished it off.

I was still on duty at the armistice talks when the operation began, and my deputy, Brig. Gen. Chang Chang Kuk was in command. ROK I Corps attacked in the most rugged, and steep terrain in South Korea, with Brig. Gen. Song Yo Chan's Capital Division on the right and the 11th Division on the left. The Capital Division seized its objective, Hill 924, and managed to drive off a series of determined enemy counterattacks.

The 11th didn't fare so well. It took Hill 884, its objective, not once but three separate times, but couldn't hold it. Each time a strong enemy counterattack pushed the division back down from the objective. Such combat is always exceptionally bloody, and the fighting here was no exception. The 11th finally withdrew across the Nam River, the major waterway in the Diamond Mountains, and left the enemy atop Hill 884 on the other side of the river.

I returned to ROK I Corps, familiarized myself with developments, and determined that the light 105mm howitzers organic to my divisions lacked the firepower to neutralize the enemy's new, covered fighting positions. I told Van Fleet we had to have 155mm howitzers if we were to reduce casualties and keep the 11th Division on its objective. His response was something like, where in hell did I expect him to come up with 155mm guns.

New X Corps commander Major General Byers was present, and so I casually suggested that X Corps might be able to provide us 155mm support. The words weren't out of my mouth before naked alarm swept Byers's face. The X Corps attack was bogging down too, he insisted, contrary to expectations, and he wasn't in a position at the moment to provide 155mm support to I Corps.

Too late. Van Fleet ordered him to do just that, and in no uncertain terms. The next day a battery of 155mm howitzers—six tubes—arrived at the 11th Division. The cloud cover lifted the same day. We placed a 155mm howitzer barrage on the enemy hill and took advantage of the improved visibility to request close air support from U.S. naval aircraft flying from an aircraft carrier in the Sea of Japan. A struggle that had delayed the ROK 11th Division for ten bloody days ended in ten minutes, and we occupied all the high ground necessary to bring the Punchbowl under direct observation.

When I left Peace Camp, I assumed I was returning to ROK I Corps temporarily and would be back at the negotiating table soon. Wrong. Ridgway and Van Fleet decided to use the opportunity afforded by my return to the front to keep me there permanently, where I could concentrate solely on combat. Having made this decision, the U.S. military side went to great lengths to implement it.

The following extracts come from *Negotiating while Fighting: The Diary of Admiral C. Turner Joy at the Korean Armistice Conference*, a compendium of notes and diary entries made by Admiral Joy during the armistice negotiations and edited and published later.

Aug. 27 (Mon): . . . Late in p.m. received msg from R. [Ridgway] that he would like to see me at Kimpo [Airfield, near Seoul] at 1815. . . . He [Ridgway] also announced General Paik would remain permanently with his Corps and not return to conference as he was sorely needed in fighting.

Sept. 1 (Sat): Muccio [U.S. Ambassador to Korea] arrived at 12:45. After lunch we discussed Paik's release from delegation and how it would be best to announce it in press. As result I sent msg to Ridgway suggesting only that appointment of Lee as alternate for Paik be announced and that no direct announcement of Paik's return to his Corps made. Muccio was afraid, and I concurred, that if announcement was made that Paik was relieved it would create misgivings in eyes of Korean people.

These gentlemen went to such lengths and obviously were concerned about my attitude because, of course, when I was appointed as a delegate to the armistice talks I had hinted that I might resign as a way of expressing my government's views. There were genuine military reasons to restore me to command at ROK I Corps, however, so it seems ironic that they were so concerned that my leaving the armistice delegation might be perceived by outsiders as evidence of discord among the U.S. and Korean delegates.

I never got an opportunity to turn over my armistice duties to my replacement, or even share my insights with him.

The armistice was signed on July 27, 1953, almost two years after I left Peace Camp. By that time I was chief of staff of the army and had to deal with the truce from that perspective.

Fighting continued along the static front during the entire time the two sides sat down at the negotiating table, and many men were to die before the guns fell silent. Surely this must stand as one of the most lengthy truce negotiations in world history.

After I returned to ROK I Corps, our sector of the front at the east coast continued in a temporary lull. By the middle of October 1951, however, U.S. X Corps on our flank was locked in fierce fighting to capture the Punchbowl and nearby valley. The U.S. 1st Marine Division under Maj. Gen. Gerald Thomas and the ROK 1st Marine Regiment under Col. Kim Dae Sik were the major players for U.S. X Corps in the battle for the Punchbowl area, and both units gave outstanding accounts of themselves.

Heavy fighting occurred at a place called Heartbreak Ridge located west of the Punchbowl and north of Yanggu. The fighting in that sector centered on the U.S. 2d Division, with the ROK 7th Division under Brig. Gen. Lee Sung Ga and the ROK 5th Division under Brig. Gen. Min Ki Sik joining in the fighting on right and left.

The battles at the Punchbowl and Heartbreak Ridge by elements of U.S. X Corps were the last battles of maneuver ever fought in the Korean War. The UN Command recaptured the crucial Punchbowl area from the enemy but paid a heavy price in blood.

The fighting proved costly because the truce talks had provided communist forces time to reorganize their units and harden their fighting positions. The negotiations granted the priceless gift of a full uninterrupted month to the communist forces, and the UN Command paid a horrendous price as a result. Thereafter, the UN Command avoided large-scale combat operations for the duration of the war.

I Corps had full responsibility for the eastern front, and even after the front stabilized elsewhere, we continued to struggle to gain every inch of ground we could.

A glance at a map will reveal that we succeeded. The armistice line, or DMZ, does not proceed directly eastward from Hyangno Peak to the Sea of Japan, the sector under I Corps control. Instead the DMZ juts almost directly northeast from Hyangno before it flattens out and runs into the sea under the Haegum River. The I Corps fought for and won that northward bulge of land for the Republic of Korea.

The east coast was the only sector of the front controlled by a ROK Army Corps at the time. Had the east coast been under direct UN Command control, the DMZ in that sector would look quite different today. The UN Command had no great interest in expanding ROK national territory.

I deployed the ROK Capital Division along the northernmost salient of our sector, and the division slowly bulled its way north, reaching a point farther north than any other on the line, and repulsing determined enemy counterattacks in the process.

Of course, a basic rule of military science is that if a unit advances ahead of units on its flanks, the lead unit becomes vulnerable. In such a case, the likelihood is that the enemy will attack the lead unit's exposed flank. To prevent this and allow the Capital Division to continue inching northward, starting in the fall of 1951 I put primary emphasis on building barriers to strengthen the Capital Division's flank, using two divisions to harden the positions. I must acknowledge that I am very lucky that the enemy did not penetrate this hardened flank before the armistice brought down the curtain on the war.

In late September 1951, General of the Army Omar Bradley, chairman of the U.S. Joint Chiefs of Staff, visited ROK I Corps headquarters at Sokcho. Bradley had come to Korea to discover whether there were other factors to consider in setting U.S. military policy at the armistice talks.

Task Force Paik Hammers Guerrillas

By the middle of November 1951, ROK I Corps had occupied all the key terrain east of the Nam River, and our front had stabilized. One day I got a telephone call from Chief of Staff Lee Chong Chan. "Be at Eighth Army Headquarters in Seoul tomorrow," he directed. "Van Fleet has something he wants to discuss. I can't get into details on the phone, but don't worry. Nothing's wrong."

The next day General Van Fleet, his chief of staff Maj. Gen. Paul Adams, his G-3 Col. Gilman C. Mudgett, Army chief of staff General Lee, and myself all met in Van Fleet's office. General Van Fleet had called the conference to discuss an operation to eradicate the communist guerrillas who infested the Chiri Mountains in the south.

The National Assembly had passed a resolution by an overwhelming vote demanding the restoration of law and order in Korea's southern districts. This lighted a fire under President Rhee, who then earnestly requested General Van Fleet to take action.

"General Paik," General Van Fleet said to me, "I'm informed that you have a lot of experience in counterguerrilla warfare. You've got to take charge of this thing. We can temporarily pull two divisions out of the line for this mission, and I'll leave it up to you which ones we use." He then laid out a map and presented an outline of the mission.

1. The ROK government would announce martial law south of Taejon for the duration of the operation.
2. One division would land at Yosu and then march north. The other division would travel overland to Taejon and then march south. The two would converge on the Chiri Mountains and attack from all sides at once.
3. The ROK Air Force would provide close air support.

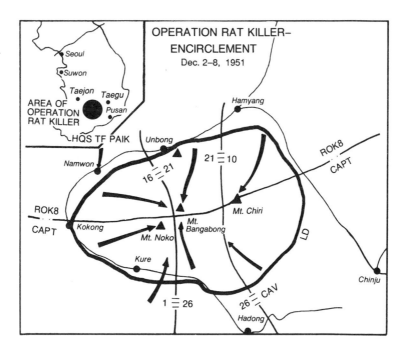

4. I would prepare detailed operations plans under the direction and with the cooperation of the ROK Army chief of staff.

5. Eighth Army and the UN Command would provide all needed support.

6. The U.S. Far East Command Headquarters in Tokyo would provide psychological warfare support in the form of broadcasts and leaflets.

I later sat down with Van Fleet's G-3, Colonel Mudgett, and worked out a detailed operational plan as Van Fleet had directed. It was very lucky for Korea that Van Fleet had served in Greece before being assigned to command Eighth Army, because the situation in Korea resemble that in Greece in many ways. As was often the case in U.S. Army units, Van Fleet's staff invariably referred to their commander as "the old man."

Mudgett told me that we should follow the directions "the old man" had laid down in the conference and asked me which two divisions should be included in the operation against the guerrillas. I said I wanted the Capital Division and the ROK 8th Division. Of course, the old ROK 1st Division I commanded so long jumped to mind first, but the 1st occupied a crucial sector of the line, and I abandoned that idea without hesitation.

Brig. Gen. Song Yo Chan's Capital Division was perfect for the mission, not only because it was experienced, but because the division could easily embark for an amphibious movement from its location near the Sea of Japan. Brig. Gen. Choi Young Hi's 8th Division was widely believed to have suppressed Korea's endemic communist guerrillas better than any other ROK Army unit involved in such operations.

On November 16, 1951, I was appointed commander of a new unit whose mission was to sweep the communist guerrillas from the Chirl Mountains. Maj. Gen. Lee Hyung Koon replaced me as commander of ROK I Corps. An Eighth Army operational order directed that the new unit be named "Task Force Paik," while the operation itself was to be dubbed "Operation Rat Killer." I was unabashedly proud that my name had been given to the unit, the first time an ROK Army commander had been so honored. At the same time, however, I was awed at the grave responsibility inherent in the operation.

The Southwest District Combat Command under Brig. Gen. Kim Yong Bae, who later served as ROK Army chief of staff, had been fighting guerrillas in the area. His force and all the Korean National Police units in the district were to be placed under my command.

I left ROK I Corps and proceeded to ROK Army Headquarters at Taegu, where I undertook the exacting task of organizing my new unit. I selected Col. Kim Chum Kon as my chief of staff, Col. Kong Kuk Chin as my G-3, Col. Yoo Yang Soo as my G-2, and Lt. Col. Chang Woo Joo as my G-4. My staff worked closely with Col. Jung Nae Hiuk, ROK Army G-3, to acquire the personnel and equipment necessary to establish Task Force Paik and accomplish the many complex chores associated therewith. Jung later served as minister of defense. We found both the U.S. Eighth Army and ROK Army to be forthcoming in their support, and we managed to complete preparations smoothly and quickly.

I must say that it was risky to withdraw two full divisions from the front and employ them in rear-area combat operations during a shooting war. Indeed, our willingness to accept that risk suggests the level of threat the communist guerrillas posed to the state.

The guerrillas could and did emerge almost any place in Korea's southern area, but the bulk of them were concentrated around Mount Chiri. That mountain jutted up at the center of a concentric circle of many rugged peaks, the whole of which amounted to a perfect natural redoubt, providing a site from which the guerrillas mounted depredations at will while enjoying the high degree of security afforded by the mountains' excellent observation and cover.

Communist guerrillas had been a growing cancer in Korea since the country's liberation from the Japanese at the end of World War II in August 1945. Rat Killer's objective was to neutralize the guerrillas' long-time Chiri stronghold without further delay.

Winter presented the optimum conditions for Rat Killer's success. The absence of foliage combined with a layer of snow to rob the guerrillas of concealment.

Our intelligence estimates suggested that the guerrillas were organized into the infamous Nambu Kundan—Southern Corps—commanded by Lee Hyon Sang. Intelligence also told us that the Nambu Kundan's main force consisted of some 3,800 fighters, who pretty much ran the Chiri Mountains as their private fiefdom. These fighters were mostly conventional North Korean troops from units that had been defeated along the Naktong River line in September 1950. These men fought side by side with guerrillas who had been core members of the South Chosun Workers' party. Headed by Kim Il Sung, the Chosun Workers' party was the communist party in North Korea. Its southern arm, the South Chosun Workers' party, disintegrated after the North Koreans invaded on June 25, 1950. Committed communist leaders of the South Chosun Workers' party found their way to the Chiri from all around the country and joined the Nambu Kundan.

Other guerrillas in the Nambu Kundan had longer roots. After months and years of accumulating their strength, even in some units of the fledgling ROK Army of the time, communist forces attempted overt rebellion in late 1948, seizing command of ROK Army units and taking control of local governments. The most successful of these attempts, called the Yosu Rebellion, occurred in October 1948 not far from the

Chiri Mountains in the towns of Yosu and Sunchon. Although the rebellion was put down, many of the rebellious communists had been living and fighting in the Chiri ever since.

The guerrillas conducted rear-area harassment missions throughout the southern districts of the Republic of Korea, seriously impairing law and order and taking a toll on UN Command transportation and communication lines as well. The guerrillas grew so adept at blowing up roads and rail lines that even the main rail link between Seoul and Pusan was unsafe. Guerrilla control was so strong, especially in the mountainous, interior areas of the south, that a popular saying of the day had it that "It's the Republic of Korea during the daytime. But it's the People's Republic of Chosun [North Korea] at night."

I finished organizing task force headquarters, now composed of two hundred officers and noncommissioned officers, and we moved first to Taejon and then on to Chonju. We camped just north of Chonju for a week and finished all preparations necessary to move into Namwon, from which city we would exercise command and control of Operation Rat Killer.

Meanwhile, the Capital Division on the eastern front and the ROK 8th Division on the central front transferred their combat missions to other divisions and withdrew from the line. The Capital Division embarked on LSTs at Sokcho and sailed to Yosu, where it landed and began to sweep northward. The ROK 8th Division traveled by truck from the Punchbowl area to Taejon and then swept south to the Chiri Mountains, encircling the enemy.

Maintaining operational security was the most crucial aspect of the mission up to this point. If security were breached, my two divisions would find nothing but empty mountains and the largest tactical maneuver ever undertaken by the ROK Army would end in failure.

At the end of November, we moved task force headquarters into a primary school building located at a key point on the road leading from Namwon to Unpong. Members of the Korean National Police and our KMAG team joined us there.

The KMAG team was composed of sixty men, most of whom were experts at operational liaison, communications, air-ground liaison, reconnaissance, or psychological warfare. The senior adviser, Lt. Col. William Dodds, was experienced in counterguerrilla warfare and had served under General Van Fleet in Greece after World War II. Van Fleet had specially selected Dodds for the mission.

Superintendent General Choi Chi Hwan of the National Police joined us at our new headquarters, where he acted as the personal representative of the National Police director. We made contact with commanders of the National Police regiments assigned to Rat Killer. Police forces in the area provided us with every possible assistance, as indeed did the directors of the police bureaus of all the other provinces.

With the declaration of martial law, the army chief of staff became martial law commander, and I became his agent for the area. This placed all administrative governmental entities and the National Police directly under my command, giving me all requisite administrative power and vastly improving the chances that Rat Killer would succeed.

The squadron of ROK Air Force Mustang fighters stationed in Kangnung were moved through Chinhae and deployed to the air base at Sachon, where the aircraft were soon ready to provide Rat Killer with close air support. We established prisoner-of-war enclosures outside Namwon and Kwangju. All my subordinate units were equipped with communications gear provided by Eighth Army. We accomplished these and other preliminary steps just as fast as humanly possible in an attempt to avoid detection by the Nambu Kundan's intelligence-collection nets.

We handled thousands of details to prepare for the operation, but we deliberately left our artillery at home. In Greece, General Van Fleet had learned that the infantry would not execute a final assault on a summit defended by die-hard guerrillas if artillery support was available.

I received a letter from Vice President Kim Song Su just before H-hour. The letter's calligraphy was elegantly done in traditional horsehair brush, while the letter itself was a paradigm of the formal, fastidious style and attention to detail that has characterized cultured, written communication in Korea for centuries. The letter was delivered in person by the chief secretary to the vice president.

> . . . the Korean people are sunk in misery. Law and order do not exist in our mountains or in our interior, and the Korean people groan under the oppression of the communist guerrillas. If that were not enough, the military and the police impose an added burden of malfeasance on the people, impairing the crucial trust the people must have for the military. I am informed, General Paik, that you will command two picked divisions and eradicate the guerrilla threat. This puts me at ease, certainly. But you must restore law and order wisely, with affection and consideration for our people. You must not inflict more suffering on them. Your operation will put the people at ease, certainly, and they will be able to get on with their lives.

The vice president's concern was not misplaced. Public criticism had flared over past incidents of egregious injury visited by the army and National Police on civilian residents of the mountainous regions the guerrillas used for sanctuary. The most staggering of these was the Kochang Massacre.

In 1949 I commanded the ROK 5th Division in Kwangju and conducted sweeps against the guerrillas. I endured an unforgettably bitter experience as the result of one of those operations.

In the fall of 1949 I rode into the field to check on my 15th Regiment, which was conducting operations against communist guerrillas around Paegun Mountain. On my way back to Kwangju I suddenly came upon a hamlet in which every building was wrapped in tongues of flame. The fire destroyed virtually all of the three hundred houses in the village. The disconsolate villagers of Hanchon stood in stunned groups or had sunk to the ground in despair.

I had the incident investigated, and the inquiry concluded that communist guerrillas had torched the hamlet and fled into the mountains. I smelled a rat. I went back to Hanchon, sought out the village elders, and asked for the full story. They told me that one of my own 5th Division units had burned the hamlet to the ground, accusing the villagers of maintaining ties with the guerrillas. I was shocked, I apologized to the villagers and promised that they could count on me to make restitution. I raced back to Kwangju and went directly to the official residence of the governor of South Cholla Province.

Governor Lee Nam Ki listened to my insistent explanation and readily promised support. The governor also agreed to accompany me back to the hamlet. The next day Governor Lee and I drove back to Hanchon. When the villagers had assembled, I knelt down in front of them. "The full responsibility for this is mine," I said. "Kill me now if you like." The villagers made no move toward me. "Winter is near," I continued. "And I will do my very best to see that you have shelter, so that you do not freeze on this desolate ground. I have brought with me 30 million won of public funds allocated to my division. It is yours. Honorable Governor Lee has pledged to rebuild your village."

Our actions revitalized the villagers, who emerged from the lethargy of hopelessness to cut wood in nearby mountains and to prepare in other ways to get through the coming winter. As good as his word, Governor Lee rebuilt the burned village, and popular sentiment in the area shifted to the government side. I was touched to learn later that the villagers pooled their resources and erected a stone monument in my honor.

My very bones told me that we had to have popular support if Task Force Paik was to win the upcoming round with the guerrillas. Indeed, I regarded popular support to be every whit as crucial as actual military operations against the guerrillas. Recalling my experience at Hanchon, I issued a tough order directing that no task force unit would bivouac near any village or hamlet during Operation Rat Killer. I ordered officers and men not to take so much as a drop of water from civilian residents in the operational area, and I directed that no individual or unit should fire at anyone who was not in the act of resisting.

Civilian residents within Rat Killer's operational area felt defensive toward, if not outright fear of, the army and the National Police. The guerrillas made these villagers the objects of their so-called "supply struggle," arrogating to themselves the right to acquire the villagers'

produce. At the same time, the army and the National Police took re-
venge on villagers who maintained communications with the guerrillas,
something most could not avoid. As a result, the civilian residents of
areas infested by guerrillas had become opportunistic to survive; harsh
experience had taught these long-suffering people to throw their support to the side they believed would win. I intended to show them that
the army was stronger than the guerrillas. I also intended to show them
that the army held all the Korean people in high esteem without exception.

Quiet Returns to the Chiri

By the evening of December 1, 1951, the units of my divisions had deployed to their respective jump-off points and were ready to launch the
attack. The Capital Division was poised to advance from Kwangyang,
Hadong, and Wonji-dong, and the ROK 8th Division was ready to push
off from Namwon, Unbong, and Hamyang. This arrangement of forces
essentially formed a huge net around the peaks at whose center Mount
Chiri loomed like a bull's-eye.

I established D-day for December 2, and H-hour for 6 A.M. We jumped
off on time, and thirty thousand troops moved out briskly toward the
peaks, closing the net. Our concept was as simple as a rabbit hunt.

The strike force was composed of the two divisions surrounding the
Chiri redoubt. Each unit on the perimeter was to attack along parallel
approaches to Mount Chiri itself. The blocking force was composed of
reserve regiments and police units positioned astride roads and escape
routes just outside the strike force's tightening net. I was determined to
pull the net closed on the guerrillas, and this blocking force was to neutralize those who managed to worm their way through the net.

As the strike force advanced, we burned abandoned structures and
guerrilla facilities we discovered in the mountains to prevent the guerrillas from using them again. We evacuated civilian residents to a relief
station.

On the first day of the operation, I set out to keep a commander's eye
on the situation, riding toward Hyongje Peak in the vicinity of Hwagae
Market, where the Capital Division's 26th Regiment under Col. Lee
Dong Hwa was engaged in a sharp firefight with the guerrillas.

Nothing distinguished the fight with the guerrillas from conventional
combat. The guerrillas even employed mortars, and the deafening thunder of gunfire sounded from everywhere.

For the duration of Rat Killer, I spent virtually every hour of daylight
flying over the operational area in a light reconnaissance aircraft. The
panorama of flight afforded me the luxury of inspecting the movements

of my troops and guerrilla forces before issuing orders to my regimental and division commanders.

I remember Rat Killer to be the single operation of the war in which it was most necessary to express frequent encouragement to my commanders. The fast-breaking nature of the battle forced task force commanders to adapt swiftly to the changes inherent in the tactical situation. The sheer velocity of change ground down the morale of commanders accustomed to more predictable operations and obliged me to counter low spirits with effusive encouragement. As our net closed on the guerrillas, they began withdrawing deeper and deeper into the web of mountains.

Because the guerrillas didn't stand and fight, we had very few concrete results to report during the first two days of the operation. Nor had we taken any prisoners. At this point, General Van Fleet visited my headquarters at Namwon. I briefed him on the operation and expressed my concern that we did not yet have positive combat results to report.

We had been able to keep Rat Killer secret until we actually launched the attack, but as soon as the operation was under way, foreign and domestic journalists descended on me in droves. They made the operation the banner press story of the day.

Under the intense press scrutiny, I felt that the lack of positive combat results reflected adversely on me, the ROK Army, and the UN Command, and I told Van Fleet as much. "Forget it. Don't worry." He smiled grimly. "I'll handle the media. You concentrate on the guerrillas." As I look back on it now, I believe General Van Fleet's kind statement may have been an example of the expansive nature of senior military officers in an open society.

The strike force continued to close the net. On day three of Rat Killer, good news began to flood in. We were inflicting terrible losses on the guerrillas everywhere, and a steady stream of prisoners began to flow into our enclosures.

The largest fraction of the prisoners proved to be conventional soldiers of the NKPA. Their North Korean accents made them easy to identify. Their attitudes helped as well, because they made no effort to mask the malice they felt for us, even when they were captured and transported to the enclosures. The other two types of prisoners were those who joined the guerrillas after working with the South Chosun Workers' party and those who had previously been residents of various regions of South Korea. The attitudes of these latter two types of prisoners differed markedly from that of the NKPA soldiers. They begged us to spare their lives and showed no sign either of malice or intransigence.

We found the guerrillas to be armed with a full range of communist weapons and with U.S. M-1 rifles and carbines and even Japanese M-99 rifles. All were dressed in rags and desperately needed haircuts. They obviously enjoyed only minimal bathing facilities, for when we put them in the warm enclosures, the fetid odor assaulted the nostrils so strongly one had to gasp for air.

The guerrillas varied in age from ten to forty, although most were in their twenties or thirties, and a large number of them were women. After initial interrogation, we transferred the prisoners to Kwangju. Prisoner interrogations were conducted by joint teams composed of representatives from the army, the National Police, and the local prosecutor. American interrogators worked with our teams as well.

As the strike force continued its work, only the summit of Mount Chiri remained open to the guerrillas. At that point, the ROK Air Force began its work in earnest, fascinating all observers.

Our strike-force units carried ground-air signal panels, which they now laid out so the fighter bomber pilots could distinguish between Task Force Paik and the guerrillas. The panels were about 5 meters long, 1.5 meters wide, and rolled up. Made of canvas, the panels were white on one side and orange on the other. The color displayed was predesignated each day in order to prevent any compromising situation.

When an air-ground liaison officer attached to one of my divisions requested close air support, flights of Mustangs took off from nearby Sachon Airfield and were over the battlefield in minutes. The Mustangs then bombed and strafed the shrinking cover left to the desperate guerrillas.

I had a literal bird's-eye view of the ROK Air Force Mustangs from my seat in the reconnaissance aircraft. The air force pilots who flew these missions, then company- and field-grade officers, were to rise to the highest positions in our air force.

On Mount Chiri today, a wilderness trail has been built along a ridge that runs from Nogodan to Chonwang Peak. The guerrillas ran out of ground on that ridge. With no place to go and with strike-force units closing in from every side, our air attacks slew them in hundreds on the ridge, their bodies piling up like cordwood.

Rat Killer caught the guerrillas completely by surprise. The guerrillas had been lulled into a false sense of security because they thought we would not pull units from the line while fighting had continued at the main battleline north of Seoul. The harvest had just ended, too, and the guerrillas had collected ample grain supplies from local villages and completed other preparations for the winter. The guerrilla leadership was overconfident.

We launched an active psychological warfare campaign as soon as our strike force began the assault. U.S. Army units at Namwon equipped with the appropriate gear started to broadcast surrender demands to the guerrillas around the clock. Soldiers equipped with portable loudspeakers were attached to every unit in the task force, and these men broadcast on-the-spot appeals for the guerrillas to throw down their weapons and surrender. We also directed broadcasts at local villagers, urging them not to aid the guerrillas. We dropped so many of the leaflets supplied to us by the Far East Command in Tokyo that the whole, enormous Mount Chiri area was covered with them. Records show that we scattered a total of 9,920,000 leaflets during Rat Killer.

The Chiri area was covered with snow during the operation, and the men encountered huge differences in temperatures, depending on the time of day and the elevation. Such conditions imposed severe privation on my men but hurt the guerrillas even more. Many of our prisoners suffered from frostbite.

I learned a few things from the operation. For example, I discovered that tearing about in a light reconnaissance aircraft above mountain masses is no picnic. The Chiri terrain is extremely rough and convoluted, and the winds above the area are strong, turbulent, and unpredictable. Every day the winds buffeted my little plane, and we plunged into dozens of air pockets and downdrafts, making me dizzy and sick as we fell dozens or even hundreds of feet each time. It was like falling off a cliff over and over again. I've flown all over Korea in light aircraft now, but I've yet to find another airspace that frightens me quite as much as the turbulent sky over the Chiri, although Taegwallyong near Kangnung and Mugyongsaejae run a close second.

Task Force Paik needed a week to sweep to the peak of Mount Chiri. When we got there on December 8, 1951, each unit turned around and continued the assault, this time retracing its steps from the central mountain to the outer perimeter. This turned the net inside out and allowed us to sweep the area once more in detail. National Police units blocking roads and escape routes ran to ground those guerrillas who evaded our web. That was the end of phase one of Rat Killer. We had destroyed the Mount Chiri fortress in this brief operation, a fortress the guerrillas had called impregnable.

Rat Killer's second phase began December 19, 1951, as we began to sweep the high ground all around the Chiri Mountains. Chains of mountains surround the Mount Chiri area itself. The guerrillas, of course, had sanctuaries and fighting positions scattered throughout these mountains. A number of guerrillas who eluded Rat Killer's net made for these nearby peaks and hid out. I assigned the Capital Division the sector east of a north-south line running through Chonju and Sunchon and gave the 8th Division the sector west of that line. We had to strike quickly, before the fleeing guerrillas had time to make good their escape.

We encountered substantially reduced guerrilla resistance in Rat Killer's second phase. It soon became evident that the guerrillas were concentrating more on escape than on combat, and nearly four hundred defected to our forces.

During the second phase of Rat Killer, near the end of December, I relieved my G-3, Col. Kong Kuk Chin, and appointed Lt. Col. Park Chin

Suk in his place. Replacing a key staff officer during an operation is, of course, highly unusual. The problem developed over a difference of opinion between Colonel Kong and my G-2, Col. Yoo Yang Soo.

At one point in Rat Killer, one of the Capital Division's regiments was scheduled to attack the high ground west of Mount Tokyu. We received intelligence information, however, that guerrillas who had been dug in on the regiment's objective had eluded the net and taken cover on Mount Tokyu itself.

Colonel Yoo recommended that we adjust the operational plan and direct the regiment to assault Mount Tokyu rather than its original objective. Colonel Kong, who had a reputation as an outstanding staff officer, disagreed.

As I reviewed each officer's position, I concluded that Kong's views did not originate from a faulty interpretation of intelligence data. He knew the guerrilla unit had escaped, but he still clung blindly to the original operations order. Kong was advocating a philosophical position. In his mind, swift changes in the situation on the ground did not justify even relatively minor changes in a division-level operations order because tactical combat situations are fluid by definition. Once we begin altering operational orders, he believed, an endless series of changes would follow, undercutting the authority and utility of our orders.

Although Kong may have had a point in conventional operations, I believed that in counterguerrilla operations, we had to place the highest possible value on flexibility and the ability to adapt to changing circumstances. If the situation changed, we must adjust operations to match.

I called in Colonel Kong and used every argument I could muster to convince him on this point, waiting for him to change his views, believing he would do so. He didn't. Even after three hours of patient argument, he remained as adamant as the granite of Mount Chiri itself. I relieved him before he left my office.

We diverted the Capital Division to Mount Tokyu, where the unit pinned down and eventually annihilated guerrilla units that proved to be the enemy's main force in the Chiri.

Colonel Yoo, who had advocated the attack on Mount Tokyu, told me later that when I relieved Colonel Kong he couldn't sleep for three days because he was afraid he'd been wrong. Had he been in error, the Capital Division would not have made contact with the guerrilla's main force units, Operation Rat Killer would have failed, and Yoo would have been responsible for the sacrifice of a fellow staff officer.

I viewed the incident at the time as a remarkable display of principle under combat conditions. Staff officers are motivated by personal convictions, and I deeply admire officers who remain true to those convictions. Thus, Colonel Kong left Task Force Paik with no sense of awkwardness, and Kong and Yoo maintained the deep friendship they had nourished before the incident.

We launched the third and final phase of Rat Killer on January 15, 1952. In six weeks of fighting, we had virtually destroyed the Nambu Kundan's structure and demolished its base camp. The guerrillas were down but not out. Intelligence determined that the commander of the Nambu Kundan, Lee Hyon Sang, had directed the surviving members of the defeated unit to assemble again on Mount Chiri. I reacted by ordering the Capital Division to conduct another sweep of Mount Chiri, repeating our original operational pattern.

The Capital Division was bone weary from long weeks of slugging up and down the severe terrain, but their attack was coordinated perfectly under the strict leadership of General Song Yo Chan. The division chased down or ambushed more and more of the guerrillas each day. Combat reports fairly brimmed with concrete results. The overwhelming success of Rat Killer finally began to dawn on the civilian population, and their attitudes began to change. They had been reluctant to aid us because they feared we would leave behind a substantial number of guerrillas who would seek vengeance on those who had helped us.

Their fears mollified, the civilians began to cooperate with us, and as they did we killed even more guerrillas. A remarkable multiplier effect took hold at this point. As we killed more guerrillas, the local citizens provided us more aid, which led to more dead guerrillas and more aid.

Smashed into small groups by Rat Killer and no longer able to rely on the assistance of the area's civilian residents, the guerrillas abandoned Mount Chiri and made for the rough terrain around Kimje. Rat Killer was over. Only minor mop-up operations remained. Task force headquarters was preparing to pull out by the end of January 1951.

Official army records show that we killed a total of 5,800 guerrillas and captured 5,700 during Rat Killer. The published history of the U.S. Army says that ROK Army and National Police units together killed 9,000 guerrillas.

During initial planning for Rat Killer, we had assumed we would confront only 3,800 armed guerrillas operating out of the Chiri itself and find another 4,000 in nearby strongholds. Our estimate was off, in the first instance, simply because many more main-force North Korean guerrillas existed than anyone had realized. We also grossly underestimated, however, the number of South Korean citizens the guerrillas had recruited to their cause and who had joined them in their difficult life in the Chiri. Many of these converts, we found, were unarmed, never having been granted fighting status.

Prisoner interrogations revealed much about the guerrillas' recruitment tactics. The communists approached young men of military age in the villages and hamlets throughout the Chiri area and promised these men that if they joined the guerrillas, the communist leaders would appoint them to prize positions in local government—such as mayors of townships, county chiefs, and heads of post offices—once a communist society had been set up in the south. Dazzled by the temptation of filling posts they regarded as highly desirable, young villagers often left their families to join the guerrillas in the mountains.

We discovered that many of these young people carried actual "Certificates of Appointment" hidden in the waistbands of their trousers. They valued these documents highly, for they regarded them as evidence that they would eventually receive the position indicated on the certificate. Once a villager joined the guerrillas, the new recruit often found that his first mission was to win his own village over to the communist cause, a process that usually involved the punishment of "reactionary elements" in the hamlet, even their assassination.

Once a recruit had committed criminal acts, he had no choice but to remain with the communist cause and, of course, could not flee the mountains and return to his village. We found South Korean citizens from all over the country who had thrown in their lot with the communist guerrillas only to undergo a change of heart. But they couldn't leave the Chiri, couldn't return home, and during Rat Killer couldn't surrender because of the crimes the communists directed them to commit in their home villages.

One shocking outcome of Rat Killer was the creation of large numbers of orphans. We were in no position to ignore pitiful children who had lost their parents, whether those parents were North Korean guerrillas or South Koreans who had joined them. With the help of the South Cholla Province governor at the time, Lee Ul Sik, my staff and I found a building in Sonjong that had belonged to the Japanese during the occupation and made it over into an orphanage. We provided aid to that orphanage for thirty-five years. Apart from our own efforts, Dr. Bob Pierce was personally instrumental in caring for a large number of orphans. Bob was then a war correspondent, and he later served as president of the World Visions Mission and its famous choir.

Many years later, Songjong was incorporated into the Municipality of Kwangju and the land on which the orphanage stood appreciated rapidly, reaching a value of several hundred thousand dollars. In the fall of 1988, after conferring with the orphanage's board of directors, including Kim Chum Kon, we donated the orphanage property to a Catholic nunnery. The nuns, we were certain, would continue handling this social responsibility.

The ROK 8th Division returned to its sector at the front in early February 1951, but the Capital Division remained in the area for another month mopping up. Rat Killer did not eradicate the guerrillas. They continued to emerge from their mountain lairs for years, even after the truce was signed in 1953, always bringing misery and misfortune to innocent villagers. But we had dealt the Nambu Kundan a fatal blow. Before Rat Killer, government administrative authority did not extend into the area under Nambu Kundan control. After Rat Killer, the Nambu Kundan virtually disappeared.

A telegram for me arrived at task force headquarters January 12, 1951. My units were smack in the middle of Rat Killer at that moment, and I was so busy I could hardly find time to sleep. The telegram informed me that I had been promoted to lieutenant general.

Two other major generals were promoted the same day, Army Chief of Staff Lee Chong Chan and Chief of Naval Operations Sohn Won Il. Before January 12, 1952, only one ROK military officer had held the rank of lieutenant general—Chung Il Kwon, who was then studying in the United States.

My chief of staff Kim Chum Kon and National Police Superintendent General Choi Chi Hwan acquired the necessary three-star insignia and did me the honor of pinning them on. Acting on his own, my orderly took my fatigue uniforms to a nearby girls' school and had a third white star embroidered on the shoulders. I was touched by these expressions of kindness from men who worked so closely with me.

As Rat Killer was winding down, Eighth Army G-3 Col. Gilman C. Mudgett secretly visited my headquarters at Namwon. I sat down with the colonel, and he said, "I've come to tell you on General Van Fleet's secret instructions that a second corps is to be created in the ROK Army." Mudgett went on to inform me that Task Force Paik Headquarters would be used as a nucleus around which to organize ROK II Corps. He said that the plan was to send my headquarters staff to train for a number of weeks at U.S. IX Corps, north of Chunchon, before being formally organized into II Corps Headquarters. If Mudgett expected me to be excited, he was disappointed. I put it plainly and simply. "I don't agree with the plan."

I was in touch with my contemporaries, of course. I fully understood that every officer in the ROK Army believed that our single large unit, I Corps, was not enough. We all felt that ROK Army must have more corps, and quickly. Dissenting views simply didn't exist. Yet here I was dissenting. I gave Mudgett an earful. I said that in order for a corps to support its divisions and be effective in combat, corps headquarters had to have organic artillery, engineer, and quartermaster assets. In those days the reality was that without U.S. Army assistance, the ROK Army could not provide such units to a corps headquarters. I said that this meant that a ROK Army corps was a corps in name only.

Mudgett smiled like the proverbial cat who swallowed the canary. "You have no reason to worry about that, sir," he assured me. "Eighth Army will work with ROK Army Headquarters to provide corps-level units with organic engineer, administrative, and supply units and to create artillery units to be assigned as organic corps-level artillery." My ears perked up.

Colonel Mudgett explained that Eighth Army planned to attach the 5th Artillery Group to serve in the role of corps artillery for the new ROK II Corps. He said that II Corps would be provided with an engineer group and a quartermaster group as well.

Six 155mm medium howitzer battalions were being trained at the ROK Army Artillery School in Kwangju. These battalions would be deployed to bolster the anemic firepower of ROK forces. Mudgett said Eighth Army planned to season these battalions quickly by assigning them to the front as soon as they completed their training at Kwangju. Then, he said, each battalion would be given a dual mission, providing real-world fire support part of the time and continuing its training the rest of the time.

As soon as Mudgett returned to Seoul, I relocated Task Force Paik Headquarters lock, stock, and barrel to a location north of Chunchon in the U.S. IX Corps sector, leaving the Capital Division to wrap up Rat Killer. My new mission was to build ROK II Corps.

Organizing II Corps: Symbol of the New Army

Task Force Paik Headquarters pitched its tents, and the key members of the two hundred officers and men on my staff began a program of on-the-job training aimed at preparing us to manage II Corps. Each key staff member spent his days at U.S. IX Corps headquarters working with his counterpart.

Brig. Gen. Lee Hyong Sok was appointed II Corps chief of staff. Brig. Gen. Won Yong Duk was appointed to serve as deputy commanding general. Both men joined us at headquarters. General Won was a military doctor trained at Severance Medical School, but he was much more the combat commander than the physician, having established an enviable combat record. His military knowledge and ability with the English language astounded the Americans. General Lee was also a gifted man, having been the first Korean ever to pass the entrance examination for the Japanese Military Academy, Japan's West Point. Both officers were ten years older than me, but neither showed the reserve or restraint that might have characterized such a relationship in Asian countries, which made my job immensely easier.

Maj. Gen. Willard Wyman, commander of IX Corps, who was in charge of our training, went out of his way to treat me with every courtesy due my new rank.

Our headquarters was at Chonjon, near the site where Soyang Dam stands today. An English translation of the village's name is Field of Springs Village, and true to its name, the ground in the entire area was soggy with water welling up from underground, making tent life miserable.

After about five weeks at Chonjon, my staff had picked up the fundamentals of U.S. Army's corps-level organization and operational procedures and also managed to write the standard operation procedures we would use in II Corps. As if this was not enough, during those weeks we also managed to organize ourselves so that II Corps could hit the ground with its infantry, communications, quartermaster, engineer, and air-ground liaison functions all operating smoothly. Needless to say, we worked virtually around the clock.

By April 1952 we were ready. ROK II Corps was off the ground. All we lacked were tanks. Our various forms of combat-support capabilities were up and functioning, and corps artillery was raring to go. My II Corps was the first ROK Army corps to have the organic capability to conduct combined-arms operations. The new II Corps symbolized the New ROK Army.

ROK II Corps Artillery (the 5th Artillery Group) was commanded by Colonel Richard W. Mayo, who had been KMAG's chief of staff, and consisted of one battalion of light (105mm) U.S. artillery, two battalions of medium (155mm) U.S. artillery, and four battalions of ROK Army medium artillery, giving the corps a total of seven battalions of howitzers.

The medium artillery was composed of the first four newly organized ROK Army 155mm artillery battalions to be assigned to combat duty. Col. No Chae Hyon received the distinction of being the first Korean artilleryman to command such a powerful unit. ROK II Corps's artillery capability was truly momentous, especially when contrasted with ROK I Corps on the east coast, which remained without organic artillery until the armistice.

On April 4, 1952, U.S. IX Corps transferred a segment of its front to my II Corps. Our sector of the front was located in an area called the Kumsong zone, which extended sixteen miles west from the Pukhan River north of Hwachon. Our sector was located just south of the area where the North Koreans are building their Diamond Mountain Dam today.

The new II Corps Headquarters was located in a place called Sotogomi, just north of Hwachon. ROK II Corps was only the second Korean unit, after ROK I Corps on the east coast, to bear responsibility for a sector of the battlefront. Located almost in the middle of the 155-mile Korean front, our sector was crucial because any enemy breakthrough in our area would immediately threaten both Chunchon and Wonju. My unit was also the first ROK corps to be deployed directly opposite Chinese Army units. If all that were not enough, our sector of the line bulged provokingly northward.

The three divisions assigned to ROK II Corps were the ROK 3d Division under Brig. Gen. Paik Nam Kwon, which had been attached to U.S. IX Corps; the ROK 6th Division under my brother Brig. Gen. Paik

In Yup; and Brig. Gen. Song Yo Chan's Capital Division, which had finished mopping up guerrillas in the Chiri and returned to the front. I put the 6th Division on the left and the 3d Division on the right, leaving the center for the Capital Division.

U.S. IX Corps sidestepped to the west to provide ROK II Corps a sector of the line. The IX Corps's U.S. 40th Division under Maj. Gen. Joseph Cleland bordered ROK II Corps on the left, while the ROK 7th Division, attached to U.S. X Corps, flanked us on the right across the Pukhan River, which flowed north to south as it crossed the front.

A National Guard unit from California, the U.S. 40th Division was committed to the Okinawa campaign late in World War II. After the Japanese surrendered in August 1945, the 40th was sent to Korea, along with the U.S. 6th and 7th divisions, as part of U.S. Army occupation forces. The 40th deployed to Pusan and later Kwangju before being withdrawn in 1948. After the Korean War broke out, the 40th was tapped once more for duty in Korea, returning to the peninsula in late January 1952 as part of the U.S. Army's program to relieve line divisions.

My corps reserve consisted of the 32d Regiment of the U.S. 7th Division and the Thai Army Battalion, both bivouacked west of Hwachon Dam. Lt. Col. Chomanan Kriangsak commanded the Thai Battalion at the time and went on to serve as prime minister of Thailand in 1978. Colonel Kriangsak sent me three bags of savory Thai rice as a gift, and I met him again when I visited Thailand in the early 1970s. He was serving as superintendent of the Thai Military Academy at the time.

The U.S. 7th Division was commanded during this period by Maj. Gen. Lyman Lemnitzer, who passed away in late 1988. Lemnitzer went on to serve as commander in chief of NATO forces as well as U.S. Army chief of staff and chairman of the U.S. Joint Chiefs of Staff. The UN Command tactical commanders on the central front in those days were a veritable galaxy of renowned soldiers; perhaps I could be forgiven for calling them a group of "shooting stars."

On April 5, 1952, a Foundation Day ceremony was held at the airstrip in Sotogomi to commemorate the official creation of ROK II Corps. The key figures of the times attended, from President Syngman Rhee and Minister of National Defense Shin Tae Yong, to Army Chief of Staff Lee Chong Chan, ROK I Corps commander Lee Hyung Koon, U.S. Ambassador to Korea John J. Muccio, Eighth Army commander Gen. James A. Van Fleet; commander of U.S. I Corps, John O'Daniel; and commander of U.S. X Corps William Palmer.

We regarded U.S. IX Corps as our parent unit. We had trained with it, and in our first combat assignment we defended a sector of the front it had transferred to us. The IX Corps commander, Maj. Gen. Willard Wyman, made the new ROK II Corps flag and presented it to me during the ceremony. Our patch consisted of a roman numeral II on a blue background, the same color as IX Corps's patch, symbolizing our close relationship to the U.S. unit. Indeed, we adopted our code name from that of U.S. IX Corps, which was called "Tornado." We became "Tempest."

President Rhee could not hide his emotions during the ceremony. It must have been a bitter pill for Korea's president to endure the disestablishment of the former ROK II Corps in the wake of the Chinese Army's January 1951 offensive and the equally bitter disestablishment of ROK III Corps after the May offensive of the same year. The creation of the strongest ROK corps yet visibly touched the president.

In the speech he delivered at the ceremony, President Rhee repeatedly made the following statement. "Our army now has the personnel and the materiel resources to fight. We must punch through the barbarians and advance north, unifying the entire country." By this time, of course, the United States had abandoned any notion of advancing north again, and President Rhee's "advance to the north" slogan fell officially on deaf ears. General Wyman, however, expressed that day his personal conviction that we should attack through Chorwon as far as Pyonggang.

After the ROK II Corps ceremony concluded, General Van Fleet shared some shocking news with us. His son was missing in action. The younger Van Fleet, a first lieutenant, was a bomber pilot. The previous night he had taken off in his B-26 from a military air base in Kunsan for a night bombing run over North Korea. He was never heard from again. Although General Van Fleet was aware of this terrible news, he not only had flown out to attend the ROK II Corps ceremony but had said nothing to anyone and remained perfectly composed throughout the ceremony.

The U.S. Army had aided willingly in the creation of ROK II Corps for a number of reasons, chief among which was the nature of the terrain in our sector of the line. That region of the central front was so mountainous and rough that the unrivaled maneuverability of U.S. units—a maneuverability depending heavily on large numbers of organic tanks, trucks, and other vehicles—was largely useless in the area. The terrain did not suit the composition of the U.S. units.

Another reason for the U.S. Army interest in creating II Corps was the situation in Europe. The United States was rapidly expanding its own military capabilities and that of its allies in Europe at this time; consequently, the U.S. Army faced a limit on the number of troops available for service in Korea.

Finally, the U.S. Army had reached the very natural conclusion that the ROK Army should assume an increased role in combat along the stabilized front. The U.S. military realized that the best way to accomplish this was to concentrate on providing training and fire support to the ROK Army.

Shortly after the official inauguration of the new corps, on May 12, 1952, Gen. Mark W. Clark replaced General Ridgway as commander in chief of the UN Command. Ridgway was appointed to serve as commander in chief of NATO forces.

During the time I commanded the new ROK II Corps, a temporary lull prevailed along the now-static front. During the lull, Eighth Army actively encouraged line units to seize enemy prisoners. This policy was based on two simple needs. First, the quieter a combat front, the more important it is to ascertain the enemy's movements. Prisoners are a key source of such information. Second, in static warfare and during lulls it is important to preserve the sense of caution active combat instills in soldiers' minds. Operations designed to take prisoners fill this need also.

The truce talks were alive. We had insisted on moving them from Kaesong in enemy territory to a neutral site at Panmunjom. At the moment, however, the talks were stalemated on the issue of prisoner exchange.

We usually sent out company-sized commando teams to bring back enemy prisoners. It was a formidable task to locate, seize, and bring an enemy soldier back to our lines alive, especially because at this stage of the war enemy troops occupied prepared positions. Thus, each such operation required intense, minute planning.

We went so far as to prepare models of enemy positions and the surrounding terrain and thoroughly familiarize ourselves with it. We then conducted repeated rehearsals of the operation using the models. Even after all that preparation, I would not authorize an operation until the unit passed a strict operational inspection. General Van Fleet personally participated in training with terrain models and as an expert on special operations provided valuable on-the-spot guidance.

The ROK 6th Division proved itself exceptionally adroit at conducting operations to seize prisoners. In one case the 6th captured sixteen Chinese soldiers in a single mission. I recall that Lt. Col. Kim Jong Pil, former president of the New Democratic Republican party, served at that time as a battalion commander in the ROK 6th Division and distinguished himself with his active participation in these operations.

Apart from worrying about operations to seize enemy prisoners, my chief concern was that the communist Chinese Army would launch a huge, localized offensive directed straight at II Corps. I had good reason to be worried. I calculated that the Chinese commanders might not be able to resist the temptation to attack once they learned an ROK Army unit had moved into the line opposite Chinese units, especially since our sector of the line bulged north. This combination had to draw the attention of the Chinese leadership like a thumb in the eye.

Because I was concerned about a possible Chinese attack, I took more than a passing interest in the unit designations of the Chinese prisoners of war we were taking. Starting in May, about a month after ROK II

Corps deployed into the line, I detected an increase in the number of units from which our prisoners were coming. This clearly established that the Chinese Army was concentrating units opposite ROK II Corps.

In mid-May, I conveyed this piece of intelligence to Eighth Army Headquarters, and very shortly thereafter I found myself taking a telephone call from General Van Fleet. "Have your artillery shoot the hell out of the areas where you think the Chinese are massing," he said. "And do it as soon as I hang up. Use as much ammunition as it takes." I called in Colonel Mayo, the corps artillery group commander, explained the situation, and directed him to prepare a massive artillery attack.

Mayo said he didn't want to do it.

Philosophically, Mayo was wedded to the notion that ammunition was made to be conserved. This idea had been ingrained into this veteran U.S. artilleryman, I suppose, during the years he had served as an instructor at the U.S. Army artillery school at Fort Sill. His credo was that no target should be taken under artillery attack until and unless that target was verified by direct observation.

In the end, of course, Mayo caved in. He had no choice, since Van Fleet's order had been a marvel of clarity. Starting that afternoon about 3 P.M., a total of ten battalions of artillery—the seven battalions of organic corps artillery, plus one battalion of 105mm howitzers from each of my three divisions, plus all the divisional mortars—delivered a massive barrage of fire at the Chinese Army. This was the most powerful bombardment ever fired by an ROK Army corps with its own assets up to that point in the war.

We not only started big, we kept it up, firing all through the night and continuing until 10 A.M. the next morning. Our mortars and 180 howitzer tubes poured twenty thousand rounds onto enemy positions along a twelve-mile front. We had no way to verify the extent of the damage this fire inflicted on the enemy, but there is no reason to doubt that the tremendous display caused the Chinese to change their minds about launching an offensive aimed at ROK II Corps. We picked up no further intelligence suggesting that the Chinese forces opposing us were preparing for a tactical move as of the time I left in July 1952.

General Van Fleet's prompt decision to launch an artillery attack of this scale was all the more impressive in view of the fact that artillery ammunition had become a political issue of the day. The U.S. Army artillery ammunition resupply system was not performing well, for one thing, and the U.S. Congress was investigating U.S. Army artillery ammunition use rates, which some claimed to be inordinately high. I had an occasion later to thank General Van Fleet for his decision. I've paraphrased his response in the following paragraph.

> The artillery barrage allowed us to steal a march on the enemy, preventing it from launching an attack. That, in turn, resulted in extra weeks of quiet on

that sector of the front, and that, in its turn, reduced the total number of friendly casualties we took in that sector. Compared with the value of these outcomes, the ammunition we expended was cheap indeed. The Chinese Army has nothing but scorn for the ROK Army. The quickest way to establish psychological mastery over the Chinese Army, then, is by providing ROK II Corps whatever it needs to intimidate the Chinese Army with sheer firepower.

General Van Fleet's belief in the transcending value of firepower produced a popular saying among American soldiers, who jocularly referred to the "Van Fleet supply rate" among themselves. This was a pun on the usual term, "regular supply rate," which set daily artillery ammunition use rates.

Senior U.S. officials developed an intense interest in the 5th Artillery Group because of its role in training ROK Army artillery battalions. While I was II Corps commander, UN Commander Mark W. Clark; U.S. Army Chief of Staff J. Lawton Collins; General Clark's friend, Britain's Lord Alexander; and General Van Fleet's friend, the chief of staff of the Greek Army, all visited to inspect the 5th Artillery Group. During his visit to Korea the following year, U.S. President-elect Dwight David Eisenhower also inspected the 5th Artillery Group despite his intense schedule.

My efforts to establish ROK II Corps taught me just how strenuous is the work of bringing a new unit on-line. The experience also caused me to realize just how valuable and how terribly important is a military unit with a long tradition.

7

THE ROAD TO FOUR STARS AND ARMY CHIEF-OF-STAFF

A New Honor

On July 22, 1952, Rhee suddenly dismissed Lt. Gen. Lee Chong Chan as army chief of staff, the top post in the ROK Army. Lee's dismissal was triggered by the so-called Pusan Political Crisis.

On May 25, 1952, two months before I became chief of staff, the government declared martial law in two dozen southern cities in South Kyongsang and North and South Cholla provinces, claiming that continued guerrilla activity made martial law necessary. The next day, however, martial law authorities arrested not communist guerrillas but National Assembly deputies.

The main military culprit was Brig. Gen. Won Yong Duk, who served briefly under me as deputy commander of ROK II Corps. Won had been transferred to the Ministry of Defense in Pusan earlier in the spring, and when martial law was declared, he was appointed martial law commander for South Kyongsang Province and Pusan, which was serving as the temporary seat of national government. Won played a leading role in what came to be called the Pusan Political Crisis when he used his martial law authority to arrest assembly deputies who championed a constitutional amendment to change Korea's style of government from an executive-centered system to a cabinet-centered executive system. Such an amendment, of course, would have limited the power of the president, something President Rhee adamantly opposed.

During the incident, Army Chief of Staff Lee Chong Chan refused an order from the minister of defense to bring army troops into Pusan to back up Won Yong Duk. Lee faced a number of problems thereafter, and President Rhee soon removed him from his post. Both ROK Army G-3 Lee Yong Mun and G-2 Kim Chong Myon were ignominiously fired for supporting General Lee in refusing to bring troops into Pusan.

Lee Ki Poong surrendered his portfolio at Defense when martial law was declared, and Shin Tae Yong replaced him as defense minister.

The U.S. Army exercised operational command of the ROK military of course, and had troops been sent into Pusan, Van Fleet and the United States would have been involved in the unfortunate political disturbance. Gen. Lee Chong Chan lost his job as chief of staff, but according to rumor, Van Fleet's influence prevented President Rhee from taking even more stringent measures against General Lee.

I was astonished to receive a message informing me that I was to replace General Lee. The message directed me to proceed to Pusan and report to President Rhee. Except for about a year I spent as the G-2 at ROK Army Headquarters earlier, I had spent my entire army career as a line commander. The chief of staff position requires skills other than those I had honed as a tactical commander, and I was very puzzled as to why President Rhee would select me to be chief. I couldn't rid myself of the nagging feeling that I would not be up to handling the politics that went with the job.

I dutifully turned over command of ROK II Corps to Maj. Gen. Yu Jae Hung, who had been serving as army vice chief of staff, and started for Pusan, going by way of Seoul.

I stopped by Eighth Army Headquarters in Seoul's Tongsung Subward and paid a farewell call on General Van Fleet. The general congratulated me on my new appointment and treated me to dinner. We discussed many things, but eventually I asked Van Fleet for any ideas he might have on how I could successfully perform my new duties.

Van Fleet was fifty-nine years old, meaning that he was one year away from the U.S. Army's mandatory retirement age. I was sure this old warrior would have plenty of advice for a man of thirty-two who had just been appointed to the top position in his army. The American general contemplated quietly for a few moments before answering. "I believe you'll be a great chief," he ventured, "because you're a tough fighter. But please don't say very much. Listen to your staff and your commanders instead of talking yourself. No matter what difficulties you encounter, don't allow yourself to be pushed into a hasty decision. Sleep on the problem and decide the next morning. When you say 'yes,' say it clearly, and when you say 'no,' say that clearly too. And never ever show anger in front of your people."

Only as time passed did I come to realize the depth and complexity of his advice. General Van Fleet was sincerely concerned about my future, one I think he knew would require me to fulfill many duties while coping with an endless war, complex internal political developments, and a maelstrom of social commotion. Bidding farewell to Van Fleet, I took a jeep out to Youido Airfield to catch a hop to Pusan. I ran into Prime Minister Chang Taek Sang at the field, and we flew down together.

As our C-47 droned through the humid summer skies, Prime Minister Chang reviewed for me the key points about the Constitutional Revision Bill and the Pusan Political Crisis. I blinked as he spoke, trying to concentrate, but I simply couldn't understand the details. I'd been in combat so long that I couldn't grasp Korea's complex, chaotic political situation at a single sitting.

What I did understand loud and clear from the prime minister's remarks was that as chief of staff I would never be able to separate the duties of my office from politics. The idea of it seemed terribly depressing.

I reported to President Rhee on July 23, 1952. The president took my hand and congratulated me on my appointment. "Its been a threatening period," he said. I believed the president was referring to the Pusan Political Crisis and was sure he spoke so telegraphically because he assumed I knew all the details. President Rhee then cited a few problems that marked the tenure of my predecessor, General Lee, and ended with, "The army chief of staff must obey the president without deviation. . . . "

As I pen these words, the political situation in Korea seems only too similar today. The ruling party has majority in the National Assembly, and the issue of moving Army troops is inextricably linked with U.S. Army operational command of ROK forces. Some say history repeats itself, and I must agree that it certainly seems to be cyclical. As I indicated above, however, I was largely ignorant of political events at that time, and I regret that I am not able to provide more details.

Army headquarters was located in a government building near Kyongbuk National University's Medical School in Taegu. As I assumed my duties there, I found I had to deal with the personal affairs of my immediate predecessors, Lt. Gens. Lee Chong Chan and Chung Il Kwon.

Lee and Brig. Gens. Park Byung Kwon, Chang Do Young, and Choi Young Hi had all been assigned to military training courses in the United States when Lee was removed as chief of staff. This was a face-saving way to ease General Lee from the scene, but for personal reasons Lee postponed his departure. I served as army chief for several weeks before Lee finally left Korea. I met with him several times before he left, and the general expressed his remorse at President Rhee's actions.

Gen. Chung Il Kwon's situation was more complex. Chung left office after a number of incidents exploded on his watch, including the Citizens Defense Force incident and the Kochang Massacre. Some of the sting had been taken from Chung's departure by assigning him and

Maj. Gen. Kang Mun Bong to attend military training courses in the United States. Chung completed a course at Fort Leavenworth's Command and General Staff College and returned to Korea not long before I was appointed army chief.

Former Chief of Staff Lee Chong Chan had decided to deal with General Chung by assigning him to command the ROK 2d Division and discussed the matter with Van Fleet and then obtained President Rhee's approval. General Chung, however, was not happy to be asked to command a frontline division. He was disappointed because he felt that as a former chief of staff it was now too late for him to command a tactical unit. When I took over as army chief, General Chung was avoiding the issue by taking a period of rest and recuperation at the home of a friend in Chinhae. General Chung, in point of fact, had served not only as army chief of staff but exercised overall command of the ROK Navy and Air Force as well. Any reasonable man would agree that Chung would be hard-pressed to assent to serve now as a division commander.

Nevertheless, some officers believed that General Chung did not have the military experience requisite to his rank. The U.S. military was particularly insistent on the precedent that officers be promoted through a series of progressively more responsible positions. General Chung had served briefly during Korean Constabulary days as commander of the 4th Regiment in Kwangju but had never commanded either a division or a corps.

President Rhee's attitude seemed to be that rather than waste General Chung's skills, he should gain command experience and again serve in senior military positions. I had to solve this problem before I could get on with my other duties, so I quickly went down to Chinhae to have a talk with Lieutenant General Chung.

Chung made no attempt to hide his dissatisfaction. "I'm going to have to leave the army and find some other way to make my living," he told me. I explained in detail the difficulties the army faced at the moment and entreated General Chung to accept the division appointment. He had already been approved to command the ROK 2d Division, I said, and I urged him to take the job as a way of pioneering new norms of conduct in the army, setting a refreshing, new example for junior officers. General Chung finally relented, and the next day he was named to command the ROK 2d Division.

I found the chief of staff post to be a strong position indeed, for as the army's senior officer the incumbent served through the defense minister as the assistant to the president for military affairs. The position was even stronger, of course, during a shooting war, especially since martial law was in force and the chief of staff executed part of the president's administrative duties under martial law.

The army chief also devoted large amounts of time to coordinating the conduct of the war with the military contingents from the sixteen sovereign countries that had dispatched forces to Korea to serve under the UN flag. Although the U.S. Army exercised operational command of ROK military forces, the chief of staff's role in managing the operational support tasks of the twelve ROK Army divisions and other units at the front and in rear areas was an overwhelming task in its own right.

The formal relationship that prevailed at the time between ROK Army Headquarters and the U.S. Army was not complicated. Eighth Army fell under the command of the UN Command and the U.S. Far East Command, both in Tokyo. Eighth Army exercised control over operational missions of ROK Army units deployed in the front area.

ROK Army Headquarters performed the operational support tasks—personnel replacement, supply, administration, and training—for the two frontline ROK Army corps and for all twelve ROK divisions. The number of ROK divisions reached sixteen by the time the armistice was signed in July 1953.

In the matter of supply, the ROK government was responsible for providing its military forces with rations, salary, part of their uniforms and basic logistic materiel, while the U.S. Army provided us with all of our ammunition, POL, equipment, and key logisitics materiel.

Newly appointed UN Command commander in chief Gen. Mark W. Clark established the Korean Communication Zone (KCOMZ) as an independent command responsible for the rear areas of the country, including the two-thirds of the Republic of Korea lying south of a line drawn between Pyongtaek on the west and Samchok on the east coast. Clark put this area under the control of a "Logistics District Command." Maj. Gen. Thomas Herren was appointed to command this unit, which was headquartered in Taegu on the site of the barracks of the former Japanese occupation forces. The ROK Second Field Army, established in 1954, later assumed most of the missions of this unit. Many believed that General Clark established KCOMZ as a means to reduce General Van Fleet's clout.

KMAG, the U.S. Military Advisory Group to the Republic of Korea, had operated on the peninsula since liberation in 1945. In its wartime role, KMAG assigned advisers to ROK Army Headquarters and subordinate units and advised the ROK Army in its staff functions. When I became army chief, the KMAG chief was Maj. Gen. Cornelius E. Ryan, who had served as Omar Bradley's G-5 in World War II.

KMAG was headquartered at the former Taegu Normal School facility near ROK Army Headquarters. KMAG assigned advisers to each of the principal staff offices at army headquarters, and U.S. and Korean personnel sat together and worked together in offices all over headquarters.

We maintained a Recruitment Division at army headquarters that operated Recruitment Command regional offices in each major administrative subdivision in Korea's rear area. The Recruitment Command was responsible for conscripting men of draft age, who were then sent for sixteen weeks of training either to the First Recruit Training Center on Cheju Island or the Second Recruit Training Center at Nonsan. ROK Army Headquarters consigned an average of 1,200 trained recruits to units on the front and in rear areas every day.

Army headquarters operated eighteen training institutions as part of the U.S. Army efforts to strengthen and professionalize the ROK Army. The U.S. military provided support to our training net, which ranged from the Korea Military Academy and the army's Command and General Staff College to service schools and branch schools for infantry, artillery, engineers, armor, communications, quartermaster, army aviation, military police, adjutant general, intelligence, troop information and education, chemical, military medicine, nursing, and the Women's Army Corps. We were training a great many officers and noncommissioned officers in the various disciplines of military science. In this area, of course, my highest priority was to increase the combat power of the ROK Army.

My first personnel action was to promote those staff officers serving at the top of their respective service branch or professional discipline to brigadier general. Promotions to flag rank had been exceptionally limited until that time. I had observed, however, that a colonel at ROK Army Headquarters who was the highest-ranking officer of his branch of service encountered difficulties when passing directions to subordinate units and when working with the Americans, whose ranks were higher for equivalent positions. I recommended to the minister of defense that they all be promoted to brigadier general, and the approval came through.

As I was settling into my new job, Secretary of the General Staff Mun Hyong Tae came to me and asked what I wanted to do with the company-grade officers working in the various offices of the general staff. A new army chief typically transferred these men elsewhere, bringing in his own men even at that level. I asked Mun whether these officers had served the previous chief of staff satisfactorily. Mun said they had been diligent workers, so I directed him to retain them all. I appointed to my staff a few men with whom I had worked closely in the past but didn't touch the lower ranking personnel at all.

In my first days as chief of staff, I established a pattern of reporting for work an hour early and ending for the day an hour early. The staff officers soon let me know in polite and gentle ways that they would appreciate it if I would maintain this schedule and not revert to the same hours as my predecessor. Apparently General Lee came to work a little late and stayed later into the evening. In the Korean army the practice is for subordinates to remain in their offices until the senior officer quits for the day. The staff didn't want me working late because that locked them into their offices until it was too late to accomplish their daily list of personal tasks. I liked getting to the office early because I could approach the issues of the day with a clear mind, and the staff loved it when I went home early because they didn't have to "read my face" as frequently to find out when I intended to go home.

Shortly after being appointed chief of staff, I brought my aged mother, my wife, and my daughter from Pusan, where they had fled as refugees, to live with me in my official residence near ROK Army Headquarters. It was pure joy to be reunited with them after more than two years.

The battlefront remained calm until the fall of 1952, but as the leaves began to fall, violent clashes broke out all along the front. The Chinese Army remained true to its solitary offensive tactic: hurl a huge mass of concentrated troops at a narrow front defended by ROK Army units.

The Chinese hit Maj. Gen. Song Yo Chan's Capital Division on September 5, 1952, striking simultaneously along the division's entire frontal sector. The division battled for the high ground, locked in bloody combat with Chinese forces for ten days, losing and retaking each hill or ridge as many as seven times. When it was over, the Capital Division's tough troops remained in their original positions, but the battle took a terrible toll on the unit.

A month later, on October 6, the Chinese attacked Maj. Gen. Kim Chong O's 9th Division at White Horse Hill north of Chorwon. The fighting was terrible, turning the hills and streams literally red with blood. In ten days of fighting, the 9th sustained some ten thousand casualties, but when the guns fell silent the plucky division remained in control of its sector.

On October 14, only eight days later, the Chinese hit the 2nd Division at Sniper Ridge, pouring an endless stream of men into the battle for six full weeks. Lt. Gen. Chung Il Kwon commanded the 2nd until November 1, when Maj. Gen. Kang Mun Bong assumed command. The 11th Division also managed to contain the Chinese assault.

The North Koreans launched a tenacious attack aimed at reducing a salient bulging northward from the ROK 5th Division's area of operations on the east coast. The NKPA fought for four months but failed to reduce the bulge. The new Korean army fought admirably, revealing to our own people and to the world that we were a different force than we had been. Our combat power could prevail.

During the fall of 1952 I received a message from Defense Minister Shin urgently requesting me to meet him in Pusan. I rushed down to the coastal city, and when I met the minister he handed me a sheet of paper. The words "Dismiss Brig. Gen. Min Ki Sik" were written on the paper, which had been signed by President Rhee himself.

The president had sent Minister Shin a directive stipulating that Brigadier General Min be ousted from the army, and Shin called me to see how to handle it. I took the document from Minister Shin and went directly to Kyongmudae, the presidential mansion in Seoul, to meet with the president. President Rhee maintained a temporary official residence in Pusan, as he had done since the Pusan Perimeter days, but he also traveled to Seoul and worked in his Kyongmudae office as the need arose.

I walked into the president's office and spoke my piece. "Your Excellency," I argued. "General Min has commanded a division since the start of the war. He's fought well. It is no easy thing to develop a combat commander of his ability. We're already terribly short of talented people. If possible, sir, let's not fire General Min."

President Rhee's face darkened as he listened, and he began to blow into his fist, a presidential habit that inevitably signaled that the old gentleman's ire was rising. He hesitated a few long moments as he thought it over, and then said, "Okay. Then what should I do?"

"Just give up on it, Excellency."

"How do I give up on it?"

I pulled the document out of my pocket, handed it to him and quickly said, "All you have to do is tear that up, sir." President Rhee tore it up as I watched.

Brigadier General Min had come to this embarrassing turn of affairs because of the so-called So Min Ho incident. Mr. So Min Ho was tried by court-martial. Three different officers served as chief judge during his trial. The first two, Choi Kyung Nok and Park Tong Kyun, stepped aside before Brig. Gen. Min Ki Sik took over and rendered a verdict. In August 1952, Brigadier General Min sentenced So to eight years of penal servitude. The problem was that President Rhee had expected So Min Ho to be given a much heavier penalty, so the eight-year sentence struck Rhee as too lenient. Thus, Brigadier General Min incurred the presidential displeasure.

Solving Ration Problems and Stacks of Other Issues

Feeding an army in wartime is a crucial problem. A soldier who eats well fights well. The Republic of Korea government was directly responsible for supplying provisions to its forces at that point in the war, yet the nation was so weak that even this task stretched us beyond our limits.

Not long after I was appointed army chief I inspected the prisoner-of-war camp at Nonsan and was startled to notice that enemy POWs ate better than the officers and men of the ROK Army. The prisoner-of-war camps were under American jurisdiction, so the prisoners were fed according to nutritional standards set by the U.S. Army. As a result they were eating until their stomachs ached while our own men went hungry.

I had my staff do a study comparing the nutritional standards at the

POW camp with those in our army. The report verified my impression; ROK Army troops consumed fewer calories of protein and fat each day than did our prisoners. I reported this astounding finding to the government but knew full well that the leaders lacked the financial ability to solve it.

I decided to try for a little help elsewhere. I reported the same information through KMAG to Eighth Army Headquarters. Somehow, the facts became known to foreign correspondents, and eventually feature articles appeared in the *Stars and Stripes* and in British newspapers under headlines like, "Korean Troops Eat Worse Than POWs."

The United States began to supply the ROK Army with soybeans as an element of military aid. At the same time, the U.S. Army began advising us to establish a central acquisition system as a way to stretch the money we spent on rations.

Under the U.S. system, the Pentagon's Central Procurement Agency would buy huge quantities of foodstuffs, say beef from Chicago slaughterhouses or oranges from California or Florida, at a season when prices were lowest, realizing savings both of scale and timing. The U.S. military then stored the supplies and distributed them to units later. This method not only stretched available dollars but reduced administrative and handling costs in the bargain.

In an attempt to emulate the American system, I directed that ROK Army Headquarters initiate a central purchasing test program for certain items, fish and vegetables among them. It didn't work out initially. We lacked both the transportation means and the storage facilities for acquisitions on an army scale, and our budget allocations were insufficient into the bargain.

The men on my staff with major responsibility for acquisition and distribution of provisions at the time were my G-4 Paik Sun Chin; Brig. Gen Lee Hu Rak, the Army's chief quartermaster who later served as director of the Korean Central Intelligence Agency; and Brig. Gen. Yun Su Hyon. These men labored for six months on the issue of central acquisition and on establishing procedures that eventually led to central acquisition for the ROK Army, especially in buying grain from the Federation of Farmers' Cooperatives, meat from the Federation of Cattle Breeders' Cooperatives, and marine products from the Federation of Fishermen's Cooperatives.

Recruit training was another crucial problem area for the army. The quality of recruit training was a major determinant of battlefield performance. When training quality dipped, our combat units suffered an almost instant degradation of performance. Moreover, the better our recruit training, the longer our soldiers survived in combat.

In the early days of the war, military police or the National Police simply grabbed young men off the street and sent them for training that lasted anywhere from a week to a month. The hapless recruits were then dispatched directly into combat. We didn't' have much choice at that perilous moment in national history.

After our January 4, 1951, withdrawal, we built the First Recruit Training Center on Cheju Island and later established the Second Recruit Training Center at Nonsan, and these facilities allowed us to bring a real replacement system on-line. We chose Cheju as the site for the First Recruit Training Center because the Chinese offensive under way at the time convinced President Rhee that he and his government might have to use that offshore island as a kind of fortress of last resort.

Once the Cheju facility was operating, ROK Army instituted a sixteen-week basic training course patterned on what the United States had done in World War I and World War II, filling the recruits' days with a full schedule of training activities. In the early period of operation, our priority was to train draftees for the Citizens Defense Force, which performed rear-area security duties, although we reverted to shorter courses and sent trainees directly to frontline units at times when the fighting favored the enemy.

The United States of America has mass production ingrained into its national psychology. Its recruit training system, like its automobile manufacturing techniques, was based on the mass-production principle. The system allowed the United States to mobilize and train 11 million men during World War II, and we adopted it for Korea.

I inspected the First Recruit Training Center and found the place to be a snarl of intractable problems. The most crucial was living accomodations for the recruits. The center received a thousand draftees a day, arriving on navy LSTs, and the men were crowded into tiny tents where they lived throughout the training cycle.

Not only were the tents crowded and inadequate, but the recruits suffered greatly from lack of water. The center had been an airstrip built by Japanese forces as a refueling stop for bombers raiding China. The Japanese had not needed to quench the thirst of thousands of parched throats as did we, and the water supply simply wasn't there.

Koreans have called Cheju "the island of three abundances" because the place had an abundance of females, an abundance of rocks, and an abundance of wind. Indeed, the wind blew so frequently and at such velocities that the LSTs bringing recruits could not land an average of ninety days out of the year. Meanwhile, the facilities at the center were downright pitiful, whether they were intended to accommodate recruits or to provide training or medical care. And finally, the procurement of side dishes to consume with the basic meal of rice had broken down. Our recruits there suffered indescribably. The Second Recruit Training Center at Nonsan wasn't quite as bad.

Apart from these challenges, we had a major problem with parents who came to the training centers to visit their sons. Our policy was to

allow a brief interview, since Korean parents are loath to send their sons
off to the army even in peacetime. They are almost desperate when they
have to turn them over to us in wartime. Lines of parents waited patiently at each training center to spend a brief few minutes with their
beloved sons.

Virtually the entire Korean population consisted of farmers in those
days, and of course Korea lacked any semblance of an American-style
social security system. To the farmers, then, a son represented not just
a beloved family member but an economic asset as well. A son and his
sons after him could continue to work the paddies, supporting aged
parents and grandparents who lived with them. Mothers regarded it as
almost a criminal act when a son had the effrontery to die before produc-
ing offspring. So we were inundated with requests for "transplant bedding" by parents who stood patiently in lines for hours in all kinds of
weather, a daughter-in-law poised shyly at their side.

We called this "transplant bedding" after our ageless agricultural
practice of sowing rice in dense rows in a transplant bed before replant-
ing the seedlings one at a time into a flooded paddy field. Officially, the
army could not condone transplant bedding, but I knew from reports I
received that parents were using every trick in the book to achieve their
purpose.

When I read my first report on transplant bedding, I hit the ceiling,
swore, and promised myself that heads would roll. But I stopped to
think about it and decided I couldn't blame these humble parents. Indeed, I began to regard it as an expression of the essential instinct for
survival of the magnificent Korean people. With tears in my eyes, I realized the transplant bedding report I had just read provided a rare
glimpse into the soul of all Koreans. Suddenly I could understand more
clearly what had sustained our people through five millennia of privation and foreign invasion.

My first move to improve recruit training was to complete the facilities
at the Second Recruit Training Center at Nonsan. I had a talk with
KMAG Chief Ryan, and he saw to it that we received the lumber, roof-
ing, cement blocks, and other materials necessary to build semiperma-
nent barracks to replace the tents in which the recruits lived. I believed
I could further ameliorate the situation by appointing training center
commanders who were mature, humane officers, and I went to some
pains to find the right men.

The First Recruit Training Center had been commanded, in turn, by
Paik In Yup, Chang Do Young, and Oh Duk Jun, tough combat infantry-
men all. I decided that the commandant of the army's Command and
General Staff College Maj. Gen. Lee Eung Joon was perfect for the job.
I entreated General Lee, the army's elder statesman in those days, to
accept command of the First Recruit Training Center.

General Lee had risen to the rank of full colonel in the Japanese Army and headed the group of men who acted as godfathers to the creation of the Korean army after World War II. He had then served as the first ROK Army chief of staff. Although he was almost sixty years old, an advanced age for Koreans in those days, after General Lee listened to my explanation about our needs at the training center, he accepted the job with the words, "I'll do whatever the country needs. I'd lay these creaky old bones down for Korea."

In return for General Lee's sacrifice, I recommended that he be promoted to lieutenant general along with his appointment as commander of the First Recruit Training Center, and this was done. The problems at the training center were too massive and difficult to be solved by any single commander, but I believe that General Lee's diligent efforts significantly improved the situation there.

Another problem facing me was that of the livelihood of my officers. I raised this issue slyly with President Rhee as I was briefing him on a different subject early in my tenure as army chief. "Your Excellency, soldiers' salaries are too low," I said. "I can barely buy enough food for my family on what I make, let alone support my family. The terrible salary we pay our officers fosters graft and corruption. Officers and non-commissioned officers sell rations and use unit vehicles illegally to make money in the private sector, disguising the usage as a 'public welfare project.' Please be aware of this issue."

The low pay scale for soldiers was a pet subject for President Rhee, and he wasn't about to give an inch. "Sure, sure! You want soldiers to learn to love money? When soldiers love money, the nation falls. Soldiers are volunteers, and their mission is to provide service." His reaction was so strong I couldn't work up the courage to raise the issue again.

Early in my tenure as chief of staff, an army truck on a so-called public welfare project picked up a load of Alaskan pollack on the east coast and hauled it across the peninsula to sell on the heavily populated west coast. The truck collided with a train in Osan. A number of similarly distasteful incidents also were reported to me.

The U.S. Army understood the realities that prevailed in Korea in those years and, of course, realized that American aid served to prop up our government. To their credit, the Americans didn't adopt a holier-than-thou attitude about such incidents. In fact, I think I could get away with saying that the Americans showed sufficient largess to close their eyes to petty sins.

Not so President Rhee. He was much too strict on petty transgressions. An illustrative incident occurred the following spring, in fact. Prime Minister Paik Too Chin, the cabinet, and the uniformed service chiefs were invited to a birthday party for President Rhee at Kyongmudae. The cabinet ministers had commissioned a mother-of-pearl–inlaid lacquerware table as their joint gift to the president. When the table was presented to him, President Rhee seized the moment to make a little speech. "I would like to thank you all for this beautiful birthday present, but if I start to accept expensive gifts like this, then all the beautiful things in the entire city of Seoul will end up at Kyongmudae as gifts for me. I'll accept this table because I do not question your good faith, but I'd like to ask you all never to do this again." The ministers and guests were humiliated; we ate a single bowl of noodles and left en masse.

ROK Army Headquarters was responsible not only for the handling of active-duty soldiers but also for the burdensome problem of disabled veterans. After two years of war, the number of veterans who had lost limbs was so great we could not count them accurately. We estimated that from twenty thousand to thirty thousand disabled veterans were accommodated at the ROK Army Hospital in Pusan and in tent villages scattered around Pusan's outskirts. We had no money to take care of these crippled heroes in any other way.

To be sure, ROK Army Headquarters had used U.S. military aid earmarked for such purposes to set up a storehouse filled with artificial limbs and crutches for disabled soldiers, and we tried to see that all these men received artificial arms and legs. Beyond that, we could do little, having the budget neither to supply these brave men with proper medical care nor even to give them room and board. As a result, disabled veterans wandered Korea's streets and byways all across the land, begging and threatening citizens for their rice. The Korean people were most unhappy with this state of affairs, of course, and the disabled veterans found little in the situation to their liking either.

One day in the fall of 1952, a clash occurred in Waegwan north of Taegu between the National Police and a group of disabled veterans. By the time rumors of the incident reached the tent cities in Pusan, they had been blown out of all proportion.

The upshot was that virtually all the disabled soldiers in Pusan had revolted. They intended to seize a train and race to Waegwan to settle scores with the police. The crippled men thronged into the plaza at Pusanjin train station and started a violent demonstration, occupying the tracks, bringing all railroad service between Seoul and Pusan to a halt, and demanding that they be provided with a train to get to Waegwan.

Defense Minister Shin sent me an urgent message at headquarters in Taegu, and I jumped into a light observation aircraft and hurried to Pusan as fast as I could. I took a jeep down to the railroad station to see for myself what was going on, learning that Pusan's top National Police official had virtually abandoned any hope of restoring order. Indeed, it took all the joint efforts of the National Police and the military police to prevent the crowd from spilling out of the plaza.

I grabbed a microphone and made a direct appeal to the veterans. "I'm Army Chief of Staff Paik Sun Yup," I said as officially as I could manage. "I've taken my life in my hands to stand in front of you folks.

I know your circumstances are lousy. But think about it. Aren't you better off than your buddies who died on those battlefields? I will take personal responsibility to solve your problems. If there are those among you who are your representatives, please send them forward and let's talk."

Tens of thousands of eyes turned on me in a second. A number of the veterans swung their crutches in my direction, and a few even threw their crutches at me. They were frustrated and full of nervous energy, and I suspect they would have beat me silly had it not been for the military police who protected me. Finally, about a dozen crippled veterans gathered around me as representatives of the group. They had blood in their eyes. I shook hands with each man in turn, and as I did I came across a familiar face. "You know me, don't you?"

"Yes, Excellency. I know you. You were my corps commander when I fought at the front. Don't you remember you gave me a cigarette on the hill?" As we spoke, I sensed the tension start to dissipate. I listened with utmost care to their problems, to which there seemed to be no end: "We can't sleep because it's too cold. We don't have blankets. Our food is terrible. Our tents are so filthy they're infested with lice and fleas." Of course, their biggest problem was psychological stress. These men had been maimed in the service of their country only to find themselves social pariahs.

I promised repeatedly that I would do all I could to redress their grievances and requested that they disperse and give me a chance. After about two hours they finally agreed. The government squeezed some money out of the budget someplace, which we allocated to each recuperation center, and Eighth Army provided twenty thousand blankets that we distributed to the men. These measures were enough to keep the lid on a boiling pot.

Luckily, Cornelius Ryan had a wealth of experience dealing with wounded veterans from his days as chief civil affairs officer for Omar Bradley during World War II. As an interim measure, I established a director of Wounded Veterans Affairs at ROK Army Headquarters and put a military medical officer in charge. The demonstration in Pusan set in train a series of actions that eventually led to the establishment of today's Office of Veterans Administration.

Korea's First Four-Star General

As I wrestled with problems like these both at the front and in the rear areas in late 1952, President-elect Dwight D. Eisenhower decided to visit Korea. Eisenhower won the November 1952 presidential election in the United States with a campaign promise to "stop the war in Korea."

To show that he intended to follow through on his campaign pledge, Eisenhower visited Korea as president-elect on December 2, 1952.

Eisenhower's visit was kept a tightly held secret until the moment he stepped off the plane at Kimpo Airport. He was taken directly to Eighth Army Headquarters in Seoul. The next morning, December 3, 1952, I attended a conference chaired by Eisenhower. In addition to the president-elect, the other attendees were Gen. Omar Bradley, chairman of the U.S. Joint Chiefs of Staff; Adm. Arthur W. Radford, commander of the Pacific Fleet; Gen. Mark W. Clark, commander in chief of the UN Command; Gen. James A. Van Fleet, Eighth Army commander; Maj. Gen. Cornelius E. Ryan, chief of KMAG; and myself.

Eisenhower walked up as we were waiting in a hallway for the conference to begin, bedecked with glittering stars and gold braid. "Good morning, gentlemen," he said, obviously in a chipper mood. "Seeing you gathered together like this reminds me of the day before the D-Day landings."

Before the meeting began, Van Fleet conveyed a greeting to Eisenhower from his son, John, who was fighting with U.S. forces in Korea. "John," Van Fleet said, "is doing a great job at the 3d Division. After you were elected, we transferred him from battalion commander to division G-2."

"That is something that falls within the purview of your responsibility," Eisenhower responded. "My only hope is that John not be allowed to fall into enemy hands." Van Fleet's son was already lost, and Eisenhower's son served as far forward as any sane person would care to be.

I had been asked to brief Eisenhower on the hour's hottest subject, the U.S. commitment to enlarge our army. I explained to the president-elect the plan to expand the Korean army to twenty divisions, laying special emphasis on the fact that we could maintain three ROK divisions for the cost of operating one U.S. division. Eisenhower listened and expressed support for the principle of expanding the ROK Army.

Later in the day Eisenhower visited Maj. Gen. Song Yo Chan's Capital Division in reserve at Kwangnung, accompanied by President Rhee. President Rhee announced that he had arranged a welcoming rally for Eisenhower by the citizens of Seoul. The Eisenhower party, however, was reluctant to attend. Not only was such an event not a part of Eisenhower's itinerary, they said, but Eisenhower could not attend on security grounds alone. They were told that one hundred thousand Seoul citizens were awaiting Eisenhower's appearance.

Refusing to take no for an answer, President Rhee betook himself to the site of the "U.S. President-elect Eisenhower Welcome Rally." Rhee sat on the stand and waited for the Americans to change their minds and for Eisenhower to show up. I accompanied President Rhee and shook from the cold, as some one hundred thousand Seoul residents waited in bitter weather, sitting on the plaza in front of the Capitol. We all waited for Eisenhower, but he never came.

I seized the moment to go up on the stand and ask President Rhee in impassioned terms why Korea had to oppose an armistice. I returned to my seat when he didn't respond, but after he realized that Eisenhower was not going to show up, he called me back, stood me up in front of the crowd, and commenced to deliver a speech. ''If the United States had a hero like Eisenhower in World War II, then Korea has a hero in this war. General Paik is that hero.'' President Rhee then outlined my battle experiences, from the Naktong to Pyongyang and beyond. And in a transport of hyperbole said that I was the soldier responsible for defending the Republic of Korea.

Eisenhower spent three days and two nights in Korea. His schedule became an issue again on the last day. President Rhee believed that with his departure now imminent Eisenhower would have to follow usual protocol and pay a courtesy call on Kyongmudae. The president summoned Prime Minister Paik Too Chin and all the cabinet ministers to the presidential mansion to stand by and sent Seoul Mayor Kim Tae Sun to Eighth Army Headquarters to use his good offices to arrange an Eisenhower courtesy call. Mayor Kim, however, was stopped at the gate to Eighth Army and not allowed into the compound. He turned around and came back.

Eisenhower's party sent word that Eisenhower had no intention of paying a courtesy call on President Rhee, partly because of security considerations and partly because Eisenhower was not the American president but only president-elect. Whatever the Americans' real reasons, this communication dealt a severe blow to the prestige of a sovereign head of state.

President Rhee and Prime Minister Paik then summoned me and directed me to proceed to Eighth Army and try once more to hammer out a compromise. I explained my mission to General Van Fleet, and he agreed to meet me. When I explained the issue to him face to face, he told me, ''I conveyed the Korean intent to General Clark but the response was negative.'' Van Fleet then recommended that I speak with General Clark myself.

Gen. Mark Clark told me that Eisenhower could not possibly visit a place the Secret Service had not approved in advance. Clark said the U.S. Secret Service, responsible for presidential security and for Eisenhower's during this trip, had no flexibility whatever. Clark could not influence them because they reported to the secretary of the treasury, not the defense secretary.

I could not imagine a greater affront to the Korean people, and I put it to Clark straight. ''If General Eisenhower does not visit President Rhee,'' I said quietly, ''you will insult President Rhee, of course, but you will also offend all the Korean people. If a meeting between the two men does not materialize, any and all future cooperation between the Republic of Korea Army and the Army of the United States of America will be jeopardized. I urge you to decide in all prudence." General Clark flushed at these words but strode into the next room, the commander's office, which Eisenhower was using. After some time he emerged and whispered, "Let's meet at 6 P.M. for dinner at Kyongmudae."

Accompanied by his son, John, and his party, Eisenhower arrived at Kyongmudae at 6 P.M. as arranged, and after trooping the honor guard, he met for forty minutes with President Rhee and his cabinet. Eisenhower then drove directly to the airport and departed Korea.

Eisenhower's team committed serious breaches of protocol, often in public, during the president-elect's visit to Korea, and Eisenhower's apparently deliberate belittlement of President Rhee doubtless had a certain political motivation. I now believe, however, that most of the problem stemmed from the fact, as the Americans themselves repeatedly claimed, that Eisenhower was traveling almost as a private citizen. Quite simply, he was not yet president of the United States.

About ten days after Eisenhower left, the politician he beat in the presidential election, Adlai Stevenson, also visited Korea. A former governor of Illinois, Stevenson was the Democratic party standard-bearer in the 1952 presidential race. Because the purpose of Stevenson's visit was to determine the real situation prevailing in the war, KMAG chief Major General Ryan and myself ended up accompanying him around the country. I was pleasantly surprised to discover that Stevenson was truly a great man, one in whom sincerity of purpose and intellectual acuity combined. He took the time to inspect every Korean and U.S. unit from the ROK 1st Division at the front to the training center on Cheju Island.

During his visit Stevenson and I stayed in lodgings provided by the U.S. Army's Visitors Bureau at what is now the Korea House in Seoul's Pil Subward. We spent most of our time traveling, of course, as I escorted Stevenson to army units all around the country. He displayed great interest in the possibility that ROK forces could be strengthened and assume missions now assigned to American units, allowing a partial withdrawal of U.S. forces.

Four years after his visit to Korea, Stevenson again ran for president against Eisenhower, and once again lost. In my view, however, if ever a man was qualified in every particular to serve as president of the United States of America, that man was Adlai Stevenson. As he left Korea after his whirlwind, three-day visit, Stevenson confided to me, "The Korean army is first-class, much better than I thought."

From Korea's viewpoint, the visits to our soil by America's two top political leaders, Eisenhower and Stevenson, provided us a golden opportunity to nail down the plan to enlarge the ROK Army. We took full advantage of the opportunity. It was vital for Korea that we have a strong, independent army, and indeed this was only slightly less crucial to the United States itself. Having decided to seek an armistice, the Americans could hope to withdraw their main-force units from Korea after the armistice was signed only if the ROK Army was strong and led by professional commanders.

The plan to expand the ROK Army was in fact fully executed. We went from ten divisions when I was appointed chief of staff to sixteen divisions when the armistice was signed in July 1953, to twenty divisions by the end of the year. An army cannot be formed simply by bringing men and equipment together, however difficult that is to accomplish. To create ten combat divisions in the brief period of a little more than twelve months required the backbreaking, day-and-night efforts of the ROK government, ROK Army Headquarters, the U.S. Eighth Army, and KMAG.

In early 1953, Gen. Mark W. Clark, commander in chief of the UN Command, began to use his good offices to arrange a summit between President Syngman Rhee and Japanese Premier Yoshida Sigeru.

Japan and the United States had normalized their post–World War II relations by signing a peace treaty on September 8, 1951, in San Francisco. A good share of the impetus for the treaty originated from the fact of war on the Korean peninsula. Having normalized relations with Tokyo, Washington saw its next step as promoting friendly relations among its allies in the Far East, now including Japan. General Clark's efforts to arrange a summit between Tokyo and Seoul were apparently aimed at providing a catalyst for a thaw in the frozen relations between Korea and Japan, although neither country was prepared to establish official diplomatic relations.

ROK Chief of Naval Operations Admiral Sohn Won Il and I accompanied President Rhee on his historic visit to Japan. ROK Air Force Maj. Gen. Kim Chung Yul headed the Korean liaison team assigned to UN Command Headquarters in Tokyo at the time, and he joined our party. President Rhee thus had his senior army, navy, and air force officers along to assist him during his talks with the Japanese. On January 5, 1953, the presidential party boarded a C-54 military aircraft sent from Japan by General Clark, departed Pusan, and arrived several hours later at Haneda Airport in Japan.

President Rhee stepped down from the stairway as he left the aircraft at Haneda to be greeted by General Clark and his wife, Japanese Foreign Minister Okazaki Kazuo, and others. The Japanese National Police and the U.S. Army shared joint responsibility for providing security, which was exceptionally tight. Many were concerned that the Chosen Soren or other communist groups might make an attempt on Rhee's life.

The summit talks between President Rhee and Prime Minister Yoshida were held the following afternoon, January 6, 1953, at Maeda House in Tokyo, official residence of General Clark. Those attending were President Syngman Rhee; Kim Yong Shik, Korean minister in Japan; Japanese Prime Minister Yoshida; Foreign Affairs Minister Okazaki; General

Clark; and Ambassador Robert D. Murphy, Clark's political adviser, a total of six men representing three nations.

Pictures were taken of the two principals, each over seventy, against the background of the setting sun, before they entered the summit conference chamber. President Rhee fairly brimmed with confidence, showing not the slightest sign of irresolution or reticence. Premier Yoshida was equally composed and obviously prepared for the meeting.

Minister Kim Yong Shik, who represented our Foreign Affairs Ministry at the session, said President Rhee did virtually all the talking while Premier Yoshida listened during the meeting's seventy minutes. I am told that President Rhee spoke first, expressing his hope that the various problems looming between Korea and Japan could be resolved amicably in the future. Premier Yoshida pledged that Korea would never again be the object of Japanese aggression and said that a revival of militarism in Japan was not possible.

Popular rumors of the day had Premier Yoshida asking President Rhee at this meeting: "Are there still many tigers in Korea?" To which President supposedly responded, "No. Kato killed them all." However much this version may appeal to the popular mind, with its trenchant reference to plunderings by Kato, a prominent Japanese general during the Japanese invasion of Korea in the sixteenth century, I understand the actual exchange went more along the following lines.

Prime Minister Yoshida said that as a young man he had been posted as minister to Antung in Manchuria just across the Yalu River from Korea's Sinuiju. Yoshida said that while serving in Antung he had heard that there were many tigers in Korea. President Rhee responded by quoting a Korean proverb. "In our country we say that a man must have a son to carry on the family name and a son to consecrate to Buddha as a priest. We say, then, that a man needs three sons, since a prudent father can't be sure a tiger won't get one of them."

I asked President Rhee about his impression of the summit in the aircraft as we were returning to Korea. "We solved nothing," he said. "It is not easy to improve relations with Japan so soon after [Korea's] liberation. It may be thirty years before Korea will be in a position to pursue contacts with Japan on the basis of equality. I don't think it can happen until new shoots grow up to replace the old rice plants that remember the Japanese occupation."

A look around Tokyo showed that postwar restoration was not yet complete, and it was obvious that what the Japanese called the "special Korean demand" occasioned by the war in Korea was pulling Japan out of the economic desolation visited on the country by World War II. I noticed large numbers of American soldiers both in and out of uniform on the streets of Tokyo.

I was promoted to full general, four-star rank, on January 31, 1953, and felt honored to be the first Korean officer ever to reach that rank. I learned about my promotion from my chief secretary, and when I reported to the Pusan presidential mansion, President Rhee pinned one set of four-star insignia on a shoulder of my uniform, and General Van Fleet pinned a set on the other shoulder. During the promotion ceremony, President Rhee had a few words for me. "If we lived in former times, you would be king of a new dynasty today. Generals as powerful and successful as you in the dynastic years weren't satisfied to serve as mere subjects to the old king. But we are now a republic, not a kingdom, so you must be content with the stars of a full general."

The U.S. Army at the time followed the principle of appointing one full general for every two hundred thousand men, and the ROK Army numbered about five hundred thousand at the time. Still, nobody, myself included, expected to see a full general in the ROK Army.

As it happened, on the same day I was promoted, General Van Fleet received an honorary doctorate of law degree from Seoul National University. General Van Fleet was scheduled to complete his tour of duty and leave Korea shortly, and many key governmental figures attended his award ceremony. I enjoyed the opportunity to shake hands with these gentlemen, all of whom congratulated me on my promotion. Korean universities were barely clinging to life in their temporary facilities in Pusan, and Seoul National University was no different. Its faculty taught classes in tents. Because the university lacked appropriate facilities, the ceremony to award General Van Fleet his honorary doctoral degree was held at the auditorium of the South Kyongsang Province capitol.

Gen. James A. Van Fleet ended his military career after having taken command of Eighth Army on April 11, 1951, at the most dismal juncture of the war. He served as a commander longer than any other officer during the war.

Van Fleet nurtured a close relationship with President Rhee, overcame endless difficulties, and made contributions of enormous value, not only in the conduct of the war itself but also in strengthening the ROK Army. In this regard, the Van Fleet legacy that would have the most impact was the establishment of the Korea Military Academy. General Van Fleet convinced President Rhee that the long-term professionalism of the ROK Army required a military academy like West Point, and he contributed immensely to the creation of the Korea Military Academy in Chinhae in April 1952.

Despite Van Fleet's efforts on its behalf, however, the Korea Military Academy was a noncombat unit and therefore was not included on the list of ROK Army units qualifying for U.S. Army aid. As a result, the ROK government had to fund the academy from its meager budget, which meant, of course, that in its early years the academy was virtually destitute.

Van Fleet undertook to raise private funds for the academy, pursuing any number of approaches to this end, and after the academy moved from Chinhae to Taenung outside of Seoul, the funds he raised were used to build a library. As I pen these lines, General Van Fleet is ninety-six years old and lives in Polk City, Florida, on a road named Van Fleet Street.

Lt. Gen. Maxwell D. Taylor replaced Van Fleet. Taylor would later serve as U.S. Army chief of staff and as ambassador to Vietnam. Taylor was a veteran soldier. He commanded in the U.S. 101st Airborne Division during the Normandy landings and in the Luxembourg operation. After the war, Taylor served as commander of U.S. forces in West Berlin during the Soviet Union blockade of that city. An artilleryman, Taylor was a brilliant man who spoke nine languages and was a past master at military government and politics. We saw his mission as arranging the political and military situation so that top priority would fall squarely on the armistice.

Soviet Premier Joseph Stalin died on March 5, 1953, immediately after Taylor assumed command of Eighth Army. The war entered a new era after Stalin's death. Stripped of Stalin's support, the communist forces began to display a hurried interest in reviving negotiations at the stalled armistice talks.

I heard the news about Stalin's death aboard the U.S. Navy battleship *Missouri* off North Korea's major east coast city, Wonsan, accompanied by KMAG chief Ryan. The U.S. Navy exercised complete control of the sea, so occasionally I would board a U.S. Navy vessel and sail to a point from which Wonsan was visible to the naked eye. In the fall of 1952, for example, I sailed on the battleship *New Jersey* and landed on the island of Yo-do, some ten miles east of Wonsan. From this vantage point I could see Wonsan's switching yard and dock facilities and had a grandstand seat for an air and sea attack on the city, courtesy of the U.S. Navy. The Americans had turned Yo-do into a fortress and maintained U.S. Navy and Marine forces there.

Vice Adm. Joseph Clark, commander of the U.S. Seventh Fleet, had invited me to visit the USS *Missouri*. Admiral Clark himself brought me the news of Stalin's death. "General Paik," he said. "The dictator Stalin died today. I think we'll see some changes in the war."

Later that day I transferred from the USS *Missouri* to a carrier, arriving just in time to witness a serious accident. An aircraft returning to the carrier landed with a bomb still clinging to its undercarriage and exploded as it touched down, opening a gaping hole in the great ship's deck. The accident was most unfortunate, of course, but I had seen much death, accidental and otherwise. What I recall vividly was that for the first time I witnessed an American commander giving his men hell.

The War Enters a New Phase

One of the tasks essential to creating more combat divisions was expanding artillery capability. Without full artillery support, our infantry divisions could never reach their potential combat power. I can safely say that the weakness of our artillery was a major reason army units found themselves fighting for their lives so frequently during the course of the war. We were deficient in numbers of tubes, of course, but we also had virtually no artillery commanders trained to a professional level.

In the early period of the war, we suffered from another basic problem. A number of our infantry commanders lacked any concept of how infantry and artillery must cooperate. For example, artillery tubes fire at targets far and near from fixed positions. In the early days of the fighting, however, some of our infantry commanders were ignorant even of this fact. These men would issue foolish orders to their artillery, like: "Come up here and fire," or "Go over there and fire." In a number of cases, the infantry commanders went so far as to punch artillery commanders who resisted such silly orders.

As chief of staff, I was determined that the ROK Army would overcome the errors and shortcomings of the past. We had to do everything humanly possible to ensure that the artillery officers and commanders posted to the newly created divisions were professionally competent. The man in charge of this effort was Maj. Gen. Shin Ung Kyun, who had been chief artillery officer at army headquarters and was now my deputy chief of staff for administration.

In fall 1952, Major General Shin submitted a proposal to create an artillery command as a way to help us expand the artillery. The wide divergence in rank between a division commander and the commander of the division artillery resulted in too many cases of disdain by the former for his top artillery officer. Shin believed we had to narrow the rank gap between these two key players if we were to have any hope for smooth, combined operations against the enemy.

Shin suggested selecting senior infantry colonels who had served as deputy division commanders to attend a concentrated artillery training course. The army would then switch them to artillery and assign them as artillery commanders to the various divisions. According to Shin's plan, these colonels would be promoted to brigadier general when they became division artillery commanders, narrowing the prevailing rank difference. I approved his idea because not only would we solve the problems Shin had in mind, but it would also solve a personnel logjam the army was experiencing among infantry colonels. The senior colonels selected for this unusual procedure included a future president of the Republic of Korea, Park Chung Hee.

The colonels were assigned to a three-month training course at the Artillery School in Kwangju on October 13, 1952, and then were posted to Brigadier General Mayo's 5th Artillery Group for on-the-job training. When the training was complete and we were about to assign the colonels to division artillery commands throughout the army, we suddenly encountered stiff opposition from the Americans. Eighth Army commander Gen. Maxwell D. Taylor sent me a message requesting an urgent meeting. I went up to Seoul and sat down with Taylor. "You can't create an artillery commander overnight," he stated flatly. He went on to say that he wanted me to abandon the idea completely, even at this late moment.

General Taylor himself was an artillery officer, and he said that although he had made artillery a lifelong study he still felt that he was deficient in artillery knowledge. I took that aboard, but I believed Taylor was underestimating the ability of our officers to perform mathematical calculations. General Taylor, of course, was only part of the problem. ROK Army artillery branch officers, as one might imagine, opposed the idea of a group of infantry colonels suddenly changing their spots and joining the artillery branch. I understood their feelings, but they angered me when a number of them secretly conveyed their negative views to Eighth Army artillery officer Brigadier General Day.

I suppressed my displeasure as I talked with Taylor, reminding him that I was responsible for personnel matters within the army and managing to convince the American general that the senior infantry colonels were officers of stature and proven leadership ability. I proposed a compromise to Taylor. I invited him to accompany me to the 5th Artillery Group, where he would be welcome to interview each and every colonel individually and make a final determination on the acceptability of each.

Taylor calmed down and allowed as how he would take me up on the offer. He didn't have time to go himself, however, but said he would have KMAG chief Ryan go in his stead, conduct the interviews, and report back to him. Ryan and I departed immediately for the 5th Artillery Group. Mayo provided us with the individual personnel records on each colonel, and Ryan conducted the interviews. I interpreted.

Ryan found every colonel to be acceptable. In fact, he said things like, "These guys are great. They're great. Where can you find officers better than this group?" Ryan confided to me that he was particularly impressed with Col. Park Chung Hee, a man that neither of us knew then was a future president of Korea.

Having dealt with the Americans' objections, I proceeded to promote the new artillery colonels in March 1953 and appointed them to various divisions as artillery commanders. Had General Taylor persisted in opposing this action, I feel sure that none of these men would have been promoted to flag rank. In that event, Park Chung Hee would not have been a major general in 1961, and very likely he would not have been able to lead the coup d'état that overthrew the government on May 16 of that year. Korean history would have developed very differently. As it was, ROK Army artillery officers rose to prominence after the coup, and this is the story behind their first step toward the limelight.

We worked hard to train artillery officers and commanders, and the

U.S. Army provided us with artillery tubes and related equipment. Before long, our army boasted a professional corps of artillery specialists.

Throughout most of the war, the typical ROK division possessed no more than a single battalion of 105mm howitzers, and the organic "artillery" available to each of our regiments was a platoon of 4.2-inch mortars. That difficult era was ending. Each army division was now equipped with a battalion of 155mm howitzers and three battalions of 105mm howitzers. The army stood as tall in division artillery as the divisions of any great power on earth. It was a grand feeling.

After Stalin's death, meanwhile, the armistice talks at Panmunjom made substantial progress. On March 28, Kim Il Sung and Peng Teh Huai accepted Gen. Mark Clark's call of a month before to exchange sick and wounded POWs first. On April 20, 1953, the two sides actually began to do so. Between April 20 and May 3, 1953, at Panmunjom, 5,194 North Korean prisoners and 1,030 Chinese prisoners were returned to the North and 471 ROK prisoners and 149 UN prisoners were repatriated to the South. Dubbed "Little Switch," the exchange of sick and wounded POWs was overseen on the ROK Army side by our team chief, Maj. Gen. Choi Suk.

General Choi sent me a report detailing his view of why so few friendly prisoners were exchanged for the thousands of communist prisoners. "I believe North Korea has very few ROK prisoners to repatriate because after our men were captured the North Koreans forced them to serve in the NKPA."

Whatever the reason for the huge disparity, Little Switch's success caused Korean officers to believe that an armistice agreement might be reached after all. At this juncture, U.S. Army chief of staff, Gen. J. Lawton Collins, invited me to visit the United States, and I accepted. The purpose of the invitation was to allow me to inspect the Pentagon and the various military training facilities located in the United States and also to let me attend an orientation course on methods for commanding corps and armies.

In mid-May I set out alone on my first trip to America. It took two days. I flew on a military C-47 from Taegu to Tokyo and then settled down in seat number one aboard a nearly empty Pan American Airlines, four-engine passenger aircraft. With stopovers at Wake Island and Honolulu, the plane seemed to take forever to reach Travis Air Force Base near San Francisco, California.

I boarded a military C-54 at Travis for the flight to Washington, D.C. Bad weather delayed my arrival in Washington for a few hours, and this proved extremely embarrassing because Korean Ambassador to Washington Yang Yu Chan had arranged a welcome reception in my honor that night timed to coincide with my estimated time of arrival. The guests were kept waiting for hours at the ambassador's official residence. Chairman of the Joint Chiefs of Staff and General of the Army Omar Bradley and a large number of U.S. military people who had participated in the Korean War attended the reception.

The next day I hosted a reception at Fort Myer near the Pentagon where many U.S. general officers have their quarters, and Gen. J. Lawton Collins and many other Pentagon dignitaries came, making it a splendid evening. Even amid the clamor of the party chitchat and the exchange of toasts, however, I couldn't overcome the uneasy feeling that Korea faced a dark future indeed. I was thinking anxiously about my talk with U.S. officials regarding the mutual defense treaty and the ROK modernization plan during my stay in the United States.

After the reception, a few of us went over to Col. Glen Rogers's home, where we had a helpful conversation. Col. Rogers had been KMAG adviser to I Corps when I commanded that unit. In this group were Capt. Nam Sung In, who was in the United States for military training and had joined me in San Francisco as an escort officer, and three other Americans who had fought with me on Korea's battlefields.

One of these was Adm. Arleigh Burke. When I commanded I Corps on the east coast, Burke had commanded Cruiser Division 5, and he and I also served on the initial delegation to the armistice talks. We had worked and fought together in those posts. At this time in mid-1953, Burke served as director of strategic plans at the Navy Department.

Another was Col. Robert T. Hazlett, chief adviser to the 1st Division when we liberated Pyongyang. Both these officers lived in Washington. And the final American was Lt. Col. James H. Hausman, my escort officer, who was then posted to the U.S. Army's Office of Assistant Chief of Staff for Intelligence. Hausman served before and during the war as a KMAG adviser to the ROK Army chief of staff.

When our discussion broke up at 3 A.M., the six of us had reached some conclusions. The first was that "the Republic of Korea opposes to the death an armistice that leaves the country sundered in the middle. Notwithstanding, however, the United States of America will very shortly sign just such an armistice." The second conclusion was a corollary of the first: "If Korea fails to obtain from the United States some form of security guarantee at the present moment, the winning of such a guarantee in the future will be in doubt, as indeed will be the future of Korea itself."

If a U.S. commitment to Korean national security was my goal, Admiral Burke urged me in the strongest terms to meet President Eisenhower face-to-face and explain the need for such a commitment. The next morning I paid a visit to U.S. Army chief General Collins and asked him to use his good offices to arrange an interview with President Eisenhower. Collins candidly said that he was reluctant to comply. "The chiefs of staff of many different countries visit Washington," he said.

"If you were to meet with the president, it would set a precedent. We would be besieged by requests from other service chiefs to meet the president, and we would find it difficult to refuse."

I was in no position to accept a rejection. "How can you compare the ROK chief of staff, whose men fight and die beside American boys every day, with the service chiefs of other countries? Moreover, I have a nodding acquaintance with President Eisenhower."

General Collins realized I was going to be stubborn on the issue and directed army vice chief of staff Gen. John Hull to call the White House and get me an appointment with the president. Hull would later replace Clark as commander in chief of the UN Command.

At 10 A.M. sharp the next morning I walked into the president's White House office. President Eisenhower and I met privately, with no third party present. The office had a huge desk, but I found the room itself to be much smaller than I expected.

President Eisenhower inquired pleasantly enough after President Rhee's health but then fairly spat out the next words. "I am well aware that the Korean people and their government oppose an armistice. But I made a campaign promise to stop the Korean War, and I'm under pressure from Great Britain and other allied countries to conclude a cease-fire."

"If we sign an armistice where the opposing armies now stand," I responded quietly, "then the opportunity to unify Korea will disappear, probably forever. I desire only that you not underestimate the intensity of opposition to an armistice among the Korean people and in our government."

"What can I do about that?"

"Mr. President, why not offer us a guarantee?"

"What does 'guarantee' mean?"

"Sir, three years of war has smashed Korea flat. Nothing remains. One thing you could do would be to consider a mutual defense treaty."

"I agree with that idea in principle," the president said. "And we have mutual defense treaties with many of the countries of Europe, but we have very few in Asia, and such treaties require Senate approval." President Eisenhower then pointedly asked me how long I was staying in Washington. I said I could stay as long as necessary, and he told me to discuss the issue with Assistant Secretary of State Walter Bedell Smith, who had been Eisenhower's chief of staff during World War II. John Foster Dulles was secretary of state at the time.

The meeting ended in a cordial atmosphere and was very productive to the future relations between Korea and the United States. The meeting resulted in speedy progress of the mutual defense treaty, thus I felt my visit with Eisenhower was very timely. President Eisenhower demonstrated his great leadership, which I appreciated.

The following day Admiral Burke and I met with Assistant Secretary

Bedell Smith and exchanged views in detail about Korea's defense and our postarmistice reconstruction plans. These two conversations very likely were the first steps down a path that led to the signing of an ROK-U.S. mutual defense treaty on November 18, 1954.

I spent four days in Washington. With my work there completed, I went up to New York where I visited West Point and U.S. First Army Headquarters. I received a seventeen-gun salute at West Point and was reunited there with John H. Michaelis who fought beside the ROK 1st Division and me in the desperate battles around Tabu-dong in the Pusan Perimeter days. Michaelis had been promoted to brigadier general and was serving as commandant of the corps of cadets at West Point. The Korean national flag I donated to West Point during that visit is still on display at the academy's museum.

During my visit to the U.S. Army Military Academy at West Point, I felt that the academy's motto—Honor, Duty, Country—was reflected in the immense self-confidence of the succession of great leaders to emerge from West Point, men like Eisenhower, MacArthur, Patton, Walker, Ridgway, Van Fleet, and Taylor.

In New York I paid a courtesy call on Gen. Douglas MacArthur at his suite in the penthouse of the Waldorf-Astoria Hotel. I also attended a reception kindly held in my honor by the Korean-American Foundation. I appreciated the warm hospitality offered me at the reception by Lee Won Soon, adviser to the Korean-American Foundation; Kim Cha Kyung, a noted vocalist; and other Koreans residing in the United States.

On the next leg of my trip, I visited the U.S. Army Signal Training Center for the military police school at Fort Gordon, Georgia. From there, I traveled to Fort Benning and the Infantry School, where I met with many Korean officers attending training courses. Indeed, several hundred Korean officers were training at the U.S. Army Infantry School. I found so many Koreans at Benning, in fact, that I felt like the ROK Army Infantry School had been moved lock, stock, and barrel to the United States. Most of the Korean officers did not speak fluent English, so interpreter-officers worked in the classrooms. I heard that our officers were benefiting hugely from the training.

My final stop was the U.S. Army Command and General Staff College in Kansas, where I was scheduled for two weeks of training myself. I was startled to find that the school commandant was Maj. Gen. Henry Hodes, a man who had traveled back and forth with me between Munsan and Kaesong as a codelegate to the armistice talks. I also found officers at the school who had fought with me. Some of them literally had fought by my side.

My concentrated orientation course had been put together especially for me and involved twenty instructors from a number of disciplines drilling a single pupil, me. About ten days into the two-week training course, I received a telephone call from President Rhee. The president's voice reached across the Pacific Ocean. "Unless the situation there is absolutely urgent," he said quietly. "It would be well if you could return." I cut short my visit and flew immediately to Korea.

When I got the presidential telephone call, U.S. newspapers already had been reporting for two days that President Rhee was about to recall me. I had already begun to speculate that something momentous was afoot in Seoul and was not surprised by the call. American newspaper reporters dogged me every step of the way during my visit to the United States. So heavily was the Korean War highlighted in the press that it crossed my mind more than once that the American press dubbed the war as if it were the "American War" rather than the Koreans' war.

One day a reporter asked, "When will the armistice be signed?"

"Only the gods know," I responded, putting into English a phrase Koreans can use to mean, "I don't know." The next day, I was shocked to see my words headlined in American newspapers, but with a very different spin: "God only knows." On one occasion a reporter even said, "Asians are short, have buck teeth, and wear glasses. Why don't you look like that?"

The trip to America left kaleidoscopic impressions on me. The United States was incomparably cleaner and more orderly in 1953 than it is now. Everyone went to church on Sundays. Air conditioners were just becoming popular, and the American people idolized John Wayne and Marilyn Monroe. If you paid for something with a hundred-dollar bill, store clerks looked at you in a strange way and asked to see your passport.

Releasing Anticommunist POWs, Startling the World

I cut short my training at the U.S. Army Command and General Staff College and returned to Seoul in early June 1953. I proceeded to Kyongmudae as soon as I landed to meet with President Rhee, who didn't really have much to say. He did not need to tell me why he had summoned me back so urgently, because the crowds of demonstrators packing Seoul's streets had already done that.

Demonstrations by Seoul citizens opposing the armistice were escalating. Crowds of demonstrators filled the streets and yelled slogans like, "Give us unification or give us death," and "Eject the Chinese Army from the Korean peninsula." Nor were the demonstrations confined to the capital city. Citizens poured into the streets all across the country. The government had encouraged the demonstrations initially, to be sure, but did not invent the issue. The Korean people were dead serious about unification, and the demonstrations were, therefore, potentially explosive.

My own vehicle was caught in the crowds of demonstrators and forced to halt as I tried to make my way to Kyongmudae and report to the president. I was obliged to leave my vehicle, and yell to the crowd. "I'm Paik Sun Yup, the army chief of staff. I have to get through to see President Rhee at Kyongmudae." The citizens clapped and cheered and made way for my vehicle to continue.

A few days after I returned to Korea, President Rhee summoned the major staff officers at ROK Army Headquarters, key army commanders, and me to a meeting a Kyongmudae. President Rhee made it a habit to visit headquarters and the divisions to encourage the men, but it was unprecedented for him to summon the army's key flag officers to Kyongmudae. President Rhee delivered an exhortatory lecture to the assembled general officers, and that was it. The meeting ended. Afterward, he called me in privately. "You know Won Yong Duk well, don't you?" President Rhee spoke in a whisper. "I've given General Won a little homework. Please help him out with it."

I was only too aware of the hidden meaning behind the president's words. Rhee was referring to an event that was now only days away, an incident in which we would startle the world by releasing anticommunist prisoners among the North Korean POWs we had taken on the battlefield. As the pace of armistice talks at Panmunjom picked up in the weeks after Stalin's death, the U.S. side began to pressure President Rhee not to impede the armistice. Little did the Americans know that President Rhee was about to throw his entire being into a final struggle against it.

I interpreted President Rhee's summoning of key army generals to Kyongmudae to mean that he wanted to be sure of our loyalty. Rhee was preparing in utmost secrecy to release the anticommunist POWs, and he was afraid he might run into a replay of the army's "failure" during the Pusan Political Crisis, when key army officers had not followed directions. He was apprehensive lest the army oppose his plans once more.

Maj. Gen. Won Yong Duk commanded the Military Police Command, which fell outside the regular organization of the ROK Army. Let me explain the origins of that command.

In early 1953, Minister of Defense Sohn Won Il called the chiefs of each military service to the National Defense Ministry, which was then located in the building in Seoul's Huam Subward (today it houses the Office of Military Manpower). Minister Sohn told us that he had received an unexpected letter from President Rhee in which the president said he wanted to create a Military Police Command. Sohn said he was not in a position to support such a move, since each service already had its own military police command. Organizing a Military Police Command, he said, would be like building a house squarely on top of an existing house. In the end, however, the Military Police Command was created and formally placed under the authority of the defense minister.

Composed of two companies of military police, this special unit reported directly to the president.

I said nothing to my staff whatsoever about the "top secret operations" of the Military Police Command and in fact pretended not to know the unit existed. On June 17, 1953, however, the ROK Army Provost Marshal, Gen. Suk Ju Am, sent me an intelligence report that claimed, "Something big is about to happen at the Military Police Command." I told Suk: "You are not to get involved in what's happening over there in any way whatever."

At precisely 2 A.M. on June 18, 1953, tens of thousands of North Korean POWs rushed out of the major prison camps across South Korea. The perimeter wire was down at the POW camps in Pusan and Masan and in Kwangju and Nonsan. Every North Korean prisoner of war who had said he did not want to be repatriated to North Korea and every prisoner who claimed to reject communism were released at the same moment.

Army headquarters had no authority over the prison camps, which fell under the control of the UN Command's Korean Communications Zone. The guards at the camps, however, were either ROK Army military police or ROK Army soldiers who operated under U.S. Army command. General Won's Military Police Command seized the camp guards, and at the predetermined moment his men cut the barbed wire and killed the camps' lights.

In a perverse reversal of roles, what essentially happened was that the Korean guards at the camps aided and abetted the escape of the prisoners they were meant to guard. More than twenty-seven thousand prisoners flooded into the blackness of the Korean night at the same moment. A few minutes after 2 A.M. that morning, the telephone in my quarters at Taegu began to ring off the hook. The first call came from Maj. Gen. Thomas Herren, commander of KCOMZ, the officer directly responsible for the prison camps. Herren protested in vehement terms that the "Korean guards have deserted their posts," and he demanded that I return the prisoners to the camps.

The next call was from Maj. Gen. Gordon Rodgers, KMAG chief, and the next came from Eighth Army commander, General Taylor. Neither man made any attempt to hide his anger. I even took two telephone calls from the UN Command commander in chief, General Clark from Tokyo, who also voiced sharp protests. Clark seemed shocked that not a single U.S. soldier, including himself, had managed to pick up a hint that such a move was afoot.

General Clark repeatedly demanded that I tell him who had directed the release of the POWs. I could not provide him with either an answer or any clarification whatever, but I began to be very concerned because the reaction from the U.S. military was much stronger than I had anticipated.

Finally, I put in a call to Kyongmudae. I have never before or since seen fit to awaken the president in the middle of the night. "Excellency," I began. "The Americans, Clark included, are declaring themselves to be very, very regretful over this incident. This one looks like it's going to be bad."

President Rhee was unconcerned. "Okay. I see. Just tell them I did it. I'll put out a press release in the morning."

President Rhee's response surprised me. Did he intend to take responsibility for this astounding incident himself? We would regard it as appropriate if the head of state were to avoid responsibility, placing it on me as chief of staff or on Maj. Gen. Won Yong Duk as commander of the Military Police Command. Indeed, I had naturally assumed that would be the case.

As a politician, President Rhee had been known to engage in a certain duplicity when necessary. If something he ordered turned out badly, for example, Rhee was not above shifting blame for the matter to someone else. His subordinates, in fact, regarded that as the proper approach and readily accepted it. Thus, I was amazed when President Rhee said he would be answerable for a case of this magnitude.

As soon as I finished talking to President Rhee, I called General Clark in Japan and told him, "The release of anticommunist prisoners was executed on President Rhee's personal authority. There will be an announcement in the morning."

As the sun rose, the U.S. Army tried to solve the problem by rounding up the escaped prisoners and returning them to the camps. But each prisoner had been assigned an administrative agency, which provided him with civilian clothes and hid him in a private home. The Americans failed to find the prisoners.

The release of the anticommunist POWs was the final card remaining to President Rhee in his high-stakes game with the United States of America. President Rhee always followed the rule, "Be a sucker in human relations and a devil in foreign relations." Even so, with the signing of the armistice agreement barely a month away, President Rhee's release of the prisoners amounted to a bold diplomatic step, taken without apology. The move pitted Rhee, one old man, in a lonely struggle against the United States of America, the world's mightiest nation. It is no exaggeration in the least to say that in this dramatic moment Rhee was struggling for virtually everything necessary for Korea's future well-being.

On June 18, General Clark flew in from Tokyo to protest directly to Rhee, but the president just shrugged it off. "Had I told my generals about this beforehand," he told Clark, "their positions would have been even more difficult. Right?"

Fearing that President Rhee's action would torpedo the armistice talks, Washington quickly sent Walter Robertson, the State Depart-

ment's under secretary for Far Eastern affairs, to Seoul as a special emissary to see if he could work out the problems. Robertson and U.S. Army
Chief of Staff General Collins arrived in Seoul on the third anniversary
of the war, June 25, 1953. They held talks with President Rhee at Kyongmudae day after day, and I was invited to sit in on the talks as necessary.

A native of Virginia, Robertson was a man of exquisite composure and
perseverance. The overall aura emanating from the members of the U.S.
delegation fairly screamed their doubt that they could ever again cooperate with a Syngman Rhee who was capable of an act as incredible as
releasing the POWs. But as the days passed, I sensed that the Americans were developing an empathy and grudging respect for the old
gentleman.

I was interested in General Clark's impression of the Kyongmudae
talks. The president amazed him: "President Rhee knows our history
better that we do!" Clark was frankly astonished at Rhee's perspicacity
in the matter of the POW release. He couldn't understand where in hell
Rhee had come up with this bold diplomatic maneuver, one that allowed him to carve out the moral high ground on the one hand while
reaping immense practical gains for Korea. Clark freely referred to President Rhee as a "great man."

During the eighteen days of the Rhee-Robertson negotiations—which
many characterized as the "mini-armistice talks"—President Rhee
elicited the following pledges from the U.S. emissary.

1. The United States would conclude a mutual defense treaty with
   the ROK.
2. Washington would guarantee long-term economic aid to Korea,
   beginning with an initial $200 million.
3. The governments of the Republic of Korea and the United States
   of America would undertake political talks after the signing of the
   armistice, which talks would be broken off if no concrete results
   emerged within ninety days.
4. The United States approved an ROK Navy and ROK Air Force
   expansion corresponding to the expansion of the ROK Army to
   twenty divisions, then nearing completion.
5. The United States agreed to hold a Seoul-Washington summit
   prior to the political talks to enunciate the joint goals of the two
   nations.

In return for these concessions, Syngman Rhee agreed to accept the armistice.

President Rhee's face reflected deep fatigue and pain, as if he had
slept very little during the days of talks with Robertson. He revealed his
tortured soul to us on the Korean side. "How can I accept an armistice

under prevailing conditions? Death itself would be preferable. . . . We must try to find life in death.''

In the wake of the release of the POWs, meanwhile, only one domestic voice was raised in criticism, that of Dr. Cho Byong Ok, who took Rhee to task for ''opposing United Nations policies and taking immoderate actions.'' Cho's criticism was picked up by the foreign press.

President Rhee was enraged with Cho. ''All the Korean people support the release. Why is he the only one who opposes it? Not only that, but I am an intimate friend of his father-in-law. He couldn't come out in open opposition like that if he had any solicitude for his seniors.'' As a result of his statement, Dr. Cho Byong Ok was beaten by hoodlums.

The American military could not throw off the sense that they had been betrayed by our release of the POWs. In many places in his memoirs, *From the Danube to the Yalu*, UN Command Commander in Chief Clark reveals great respect and praise for President Rhee as a Korean leader, but he also notes that right up until the day he finished his assignment and left Tokyo any mention of the release of the POWs in Korea caused him a fit of uncontrollable physical trembling.

The release of the prisoners made the Korean people forget General Won's involvement in arresting National Assembly deputies during the Pusan Political Crisis. He became a hero to the Korean people overnight and was even promoted to lieutenant general. The American military, however, made him the object of incessant, unfair complaints.

Immediately after the armistice was signed in September 1953, a brigade from the Indian army landed at Inchon harbor. Its mission was to assume responsibility for communist POWs who did not want to be repatriated to their home country. Gen. Won Yong Duk revived the Americans' nightmares by blocking the rail line in an attempt to prevent the Indian force from traveling to Panmunjom and performing its mission.

The Americans convened a conference at Eighth Army Headquarters to discuss this incident and especially the issue of General Won himself. I attended. General Clark and General Taylor regarded Won's actions as inappropriate in the extreme. ''This man obstructed a UN Command operation. We can't simply close our eyes to it.''

The American officers were openly worked up and had no compunction at all about using such extreme terms as ''anti-American,'' and they openly characterized General Won as ''a nasty fellow.'' I had to try to convince the excited Americans otherwise. ''General Won is not the kind of man you think he is,'' I told them. ''He's a medical doctor, a graduate of Severance Medical School, and his father was a Christian minister. He has done what he has done because his strong sense of patriotism causes him to loyally obey his president.''

Clark wasn't buying. ''Why are you defending General Won? Can you guarantee that this kind of thing won't happen again?'' In the end,

I placated them with repeated pledges that I would indeed prevent such cases from recurring, but it was a close thing.

The Military Police Command had become the subject of intense controversy, and I agreed to bring the unit under the regular army organization and to place it on the list of units qualifying for U.S. Army support. This allowed the Military Police Command to receive equipment and POL support from the U.S. Army.

Whatever else President Rhee accomplished by using the Military Police Command to release the POWs, his creation of a unit without conferring with the U.S. Army violated the pledge Rhee himself suggested and signed in the Taejon Agreement of July 1950 in which Rhee transferred operational command of ROK military forces to the UN Command.

In April 1960 as President Rhee was falling from power, he failed to win any help from the United States. I cannot rid myself of the strong belief that the Americans withheld aid out of a distrust for Rhee that deepened immeasurably after his unilateral release of the POWs.

Meanwhile, declassified documents of the U.S. Defense Department reveal that a plan existed in 1953 to remove President Rhee from power. Dubbed "Operation Everready," essentially the plan called for Washington to win Rhee's support for an armistice by pledging to deliver a long-term defense treaty, sufficient military assistance to maintain twenty divisions, and hundreds of millions of dollars in military and economic aid. If this arrangement proved unsuccessful, then under phase two of Operation Everready Washington was to renounce these pledges and threaten to withdraw all U.S. forces from Korea, turning up the heat on Rhee. If this second option also failed, the plan's third option involved arranging a coup d'état to overthrow President Rhee and forming a new government under Prime Minister Chang Taek-sang.

Operation Everready was drafted originally at Eighth Army Headquarters. General Clark approved it and submitted it to Washington. The documents reveal that Washington put responsibility for executing the plan back on Clark, vaguely tasking him to take necessary action in case of a serious emergency. Details of Operation Everready appear on page 636 of *Korea, The Untold Story of the War* by Joseph C. Goulden (published in 1982), and on page 974 of *The Forgotten War* by Clay Blair (published in 1987). There is no way to know, however, whether the United States created this secret plan as part of its planning for worst-case, hypothetical scenarios or whether Washington actually intended to execute the plan.

Clutching for the High Ground

One would expect the fighting to ease up as the armistice approached, but the opposite was the case. The communist forces wanted to seize a number of key terrain features along the front before the armistice froze the lines. Their purpose, of course, was to lend credence to their propaganda claims that they had won the war.

As the communist commanders looked across the 155-mile Korean front, two terrain features grabbed their attention. One was the northward bulge in the line at Kumsong in the central front, and the other was the area around Hill 351 on the east coast, where the front curved farthest north. As it happened, these areas had fallen within my area of operations when I commanded ROK I Corps and ROK II Corps. The enemy would feel distinctly embarrassed should the armistice be signed with these two protrusions remaining in our hands.

Over a span of days in late May and early June 1953, the Chinese Army seized the eastern side of the Kumsong bulge, which was in the operational area of responsibility of Lt. Gen. Chung Il Kwon's ROK II Corps. The Chinese pushed back two-and-a-half miles of the eight-mile front centered on Capital Hill and Finger Ridge. At the same time the NKPA launched a fierce attack against Hill 351 in the ROK 15th Division's operational area on the eastern front. The 15th was subordinate to ROK I Corps under Lt. Gen. Lee Hyung Koon.

During this latter fighting I rushed up to ROK I Corps and convened a conference with ROK I Corps commander Lee; Admiral Clark, commander of the U.S. Seventh Fleet; and Col. Richard G. Stilwell, KMAG adviser to ROK I Corps who rose to the rank of full general and was commander in chief of the UN Command during the axe murder incident in which a U.S. Army officer was killed by a North Korean security guard at Panmunjom in 1976. At General Lee's request, I ordered my brother, Paik In Yup, to take temporary command of the ROK 15th Division.

General Taylor didn't leave the appointment of corps-level advisers strictly in KMAG's hands. He insisted that he play a role, and his conviction was that only senior colonels who had finished regimental command in the U.S. Army could be candidates. Indeed, as in the case of Colonel Stilwell, General Taylor's rule of thumb was, "Don't send anybody who isn't general officer material." Colonel Stilwell and others, therefore, contributed immensely to ROK Army corps-level operations. Major General Paik had commanded the ROK 6th Division until a few days before; he had left that assignment to prepare to depart for the United States, where he was to undergo military training. When the enemy suddenly turned up the heat along the front, we found ourselves in desperate need of division commanders with extensive combat experience, so we sent Paik back into the line.

The U.S. Seventh Fleet provided excellent fire support as we worked to contain the NKPA attack. The battleship *Missouri* and other lesser vessels took up offshore positions and pounded the enemy with their naval guns.

I found a hill near the fighting and climbed up to get a better view of the situation. I observed a continuous rain of explosions as shells from the fleet rained down on the hapless North Korean assault. I realized at the same time, however, that the NKPA force was mounting an organized, stubborn attack, quite distinct from the desultory efforts we had come to expect from them. Admiral Clark was amazed, too. "We're giving them hell with our guns," he said, shaking his head. "But they keep on coming." Just as the ROK Army had matured into a professional force, I learned that day that after its virtual destruction along the Naktong River line in 1950, the North Korean People's Army had grown into a substantial military machine.

ROK I Corps rose to the challenge, managing to hold the line, but only after tough, violent fighting. Thanks to this success, the Haegum River in North Korea is visible today from the observation deck of the Unification Tower we later built near the site of the battle.

We survived the June crisis, but by the second week of July, the Chinese Army had finished preparations for a final, decisive battle. The Chinese high command was still fixated on the Kumsong bulge. The command had managed to seize ridges in the area in early June, and these minor successes had whetted their appetites. They spent almost a month massing forces in the area, and this time they intended to reduce the bulge entirely.

On the evening of July 13, 1953, the Chinese Army launched its largest, most violent attack since the Spring Offensive of May 1951. We came to call it the Battle of Kumsong. The Chinese commanders threw no fewer than five of their armies into the surprise assault, the Twenty-fourth, Sixty-eighth, Sixty-seventh, and Sixtieth already at the front and the Fifty-fourth brought up from the rear. The 150,000 men in these units focused on a relatively narrow, twenty-mile sector of the front defended by six ROK divisions, the 6th, 8th, 3d, and 5th from ROK II Corps, and the Capital and ROK 9th attached to the adjacent U.S. IX Corps under Lt. Gen. Reuben Jenkins. Just as in every other major Chinese attack, the July offensive rammed headlong into ROK Army units, while U.S. divisions on the right and left flanks remained unengaged.

The Eighth Army had acquired information on the Chinese Army's intentions in this area. American military intelligence learned that the Chinese Fifty-fourth Army had moved from its bivouac area in North Korea's South Pyongan Province to the central front. The intelligence specialists had verified that the Chinese were building a road along the Pukhan River, a road that pointed south. The problem was, however, that the U.S. Air Force had a very limited ability to attack these targets at the time because weather factors combined against our fliers. For one thing, the terrain features in the area caused it to be blanketed by dense fog each morning. And the annual monsoon season had settled in with a vengeance, bringing low cloud cover around the clock day after frustrating day.

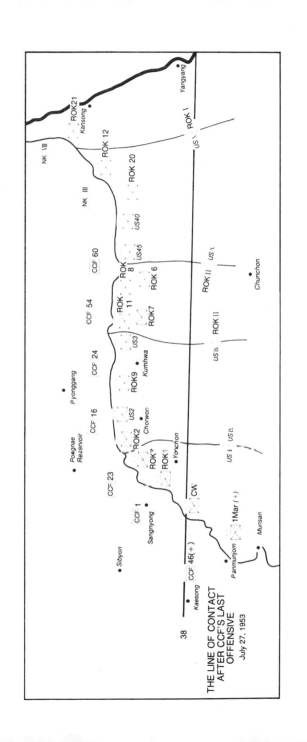

THE LINE OF CONTACT
AFTER CCF'S LAST
OFFENSIVE

July 27, 1953

The Chinese commanders assembled major forces on both sides of the Kumsong bulge and intended to exploit their skill at infiltration and bypass to cut off the rear areas and isolate our forces in the bulge. When the Chinese launched their assault, all twenty-one of our strong points in the Kumsong Salient reported that they were under Chinese attack at exactly the same moment.

The Chinese punched through ROK Army units all along the twenty-one miles of front. The tactical surprise, the darkness, and the overwhelming enemy numbers worked the usual Chinese magic. Before we knew it, we faced a situation that required our immediate withdrawal.

I was tracking the battle through situation reports relayed to ROK Army Headquarters in Taegu. I called the Eighth Army commander, Gen. Maxwell Taylor, during the afternoon of July 14 and asked if there was anything I could do to help. Taylor said he was still sorting out the situation and asked me to wait a while. That evening, however, I received an emergency message from Taylor: "Proceed immediately to ROK II Corps and aid in resolving the situation there. I have sent an aircraft to Taegu to pick you up."

Rain had been falling in spectacular sheets throughout the nation for days, as it often does in the monsoon season, and no light aircraft could possibly land at Taegu. So Taylor sent a twin-engined, all-weather, C-47 transport plane to pick me up. Accompanied only by my aide, I left Taegu about midnight, landed at K-16 Airfield in Seoul, jumped into a military police jeep, and charged all night long from Seoul to Chunchon and beyond to II Corps Headquarters near Hwachon.

Arriving at daybreak, I was greeted by II Corps commander Chung Il Kwon. Sick as a dog, Lieutenant General Chung was running a high fever, and his color was horrible. "I'm sorry," he said. "We lost a lot of Korean ground last night. . . . " II Corps faced a desperate situation, but General Chung's fever had such a tenacious hold on him that he retained only partial use of his hands. Chung was inconsolable over his physical condition. I tried to cheer him up, saying, "Hey, don't worry about losing ground last night. The armistice is only weeks away, and we've got to beat these guys even if we have to fight to the last man." I quickly began to survey what had to be done.

Temporary ROK II Corps deputy commander Maj. Gen. Samuel Williams, who served later as commander of U.S. forces in Vietnam, was in a helicopter flying to the front to direct the fight there. This was the first and last instance in the war in which an American general officer served as the deputy commander of an ROK Army corps. The ROK II Corps sector of the front was so crucial that General Taylor had specially dispatched General Williams, commander of the U.S. 25th Division, to help resolve the situation. General Williams was a soldier with an exceptionally fierce personality. He had commanded the stockade where war criminals were incarcerated during war-crime trials in Nuremberg after

World War II. He had come away from that assignment with the grim nickname of "Hanging Sam."

As army chief of staff I was in charge of administration and logistic support, of course, and was not in the combat chain. The combat command structure ran from the division commander to the corps commander and on to the commander of Eighth Army.

Col. Kim Chong Hwan, ROK II Corps G-2, briefed me on the situation. He later served as chairman of the Joint Chiefs of Staff and as home minister. The ROK divisions that had been broken through withdrew south of the Kumsong River, having suffered enormous losses of personnel, and equipment. After the briefing, I proceeded as far as Sabang Kori, a road junction, where I huddled with three regimental commanders, Cols. Yang Chung Ho, Kim Hui Chun, and Ko Paek Kyu, and saw what I could of the fighting. I discovered that the colonels had not yet determined what the enemy intentions were. They told me the situation remained fluid and unclear. We just didn't know what the enemy was after.

I immediately ordered that a reconnaissance platoon be sent north to determine in detail what the enemy was doing. I waited with the colonels for three or four hours until the platoon returned. I had witnessed too many instances in the war where ROK and American units had withdrawn farther than necessary because they had failed to keep themselves apprised of the enemy's precise location and intentions.

The reconnaissance platoon reported that Chinese Army forces had surged quickly up to points north of the Kumsong River, but only small enemy units had infiltrated south of the river. I judged from this information that the enemy commanders had not yet decided to stage a full-scale assault across the Kumsong. Taking my views as a working hypothesis, the artillery, infantry battalion, and regimental commanders in the area quickly set about strengthening their positions rather than preparing to withdraw.

I sought out and met individually with the commanders of each and every division in the battle, and each of them made emergency requests for more men and equipment. I began to appreciate that the ROK Army was very much a different animal from what it had been. Some might doubt my sanity for making such a statement after we had fallen back in the face of the Chinese assault, but I believed our forces were doing well. One can judge the strength of units better by observing them in the defense than by watching them in the attack.

In each of the previous six major enemy offensives, the Chinese Army aimed its main thrust at ROK Army units, which then lost the will to resist in the first moments of the Chinese onslaught, their officers flustered, their men running aimlessly about. I saw no such reactions on this occasion. The overwhelming weight of the Chinese attack had penetrated our lines, to be sure, but our units quickly reorganized themselves, morale remained high, and everybody was sure we could prevent the Chinese from breaking through into the rear areas. In short, the situation caused me to believe that we could prevail if we could find ways to replace the losses in men and equipment swiftly.

I contacted Vice Chief of Staff Yu Jae Hung and Deputy Chief of Staff for Administrative Affairs Chang Kuk Chin at ROK Army Headquarters and directed them to deploy every vehicle they could get their hands on to rush replacements and supplies to the combat zone. Then I called the KMAG chief, Maj. Gen. Gordon Rodgers, and asked him to meet me at the front as fast as he could get there. I could order the ROK Army to do things, and they would get done very quickly indeed. But I needed Rodgers's help if I wanted to distribute emergency arms, ammunition, and other crucial materiel stored in Eighth Army warehouses.

By the next morning, a veritable flood of replacements, supplies, and equipment began to arrive in the ROK II Corps sector. I couldn't help but be impressed myself at our newfound ability to reconstitute combat strength. The army could not have hoped to accomplish such a feat in the past.

General Taylor also placed top priority on the swift replenishment of combat strength, making a series of bold decisions in the process. He first swapped the U.S. 3d Division for the ROK Capital Division, which had suffered enormous losses in the first hours of the attack. He then flew the 187th Airborne Regimental Combat Team from Japan to Kimpo Airport and deployed it swiftly to the II Corps area, where the unit provided backup for the ROK 9th Division. The 187th's commander was Brig. Gen. William Westmoreland, who rose to four-star rank and commanded all U.S. forces in Vietnam.

Taylor detached the ROK 7th Division under Maj. Gen. Kim Yong Bae from Lt. Gen. Isaac White's X Corps, which was deployed directly to the east of the battle, and sent the 7th to Hwachon to serve as a reserve force.

Taylor also directed the ROK 11th Division under Maj. Gen. Lim Bu Taek, which was in Eighth Army reserve on the east coast, to move on an emergency basis to the battle area, where it replaced the ROK 6th Division which also had sustained severe losses. General Taylor arranged the move of the ROK 11th Division with boldness and verve. To reduce the lengthy period required to deploy a division-sized force, Taylor mobilized every L-20 aircraft in the hands of the U.S. Army in Korea and moved elements of the ROK 11th by air even as other division elements moved overland.

Dozens of L-20s landed and took off throughout the day at the ROK II Corps airstrip, and a completely equipped ROK 11th Division was inserted into the lines as fast as it could possibly be done. The Americans commonly called the L-20s "Beavers." The Canadians had originally developed the planes to carry mail, and the sturdy little aircraft were large enough to accommodate only one squad per flight.

The crisis passed on the third day of the battle. After that, ROK Army counterattacks began to hurt the enemy. We pushed them back until a new front formed on July 19 at a point where the Kumsong River turned to run north and south, bifurcating the bulge into east and west. The fighting died down. With only a week left before the armistice, we had managed to recover only about five of the nineteen miles the enemy had chopped out of the bulge.

Had the Chinese offensive carried as far Sabang Kori or Hwachon, General Taylor had completed preparations to launch a counterattack aimed at Kumsong. This assault would have been accomplished with the help of the additional forces Taylor had massed in the area, the 187th Regimental Combat Team, the U.S. 3d Division, and the ROK 11th Division from the east coast. Whether luckily for Korea or not, however, we contained the Chinese attack at the Kumsong line, preventing them from reaching Sabang Kori or Hwachon, and Taylor did not order the counterattack.

President Syngman Rhee exercised no such admirable self-restraint. He screamed for unification via another invasion of North Korea and clung persistently to his opposition to the armistice until the last moment. The outcome of the Kumsong battle, then, dealt a serious blow to the president's prestige.

The objective of the Chinese Army's final offensive was twofold. The Chinese had wanted to reduce the pocket bulging into their territory, of course, but they also had a psychological objective. They had intended to crush the morale and spirit of a reborn, confident, and strengthened Republic of Korea Army, hoping to send us into the armistice in disgrace. To accomplish these relatively modest objectives, the Chinese Army paid a terrible price: sixty-six thousand men dead and wounded. Even then the Chinese succeeded only partially at the first objective and failed abjectly at the second.

On one score, however, the Chinese July offensive cut me to the quick. Its timing could not have been worse for me. In early June, a number of senior officers returned from training in the United States—Lt. Gen. Lee Chong Chan; Maj. Gens. Choi Young Hi, Chang Do Young, and Park Byung Kwon; and Cols. Ahn Kwang Ho and Jung Nae Hiuk. I had to select generals to replace these men in the American training centers, and the selectees, in turn, needed time to prepare to travel overseas. Thus, I was obliged to execute an extensive personnel reshuffle, especially at the division commander level.

In II Corps, I replaced the commanders of the ROK 8th Division, Maj. Gen. Song Yo Chan, ROK 6th Division, Maj. Gen. Paik In Yup, and ROK 5th Division, Maj. Gen. Kim Chong Kap. Each officer turned over his division to a replacement. When the Kumsong battle began, then, General Taylor could not trust these new commanders, and he first asked me to replace a few of them. A day or two later he requested that I recall Maj. Gen. Song Yo Chan and all the other original division commanders.

I could not see the logic of recalling the old commanders at that late moment in the game. I realized, however, that the battlefield situation was precarious, and I was quite sure that this would prove to be our last major battle, so I acceded completely to Taylor's request. In Gen. Song Yo Chan's case, I had to tramp the streets of Seoul for hours in the company of military police, turning the city upside down before I found him and got him back to the front.

This shuffling and reshuffling of division commanders caused a number of anomalous situations. I knew that as soon as the armistice was signed, the commands would revert to my replacements, so in some instances I doubled up on division commanders, with two assigned to the same division at the same time. In these cases, we simply called one an "administrative division commander" and the other an "operations division commander."

In a departure from the policies of his predecessors, Gen. Maxwell D. Taylor started to stress the necessity of economy in pursuing the war. He began to impose stringent limits on ammunition and materiel use rates. It was no accident that he matured into a political-military leader of the first water, that he served both as U.S. Army chief of staff and chairman of the U.S. Joint Chiefs of Staff, that he became U.S. ambassador to Vietnam during the war there, or that he became a key member of Defense Secretary Robert McNamara's team in the Kennedy administration. In view of Taylor's emphasis on saving money, I was all the more impressed when he promptly made the "expensive" decision to transport a ROK infantry division by light aircraft.

Nevertheless, I could not be satisfied with the outcome of the Kumsong battle, because we lost the bulge, or much of it. As soon as the battle ended, I held a conference at ROK II Corps Headquarters for division and corps commanders who had participated in the fighting. Maj. Gen. Kim Chong Kap, his face red, fairly exploded in anger. "General Taylor didn't utter a single word of encouragement to us. The man's as cold as ice!" Although I said nothing, I was amazed at this news, and after the conference I went to see General Taylor. "What do you think about taking some time and shaking hands with the division commanders who will be going to the United States for training?" I asked him.

"Why do I need to shake their hands?" he countered. I have witnessed only two examples of refusals to shake hands in my life. One was General Taylor's decision in this case. The other was Charles de Gaulle. While I was serving as Korea's ambassador to France, de Gaulle refused to shake hands with the president of the French Senate, who had opposed de Gaulle's policies, and the incident was highly publicized in the press.

The Kumsong battle served as a test bed for the ROK Army's new resupply and transport capabilities. We ferried reinforcments from the training centers to Seoul and on to Chunchon by train, then trucked them to the battle area, supplying them to line units faster than we had ever done before.

The ROK Army lacked the transport capacity to handle the daily resupply requirements of the many units that fought at Kumsong, requirements that reached as many as thirty thousand artillery shells alone, not to mention other types of ammunition and supplies. We had no choice but to resort to requisitioning civilian vehicles in Pusan, Taegu, and other cities. The roads leading toward the battle area were literally packed with military vehicles and requisitioned civilian trucks.

Brig. Gen. Paik Sun Chin served as ROK Army Headquarters G-4 at the time and was in charge of transport. He was scrambling, though, to find enough civilian trucks for our needs. I was reliably informed later that General Paik donned the uniform of a special services sergeant and personally plied Pusan's streets, looking for trucks to requisition.

Brig. Gen. Lee Yong Mun was on my original list of officers to be sent to America for military training, but General Taylor scratched his name. General Taylor excluded Lee from training in the United States because Lee had been quoted in the foreign press as saying, "The ROK Army does not receive sufficient supplies of ammunition." General Taylor crossed Lee's name off with the comment, "The United States can't train officers who make political statements." General Lee continued to serve as commander of the Southern District Combat Command and was unfortunately killed in an aircraft crash in late June 1953.

8

THE WAR ENDS AT LAST

Did the War Make Unification More Remote?

The Kumsong battle was the final enemy offensive. The communists came to the armistice talks at Panmunjom on July 19, 1953, with a new attitude. Despite our release of the anticommunist POWs, the communists showed themselves prepared to conclude an armistice.

Meeting at Panmunjom, the liaison officers of the two sides agreed to establish a military demarcation line at the present location of the front, including the recent changes resulting from the Chinese offensive at Kumsong, and to sign the Armistice Agreement itself on July 27, 1953.

President Rhee summoned me to discuss the issue of whether a Republic of Korea military representative should attend the signing of the armistice. After a brief discussion, Rhee made his decision. ''I think it best that you not go, Chief.'' Therefore, no representative of the ROK armed forces attended the signing ceremony at Panmunjom, but we sent ROK Army armistice delegate Choi Duk Shin to Munsan's Peace Village to observe as the UN Command commander in chief, General Mark W. Clark, penned the final signatures on the documents. President Rhee did not want an ROK representative to sign as a party to the Armistice Agreement because he wanted the UN Command—that is, the United States of America—to be responsible for whatever followed the cease-fire.

At 10:00 A.M. on July 27, 1953, the Armistice Agreement documents were signed and exchanged, and the cease-fire became effective twelve hours later, at 10:00 P.M. The fighting was over at last.

An urgent call had woken me at home on the morning of June 25, 1950. I really didn't have the heart for what followed. I dashed from my home to the 1st Division, then south to the Naktong River, then north to the Chongchon River, then back and forth in between—fighting bloodily all the time. The war managed to exchange the "38th parallel" for the "DMZ" and drench mountains of Korean soil with oceans of blood; it had not done a hell of a lot more.

Once the armistice was a fait accompli, President Rhee accepted it almost casually.

The cease-fire caused a measure of anguish in the officers and men of the Korean army, because it perpetuated the division of our nation. The lengthy armistice negotiations had given us enough time, however, to accept the reality that we could do nothing at all about it. Indeed, I saw General Clark in Seoul right after the armistice was signed and he seemed more distressed over the cease-fire than I did. I couldn't understand it at the time; after all, Clark had helped his nation achieve a major national goal, ending the war in Korea. I learned the reason for his distress much later from his book, *From the Danube to the Yalu.* He had become, he said, the first American commander not to accept surrender from the enemy.

I had faced the bitterness of leaving my home behind and moving into South Korea, only to face the horror of another split in the nation. I felt like unification was more remote now than ever before. The return of peace to Korea, even the impermanent peace of an armistice, was most providential in one way, however. The killing stopped at last. So many of my subordinates had been killed that I literally could not count them. Nor could any mind hope to grasp the immensity of the suffering these deaths brought to so many fathers, mothers, brothers, sisters, and wives. The bombing and the barrages were still. Our people would die in the terrible explosions no more.

I had no regrets about our soldiers. They put their lives on the line with no hope of reward, and they fought the communists to the death But I had a few regrets as a commander. I was on the battlefield virtually the entire war, first as a commander of a division, then a corps, and finally as chief of staff. And I believe we could have fought a little better.

We faced enormous deficiencies, to be sure. We were a fledgling force, dreadfully inferior in training. We lacked the equipment of a modern army, and our commanders were often incompetent. These inadequacies made it all but impossible for Korean units to be tough enough to maintain our defensive positions. But this situation had nothing to do with the quality of our soldiers. If there was a lack of will, then we must turn to our commanders to find it.

Coordination between ROK Army units was lousy, and we relied too much on U.S. artillery and close air support. We lacked the toughness of spirit to rely on our own crew-served weapons and resist to the death. Air and artillery support are crucial elements, of course, that often determine whether a battle will be won or lost. But both are subject to the limitations imposed by weather conditions such as wind and rain, cloud cover, and fog. The ultimate arbiter of victory or defeat are the ground forces—especially the infantry, with its toughness of spirit—under exemplary leadership willing to stand at the vanguard and inspire every level of command.

I was busier after the armistice was signed than I was during the fighting before the cease-fire. During the 1,127 days of war we had neglected anything that didn't promote victory. Now this neglect reared up with a vengeance, and combined with the destruction and dislocations of the war, to confront ROK government leaders with a tangled, mountainous stack of thorny problems. We left the war era and entered the era of reconstruction.

We were worried that if Korea failed to live up to the burdens of the armistice, the war might break out again. For me, the burning issues of the day were the POW exchanges, fortifying our new fighting positions along the DMZ, and expanding and reorganizing the army and its chain of command as U.S. forces withdrew from Korea.

The exchange of POWs was the highest priority item on my list. I took a jeep up to Panmunjom to help greet the Republic of Korea prisoners released by the North. I awaited along with a mobile surgical hospital and the army band for the prisoners to arrive at the temporary tent village put up to accept our POWs. When at last they came, they dismounted the vehicles in dead silence, their faces masks of pain and suffering. Once they were convinced they were really on our side of the lines, once they believed they were home, their sense of relief was immense. They cried, and we cried with them.

Doctors and medics checked the POWs over, sprayed them with disinfectant, gave them new clothes, and immediately evacuated those who were ill or injured.

We found almost no officers among the repatriated POWs. The communists singled out the officers for persecution, and the only ones to survive captivity were those skillful enough to pretend to be enlisted men, and maintain that fiction throughout long months of captivity.

A number of dignitaries were on hand to welcome our POWs, including Secretary of State John Foster Dulles; Gen. Mark W. Clark, commander in chief, UN Command; Gen. Maxwell D. Taylor, commander of the Eighth Army; and Defense Minister Sohn Won Il.

Our army band was playing only Western marches, so I approached the bandmaster and asked him to "play some folk songs for these brave men who have been away so long and are so homesick." The strains of our famous folk songs "Arirang," "Toraji," and others soon reverberated in the DMZ, and hardly a Korean eye was free from tears.

The communists returned about 7,800 Republic of Korea soldiers and some 4,700 UN POWs. We repatriated some 60,000 North Korean prisoners and about 5,600 Chinese POWs.

The Neutral Nations Repatriation Commission, headed by Indian Army Lieutenant General Timaya, deliberated the cases of prisoners who desired repatriation to neither North Korea nor South Korea. (Timaya went on to become chief of staff of the Indian Army.) The Repatriation Commission sent those who passed its screening to neutral nations like India, Brazil, and Argentina.

Some twenty thousand Chinese communist soldiers refused repatriation. We sent these men to Taiwan. Republic of China Air Force Maj. Gen. Lai Ming-tang was in charge of the operation, which involved putting the communist Chinese POWs on Republic of China LSTs at Inchon for the trip to Taiwan.

The ink was barely dry on the Armistice Agreement when the U.S. Army began to withdraw, in the fall of 1953. We were hardly caught unawares. I conferred frequently with General Taylor and other top U.S. military officials to prepare the ROK Army to assume responsibility for the sectors of line that would be vacated by departing U.S. units.

When the cease-fire went into effect, three U.S. Army corps and two ROK Army corps shared responsibility for the 155-mile DMZ. We knew from our combined planning, however, that the Americans would withdraw two corps on a phased basis, ultimately leaving a single corps on the western front. We had to create two corps on a crash basis to fill the gap.

We did it the same way I had created ROK II Corps in 1952. We selected the corps headquarters staff personnel and sent them to an American corps, where they worked with their U.S. Army counterparts daily. We timed this on-the-job training so that the Korean unit was ready to take over the DMZ sector just as the U.S. unit was ready to return to the United States.

In May 1953, shortly before the armistice was signed, Maj. Gen. Kang Mun Bong and his selectees to staff a new ROK III Corps deployed to Kwandae and started on-the-job training with U.S. X Corps. In October, when X Corps withdrew, ROK III Corps assumed its mission, defending along the east-central front from the Pukhan River to the Punchbowl.

This process was repeated when Maj. Gen. Choi Young Hi's ROK V Corps team began training at U.S. IX Corps Headquarters. Our new ROK V Corps assumed responsibility for the DMZ in the Chorwon area in early 1954. By that date, four ROK Army corps were in place and defending along the eastern and central DMZ, leaving U.S. Army units on-line only on the western front. We were soon accountable for half of the western front as well. Maj. Gen. Lee Han Lim's ROK VI Corps team completed training at U.S. I Corps and took over the eastern half of the U.S. unit's DMZ sector in mid-1954.

American and other foreign troops under the UN flag flowed out of Korea through the harbor at Inchon very quickly, reminding one of the surging Inchon tides on which they sailed. A few of the troops left via

Pusan, and some flew out in huge, four-engined military transport aircraft from Kimpo Airport. Most were gone within six months of the cease-fire. For its part, the U.S. Army withdrew in a very orderly, logical fashion, starting with its easternmost units and moving step by step toward the west.

The ROK Army's swift expansion to five corps forced changes in our chain of command. These changes were symbolized by the creation of the First Field Army. To set the stage for these changes, President Syngman Rhee conducted high-level army personnel shifts on February 14, 1954. The president promoted Chung Il Kwon and Lee Hyong Koon to full general on the same day, appointing General Chung to be chief of staff for a second time, assigning General Lee to the new post of chairman of the Joint Chiefs of Staff, and making me the commander of the new First Field Army.

The mission of the chairman of the Joint Chiefs was to establish national defense strategy in consultation with the ROK Army, Navy, Air Force, and Marine Corps and to manage the task of planning and directing multiservice operations.

The U.S. practice when promoting officers to full general was to leave at least a day's difference in the date the rank changed so as to clearly indicate relative seniority. This practice was not followed when Chung and Lee were promoted. I was informed that the simultaneous promotions were not undertaken lightly. The decision was reached that neither general should be senior to the other. This approach was adopted as a means of boosting the authority of the fledgling JCS chairman. Indeed, the chief of staff position was to remain the stronger for decades to come.

These changes at the top of the army pyramid occasioned shifts in their wake. Lt. Gen. Kim Chong O was appointed to command ROK I Corps, and Lt. Gen. Chang Do Young was tapped to command ROK II Corps.

My new command, First Field Army, did not yet exist, but work was under way to establish it even then. Maj. Gen. Kim Ung Soo passed command of the ROK 2d Division to Maj. Gen. Kang Young Hoon, Korea's former prime minister, in December 1953. Kim then was designated to be the first chief of staff of the new First Field Army and led a preparation team to U.S. X Corps Headquarters for training.

U.S. Eighth Army did its part to prepare X Corps to train my new First Field Army staff. General Taylor appointed Lt. Gen. Bruce C. Clarke to command X Corps and made Col. Creighton W. Abrams Clarke's chief of staff. General Taylor was blunt about it. "We have no officer in the U.S. Army better at training than Bruce Clarke." The Americans were pulling out the stops to help us get First Field Army up and running.

Indeed, Clarke was to rise to the rank of full general and serve as commander in chief of NATO forces in Europe. As for Abrams, he was a sensational officer who had earned fame as a tank battalion commander under General Patton in World War II. He went on to replace General Westmoreland as commander of U.S. forces in Vietnam and then as U.S. Army chief of staff. America's newest tank, the M-1, was named the Abrams after this outstanding officer.

Free of chief of staff duties, I moved to the U.S. X Corps area and turned up the fire under preparations to create the First Field Army. I participated in the training conducted by Clarke and Abrams myself, although as a full general who had completed a tour as a service chief, I outranked them both. But I had to learn what was required to command a field army, because we had never had a unit that size in the ROK Army.

The First Field Army was officially inaugurated in May 1954, and four corps were assigned to it: I, II, III, and V corps. We assumed responsibility for the entire central and eastern fronts and for command and control of no fewer than sixteen divisions. We took great pride in the fact that the First Field Army was one of the largest field armies anywhere in the world.

As a corollary to First Field Army, U.S. I Corps Group was formed on the western front and given control of U.S. I Corps, with its three divisions, and of ROK VI Corps, with four more. U.S. I Corps Group was the parent of today's ROK-U.S. Combined Field Army in Uijongbu.

The government moved from its temporary home in Pusan back to Seoul in 1954. Eighth Army moved its headquarters to Yongsan in southern Seoul at the same time, opening the way for Seoul National University to return to its Tongsung Subward facilities. Eighth Army Headquarters continued to exercise operational control over U.S. I Corps Group and First Field Army.

ROK Army Headquarters also returned to Seoul and remained responsible for providing administrative, educational, training, and logistical support to ROK Army corps, including VI Corps attached to I Corps Group and to divisions of the First Field Army.

The next logical step was the formation of the Second Field Army, which was accomplished in July 1954 at Taegu under the command of Lt. Gen. Kang Mun Bong. The newly established Second Field Army assumed the missions of the Korean Communications Zone, becoming responsible for the two-thirds of the nation farthest removed from the DMZ.

All this reorganization and expansion took place a mere eighteen months after the cease-fire. The far-reaching changes made in that brief period put the army of 1954 well on the way to being a modern, twentieth-century force at the front and in the rear areas.

Chief of Staff Again

The assassination of Maj. Gen. Kim Chang Yong, chief, ROK Counterintelligence Corps, shook the army, triggering a round of personnel changes among the army's top leadership. On the morning of January 30, 1956, assassins shot Kim as he was on his way to work. The case was an immediate media sensation, dominating the news like no past story about the Army. It represented the worst violation of military discipline since the founding of the Army and revealed the ugly discord boiling beneath the surface among high-ranking Army officers. Arrests followed on the heels of the murder, and the men who had actually fired the pistols were arrested.

On May 18, 1957, JCS Chairman Gen. Chung Il Kwon retired and accepted an appointment as Republic of Korea ambassador to Turkey. Gen. Lee Hyong Koon was removed from the chief of staff post and not given another assignment, forcing him into obscurity. I had completed thirty-nine months as commander of First Field Army and was once more assigned as ROK Army chief of staff. My first tour as army chief lasted from July 1952 to February 1954. The May shifts left me as the only full general on active duty.

The most pressing issue on my new desk was the army modernization plan. After the war the Korean armed forces grew to more than seven hundred thousand men, but qualitatively we were barely marking time.

After the cease-fire was declared, departing U.S. units transferred a wealth of materiel and equipment to the ROK Army, but this equipment was World War II vintage and now antiquated. Moreover, five years had passed, and the equipment was wearing out fast. Meanwhile the North Koreans had been building up their army and navy at unprecedented rates every year since the armistice was signed. As a result, our relative military strength actually was declining.

The Americans had been providing military aid for years, now, and they were considering measures to reduce the ROK Army manpower ceiling. Because military aid was linked to the number of personnel on active duty, a lower manpower ceiling would decrease the military aid burden shouldered by the Americans.

Thus, both we and the Americans wanted to modernize the army's equipment, the Americans because modernization would lower the manpower ceiling, the Koreans to redress the balance of power favoring North Korea. Both sides wanted to increase the quality of the army while decreasing its size.

I left for the United States on March 3, 1958, accompanied by Assistant Minister of Defense for Logistics Maj. Gen. Paik Sun Chin and ROK Army Headquarters G-3 Maj. Gen. Jung Nae Hiuk. I briefed decision makers from various U.S. government agencies for two hours in a crowded Pentagon conference room on the essence of the ROK Army modernization plan.

Afterward, I paid a courtesy call on President Eisenhower at the White House and explained the modernization plan to him. Compared with my visit with President Eisenhower in the urgent days just before the armistice was signed in 1953, I felt much more relaxed, and the visit went very smoothly. President Eisenhower said he had no particular objections to the modernization plan himself, but asked, "Are you discussing this modernization issue with the Pentagon?"

The essential points of the modernization plan were to acquire new tanks, increase artillery strength, establish airborne units, acquire destroyers, and strengthen air-defense capability.

We encountered no snags when we began to implement the modernization plan. We organized tank battalions with the M-48 tanks we acquired and assigned one battalion each to frontline corps. We used the 105mm and 155mm howitzers we acquired to expand the number of tubes in our artillery units. We also acquired new tubes and other replacement artillery parts under a different program, allowing us to upgrade our older artillery pieces.

The Americans provided us with the parachutes, special weapons and equipment, and training facilities we needed to create an airborne unit. Using these acquisitions, we established an airborne training center at Kimpo and activated an airborne battalion, upgrading this to a regiment in short order. We selected personnel to fill the airborne unit on very strict criteria, administering both a physical examination and an aptitude test to volunteers from all over the army. The battalion we created grew into today's Special Warfare Command.

The ROK Navy took transfer of two DD class destroyers, fulfilling a long-cherished navy desire. The navy had operated only DE class destroyer escorts previously, so the new destroyers strengthened both the navy's firepower and its antisubmarine warfare capabilities.

The ROK Air Force acquired F-86 all-weather fighter-bombers for the first time. Our air force had suffered a serious lack of relative power since the armistice in 1953, when U.S. air assets left the area, and the F-86s partially compensated for our relative weakness vis-à-vis North Korea.

During my second tour of duty as chief of staff, I emphasized two programs, the army modernization plan and improving the army logistics system. As a part of the army's logistic restructure, we activated the Logistics Base Command in January 1960. Its first commander was Maj. Gen. Park Chung Hee.

My deputy chief of staff for logistics, Kim Ung Soo, recommended that Park Chung Hee be appointed to command the Logistics Base Command. But when Park led a coup d'état on May 16, 1961, Kim was commanding VI Corps and refused to support the military revolution. Kim later went to the United States, where he became a professor of economics at Catholic University in Washington, D.C.

I felt keenly that the social and political milieu of Korea had altered significantly since I completed my first tour as army chief. At that time, the chain of command was well respected. I had full authority to lead the army by the light of my own convictions.

The situation was completely different during my second tour as army chief, which came in the final period of Syngman Rhee's rule. The eyes of many army generals had begun to turn toward a few Liberal party politicians, especially Assembly Speaker Lee Ki Poong. Presidential aides and presidential security personnel at Kyongmudae had begun to interfere in the army's internal affairs. Discipline in the army was being eroded by outside forces.

These unfortunate trends appeared when President Rhee, who wanted a son, adopted Lee Ki Poong's son, an act that amounted to making Lee the heir apparent. At this crucial juncture for Lee Ki Poong, however, he became ill. His leg bothered him, and he suffered a speech impediment. Lee lost his previously uncanny ability to read the pulse of the country and indeed became a burden on President Rhee.

I was lucky to enjoy President Rhee's confidence and was able to deflect many of the problems the changed situation caused me as chief of staff. But I could do nothing about the larger social problems, standing by helplessly as I watched the society begin to unravel.

On February 23, 1959, I was appointed to serve as JCS chairman. An incumbent JCS chairman had a lot of extra time on his hands in those days. The position had little authority, and I recognized my demotion. I was to witness the last days of a fading Rhee regime from this post behind the scenes of history.

EPILOGUE

I retired in 1960 while serving as chairman of the Joint Chiefs of Staff and while Korea was caught up in the throes of a political transition triggered by the resignation of President Rhee in April of that year. The president stubbornly advocated a march to the North to unify the Korean peninsula, but he was a lifelong patriot of the most luminous sort, a staunch anticommunist, and my commander in chief.

After I left the army, I was posted as Korean ambassador to R.O.C. (Taiwan) for a year, to France for four years, and then to Canada for four more, returning to Korea in 1969. I found that Korea had been surging ahead economically since 1964, guided by an infusion of managerial knowledge provided by people who had served in the ROK Army.

I was appointed to serve as minister of transportation when I returned and found our railroad system to be a singularly tough nut to crack. Later I was appointed to serve as president of the Korea General Chemical Corporation, a quasi-governmental firm that manufactures chemical fertilizer and acts as a holding company for the various multinational joint-venture firms in the chemical sector.

My children are grown and married now. I visit with ROK Army and American servicemen as often as I can and always remind them that they are themselves part of army history. I keep myself busy writing a series of articles on counterinsurgency operations in Korea in those early years. The government sees to it that I stay active, too. I'm overseeing the construction of a Republic of Korea War Memorial Museum in Seoul.

During the war, I thought we would be able to unify Korea by force of arms. That ardent desire, shared by sixty million Koreans to this day, was not to be, evaporating beneath the interminable talks at Panmunjom. We gained no victory, true enough, but we staved off a defeat that the infamy of surprise attack had nearly made a sure thing, and we established the cold war policy of containment by bringing the enemy's predatory aggression up short.

My memory shall never expunge the scenes of Korean soldiers, soldiers sacrificing their lives to place explosives on enemy tanks in the first days of the war, soldiers who fought with grenade and bayonet and died in the rugged mountains within the Pusan Perimeter, soldiers who fought desperately to gain every possible inch of ground before the armistice brought the curtain down. These heroes will live always in my heart.

Index

About the Author

Paik Sun Yup was born in 1920 near Pyongyang. The second of three children, he graduated from Pyongyang Normal School, and in 1941 from Manchuria's Mukden Military Academy and was commissioned a second lieutenant in the Manchurian Army, in which he served until the end of World War II. Just ahead of the onrushing Soviet Army, Paik made his way back to Pyongyang, where he assisted Cho Man Sik, a leader of Korea's fledgling national liberation movement.

Realizing in 1946 that a communist takeover of the North was inevitable, Paik fled south for a new life and was commissioned a first lieutenant in the South Korean Constabulary (later the Republic of Korea Army). When North Korea invaded in 1950, Paik was a colonel and commander of the ROK 1st Division. During the course of the war, he rose to become South Korea's first four-star general and was his country's representative at the peace talks. Following the armistice, he served twice as army chief of staff (founding South Korea's first field army between terms) and was chairman of the Joint Chiefs of Staff. One of the most highly decorated officers in the ROK Army, he earned two Taeguk Medals (Korea's highest award), as well as seven U.S. medals, including one Silver Star and four Legions of Merit.

General Paik retired from the army in 1960 to begin a second career as a diplomat. He served as ambassador to R.O.C. (Taiwan), France (and concurrently sixteen other European and African nations), and Canada. Paik left the diplomatic service in 1969, was minister of transportation until 1971, and then was president, until 1980, of Korea General Chemical Corporation, South Korea's largest chemical company. Currently he serves as honorary chairman and adviser to various government and private organizations. Residing in Seoul, General Paik and his wife of forty-eight years, In Sook, have four children—three living in the United States—and five grandchildren.

Potomac's
MEMORIES OF WAR
Series

ıt illustrate the personal realities of war as experienced by combatants and civilians alike, in
s those of the distant past. Other titles in the series:

American Guerrilla: My War Behind Japanese Lines
Roger Hilsman

B-17s Over Berlin: Personal Stories from the 95th Bomb Group (H)
Ian Hawkins

Escape With Honor: My Last Hours in Vietnam
Amb. Francis Terry McNamara with Adrian Hill

Hitler's Prisoners: Seven Cell Mates Tell Their Stories
Erich Friedrich and Renate Vanegas

Lieutenant Ramsey's War: From Horse Soldier to Guerrilla Commander
Edwin Price Ramsey and Stephen J. Rivele

Medal of Honor: One Man's Journey from Poverty and Prejudice
Roy Benavidez with John Craig

The Gulf Between Us: Love and Survival in Desert Storm
Cynthia B. Acree with Col. Cliff Acree, USMC

Under Custer's Command: The Civil War Journal of James Henry Avery
Karla Jean Husby and Eric J. Wittenberg

Wake Island Pilot: A World War II Memoir
Brig. Gen. John F. Kinney, USMC (Ret.), with James M. McCaffrey

War in the Boats: My WWII Submarine Battles
Capt. William J. Ruhe, USN (Ret.)

White Tigers: My Secret War in North Korea
Col. Ben S. Malcom, USA (Ret.), with Ron Martz